Additional Praise for *Goliath's Revenge*

"A must read for how companies can successfully develop a digital program to defend their core franchises and grow with new digital services."
—Bill Ruh, CEO, GE Digital

"There has never been a more important time for boards to be aware of digital disruption. *Goliath's Revenge* lays out the key elements that boards and leadership teams should focus on."
—Peter Gleason, CEO, National Association of Corporate Directors

"Traditional boundaries in retail are breaking down. Hewlin and Snyder show how to accelerate digital innovation around experiences that meet the needs of today's consumer."
—Chris Gheysens, CEO Wawa

"*Goliath's Revenge* provides the roadmap that established companies need as they put their data to work and run the Silicon Valley playbook for themselves."
—Doug Merritt, President and CEO, Splunk

"*Goliath's Revenge* lays out the courageous journey every leading company must take to stay on top. Hewlin and Snyder provide the rules for reinventing your company and yourself."
—Krishnan Rajagopalan, CEO Heidrick & Struggles

"Digital is changing how healthcare is delivered and empowering patients to be more involved in their care. *Goliath's Revenge* lays out how to shape this transformation."
—Madeline Bell, CEO Children's Hospital of Philadelphia

"Hewlin and Snyder have provided a great guide for any entrenched company to win in today's data rich world while staying ahead of disruption."
—Mark Vergnano, CEO, Chemours

"We are well into the digital revolution in healthcare. The rules in *Goliath's Revenge* will separate the disruptors from the disrupted."
—Lynnette Cooke, CEO, Kantar Health

Goliath's Revenge

HOW ESTABLISHED COMPANIES TURN THE TABLES ON DIGITAL DISRUPTORS

TODD HEWLIN   SCOTT SNYDER

WILEY

For our kids—Zachary, Emma, Morgan, Lindsey, Evan, and Carson. We learn every day from your unfiltered, digital-native viewpoints and optimistic, change-the-world energy. Digital disruptors are never going to create enough interesting jobs for your generation.

For our friends who are transforming Goliaths into future disruptors. Your courageous spirit and innovator's mindset are what really make elephants dance. Your stories inspired us to write this book.

Contents

Foreword

E verybody gets that digital disruption is radically changing the landscape of every economic sector, public or private. There is scarcely a board of directors or management council that is not pounding the table for digital transformation. We all know we need to get going. The question is, where to?

You can't transform yourself if you don't have a clear idea of who or what you need to be in the future. Unfortunately, the only role models established enterprises have today are the very digital disruptors that are putting their franchises at risk. But the disruptors simply cannot be good role models for you. If you copy them, you are taking a me-too approach to a game that they themselves invented. How dumb is that?

What you need, what we all need, is a crystal ball to look into the future and see what it might look like for us to play a valuable and vibrant role, one that leverages our unique heritage and assets. In other words, we need to stop focusing on the present threat of *them* and start focusing on the future potential for *us*.

And that is precisely what *Goliath's Revenge* sets out to help you do. Todd Hewlin and Scott Snyder have been working with established companies at the cutting edge of the digital revolution for more than a decade. I have had the privilege of working alongside them on multiple projects, and I can personally vouch for their experience and their acumen. Both share the extraordinary abilities to extrapolate beyond present circumstances, to envision a variety of possible future states, and to guide their clients in sifting through a raft of possible scenarios and help them home in on their most promising paths forward.

Goliath's Revenge capitalizes on these abilities. It presents a set of scenarios across multiple industries, each with its own Goliath, each facing a daunting attack from a dangerously agile David. Some of these contests are unfolding right now and provide insightful lessons about what to do and not do in pushing back against digital disruption. Others are just over the horizon and represent the early warning signals that established companies need to be alert for now.

In other words, regardless of the disruption's time horizon in your industry, *Goliath's Revenge* will provide you with valuable case studies to reference. In each one, the insights and principles that Todd and Scott extract are not only fascinating, they are directly applicable to the challenges your company is, or soon will be, facing.

As leaders in the private and public sector, it is imperative that we galvanize our established institutions—the ones that operate at scale today, the ones that have already earned the trust of millions and millions of people—to play an active role in shaping the future of our society as it absorbs the shock of digital transformation.

There is not enough time or money to rebuild everything from scratch. We need instead to refresh the incredible legacy of assets we have been gifted with so that they can in turn be passed on to the next generation. This requires not only courage and intelligence, but creativity and imagination as well. We are fortunate to have books like this one to help us envision the possibilities.

—Geoffrey A. Moore
Author, *Crossing the Chasm*
and *Zone to Win*

Chapter 1

How Much Time
Do You Have?

How did you go bankrupt?
Two ways. Gradually, then suddenly.

—*Ernest Hemingway, author*

What company is this? Early private investor in a major ride-sharing leader. Licensed to test more fully autonomous cars on California roads than any other company. Builder of a business model that can prosper in a future where many people own cars but do not drive and others don't want to own a car at all. Recognized as the first company delivering a long-range, sporty electric car that the average person can afford. Willing to pay a massive premium to acquire Silicon Valley–based talent in order to win the long game of digital disruption in the automotive industry. Just received an investment of $2.25 billion from famed dealmaker Masayoshi Son at SoftBank.

Google? Apple? Tesla? Amazon? Uber? Those would all be excellent guesses. The company is actually General Motors. A company that just 10 years ago required a US government bailout to survive the global financial crisis. Today GM is thriving in spite of the global automotive industry being rapidly transformed by the trifecta of digital innovation: electrification, autonomy, and sharing.

Rewriting David versus Goliath

If the business world actually reflected the biblical story of David versus Goliath, established companies built over generations would struggle valiantly against the digital upstarts but would be so visually impaired and unimaginative that they would not be able to see the rock coming. Unicorn private companies from San Francisco, Shanghai, Berlin, and Tel Aviv would upend the status quo in industry after industry, leading to bankruptcy for established companies and unemployment for their workforces. In this updated version of the historic story, David's sling would be an artificially intelligent robot. We would all know how the story ends but still enjoy reading about the heroic struggle these established companies mustered before their eventual demise.

For some established companies, that is actually how the business version of David versus Goliath is playing out. Digital disruptors such as the companies listed above are well funded, well staffed, and heavily armed. They are not to be taken lightly. This is true whether the established Goliath is a global industrial titan with 100,000 employees or a local company that has been the lifeblood of a family for years with 10 employees. We've all seen that Blockbuster was destroyed by Netflix, Nokia was beaten by Apple, and that thousands of retail entrepreneurs "retire early" as Amazon gradually takes their customers away. This outcome is predictable if the news articles you read are to be taken at face value.

We think something much more interesting is afoot. We call it "Goliath's Revenge." Established companies are getting wise to David's strategy, tactics, and tools. They have seen some of their traditional competitors succumb to the digital attackers that are resetting the rules for their industries. Instead of waiting for their businesses to be disrupted by some Silicon Valley whiz kid, they are saying, Why can't we use those same strategies, tactics, and tools for ourselves? Some are setting their sights even higher. They are simultaneously protecting their core businesses from digital disruption while also running the disruptors' playbook to expand into high-growth adjacent markets.

Goliath's Revenge is not just playing out within these established companies; the script is also being rewritten for the people who work in them. Senior executives, managers, and front-line staff alike are proactively reinventing themselves to ensure that they have lifetime employment, even in this period of disconcerting and rapid change. These employees are offloading routine tasks to computers instead of clinging to them. That mindset shift is allowing them to finally take on the higher-value activities that they've never had the time to get to. These enlightened employees are stretching themselves to build the new skills their companies will require for a digital future but may not even know to ask for yet.

Before we jump into the new rules that govern how these established companies and their workforces are achieving Goliath's Revenge, let's dig deeper into how GM has been able to pull off the remarkable comeback referred to earlier.

The Resurgence of General Motors

There is no substitute for making mistakes early to build the breadth and depth of institutional knowledge required for long-term market leadership. Think about the Newton that was designed by Apple Computer and launched to much fanfare in 1993. It was both an unmitigated failure and the ancestor of what would become one of the most important products ever made: the iPhone. Apple has gone on to sell over one billion iPhones. That business now represents almost two-thirds of the company's revenue. The second time really was the charm. Steve Jobs was so confident that the iPhone would be a hit that he dropped "Computer" from the company name on the day the iPhone launched.

Around the same time Apple was working on the Newton, GM was developing the EV1—the world's first modern electric car built by a major automotive manufacturer. It was a bold bet that came to market in 1996, seven years before Tesla was founded and 16 years before Tesla's first internally developed car, the Model S. The EV1 proved to be GM's Newton—unsuccessful in the near term, quickly discontinued, and essential to the long-term success of the company.

Detroit's history with electric cars actually goes back to the early part of the twentieth century. Samuel Clemens, better known by his pen name Mark Twain, once observed, "History doesn't repeat itself, but it does rhyme." This is still the case today. Figure 1.1 shows a 1917 advertisement for a car called the Detroit Electric that uses the rising price of gas and moderate price of electricity to promote Detroit-built electric cars.

GM did not realize it at the time, but the EV1 was an essential step on the path to achieving Goliath's Revenge. The automotive industry is beset with digital Davids—Tesla, Google, Uber, Lyft, Apple, Zipcar, and BYD Auto, along with many lesser-known players—all trying to shape the future of the automotive industry through electrification, autonomy, and sharing. You can likely name an equivalent set of digital disruptors in your industry and country.

What the EV1 did was whet GM's appetite for how electrification could reshape the automotive industry. It inspired the gas-and-electric Chevy Volt in late 2010 and the wholly electric Chevy Bolt in late 2016. The Bolt was recognized as Car of the Year by *Motor Trend* in 2017 and beat Tesla's Model 3 to market by nearly a year. In short, GM's credibility with end customers, dealers, and shareholders with respect to electrification is well earned.

In terms of autonomous vehicles, GM did not have the luxury of such long-term, institutional knowledge. This required the company to make

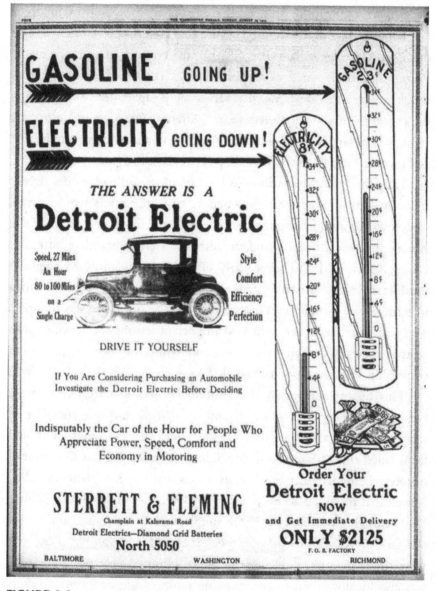

FIGURE 1.1   Detroit Electric Ad from 1917

a bold bet through the acquisition of Cruise Automation in early 2016. Headquartered in San Francisco, Cruise was just three years old when GM acquired it. More shocking was the price—a reported $1 billion—valuing the startup at nearly $25 million for each of its roughly 40 employees. For context, GM itself is valued at just $0.3 million per employee. Bets don't get a lot bigger than that. GM had the confidence to make such a major acquisition—what we will refer to as a "Big I" bet—as its own customer research demonstrated that self-driving capabilities were crossing the chasm from science project to key differentiator. Getting autonomy right was declared a must-win battle and an area in which entirely new skills would be critical to GM's long-term success.

The final shift—sharing—was the most difficult one. Every traditional automaker wanted to believe that consumers would always value owning and driving their own cars. It felt like a core tenet of the American Dream and a foundational basis of GM's brand, culture, and values. Again, GM had some early efforts to draw on. GM acquired the Hertz Drive-Ur-Self System all the way back in 1926 as its entry into the rental car market. That was 83 years before Uber was founded. The rental car business taught GM important lessons about which jobs customers wanted their cars to do and which of those required car ownership versus temporary vehicle access.

This history gave GM the confidence and experience to make two additional big bets—one around car sharing and one around ride sharing. For its car-sharing bet, GM acquired the assets and select staff from failed ride-sharing company Sidecar in January 2016. GM immediately relaunched that business as a new car-sharing platform called Maven that provided access to select GM vehicles on an hour-by-hour basis through a mobile app. Think simple, hourly car rentals and you're not far off—GM's version of Zipcar. Perfect for people who want to drive themselves but only need a car for a limited time period. Maven was also ideally suited to the growing ranks of gig economy workers driving in scheduled shifts for companies such as Uber, Instacart, and Door Dash.

Two months later GM took the bold step of investing $500 million in ride-sharing company Lyft, which then had a private market valuation of $5.5 billion. This gave GM a front-row seat for the millennial-powered transition from buying cars to purchasing rides. To GM shareholders, that investment looked expensive until Google put an additional $1 billion into Lyft, which was valued at $11 billion just 21 months later. On paper, GM had doubled its money in under two years.

There are obvious synergies between the Maven and Lyft investments. One of the critical gating factors in Lyft's growth has been its contract drivers' access to reliable, late-model cars like the ones Maven now rents on an hourly basis. GM's balanced portfolio of adjacent internal innovation initiatives and external acquisitions and investment has the company best positioned of the major automotive companies for a digital future.

GM's company-wide commitment to achieving Goliath's Revenge comes straight from the top. In an interview late in 2016 with Business Insider, GM CEO Mary Barra said, "We are in the midst of seeing more change in the next five years than we've seen in the last 50 years." GM is augmenting its decades of institutional knowledge of electrification, autonomy, and sharing with bold bets to bring in entirely new domain-specific skills, business models, technology platforms, supplier ecosystems, routes to market, and customer segments.

GM shareholders have been amply rewarded. Since the beginning of 2016, GM's stock price has increased by nearly 50% and the company now has an enterprise value of over $140 billion. While much remains to be done, GM's progress was recently rewarded by a $2.25 billion vote of confidence from the SoftBank Vision Fund.

But this is not a story about any one company. In industry after industry, a similar trend is unfolding. Established companies of all sizes, and the people who work for them, are taking bold steps to shift from being disrupted to becoming disruptors. They are shifting from a mindset of "Defend the way we do things for as long as possible" or "I just hope I can retire before this really hurts my business" to one of "We need to move aggressively now to leverage our unique capabilities in a way that disrupts the disruptors."

The Six Rules of Goliath's Revenge

Six rules govern how established companies and their teams are adjusting their vision, strategy, and execution to achieve Goliath's Revenge. The eventual split of mind share and market share between established companies and digital disruptors will be governed by how well individual companies respond to these new rules. These new rules will also determine your career prospects as the industry you work in undergoes its digital transformation.

Let us preface the new rules by highlighting that we know you and your company have already taken some steps to deal with digital disruption. You've most likely announced a digital transformation project, hired a big-name chief digital officer, done some digital coinnovation projects with your best customers, or paid a king's ransom to a major technology company to upgrade your IT systems. You might have done all of the above. You are not alone.

Digital disruption is not new. RFID (radio-frequency identification) started changing how packaged consumer goods are inventoried and distributed 15 years ago. Online banking opened the range of competitors in retail banking 20 years ago. Amazon started attacking Borders, Chapters, and Barnes & Noble with its online book sales almost 25 years ago. This has given you enough time to try to address digital disruption and maybe even get frustrated with the modest returns so far on those investments.

We have two bits of good news for you. First, you are not alone. Nearly every company, large or small, in your industry has done what we call the digital head fake—that is, an announcement such as "We get digital" or "We are going online" without enough substance behind it to make a material difference. You are just not that far behind your contemporaries. Second, you can chalk up all of what you've tried to that development of institutional knowledge that GM is seeing such positive returns on now. Think of all those past initiatives as your Newton or EV1—the attempts that may not have succeeded in their own right but are the basis for your long-term success.

So how do you ensure that the majority of your efforts to turn the tables on digital disruptors are successful going forward? We are as impatient as you, so we put the answer right up front. This is a little like going to take the SAT (or your country's standardized test for college admission) with the grading sheet in front of you. Time really is of the essence in refocusing your digital transformation, for both your career and your company. As you read the following six rules, think through which of your current attempts fit within them and which should be stopped or refocused immediately.

Rule 1: Deliver Step-Change Customer Outcomes

A little better than last year is not good enough.

A key lesson from the Davids of Silicon Valley is to aim for what venture capitalists call "10X" customer outcomes—offers that are 10 times better than the status quo. These are the opposite of the "slightly better than last year" improvements that established companies are so good at delivering. Digital disruptors are focused on game-changing customer impact. Tesla designs cars that are radically different than gas-powered ones, Apple and Android smartphones are at least 100 times better than our old Motorola and Nokia cellphones, and Netflix delivers entertainment anywhere you want it while Blockbuster required you to physically go to a store (and pay a big late fee if you didn't return your video soon enough). You get the idea.

Delivering step-change customer outcomes is the first rule for a reason. If you fail to focus on customer outcomes or you aim too low and settle for "a little better" then none of the rules that follow are going to matter.

In Chapter 4, we will give you a tool for innovation portfolio management that will focus you, your team, and your company on delivering these step-change customer outcomes. Cisco and General Electric have implemented versions of it and we believe it can help your business too.

Rule 2: Pursue Big I and Little I Innovation

Innovate both top-down and bottom-up.

John Chambers, the famed CEO of Cisco, talked a lot about the "power of and." It means that sometimes you don't get a choice as you prioritize your innovations. There are times when you might even have to be great at two seemingly contradictory things simultaneously. Achieving Goliath's Revenge requires just such a feat. Established companies have to be great at Big I disruptive innovation as well as Little I incremental improvements.

Big I requires CEO-level big bets, such as the IoT platform Predix at GE Digital or the massive investment in Digital Banking at BBVA. These top-down, bet-the-company innovations need to be governed by a company-wide Big I relay-race approach that ensures they are given every possible chance to succeed. Both financially and politically, established company leaders can only afford a few of these Big I bets, so their hit rate has got to be very high.

Little I is different, but equally important. It taps into the wisdom of crowds to act on opportunities that senior leadership teams may not even perceive exist. Little I empowers employees and installs an institutional innovation culture. General Mills' Lemonade Stand program, the Pfizer Dare to Try initiative, and Adobe's Kickbox process have allowed these companies to make substantial progress in harnessing this bottom-up, every-employee-involved form of innovation.

In Chapter 5, we will show you how to balance Big I and Little I innovation for you and your company.

Rule 3: Use Your Data as Currency

You own your data, so use it.

There was a phrase in the consumption-obsessed days of the 1980s: "He who dies with the most toys wins." Today that might be rewritten as the company with the most data under management wins. Established companies are waking up the real option value of data and the potential for that treasure trove to help them turn the tables on the digital disruptors within their industries. They've learned about the virtuous cycle of data: the more data you have today, the greater your algorithmic advantage tomorrow, and thus the more data you will attract the day after that.

The key is that data is the raw material of both defending your current businesses from digital insurgents and leveraging algorithmic advantages to grow into adjacent markets over time. Data will become your most valuable currency as you seek to deliver the step-change customer outcomes we discussed in Rule 1. Our bet is that you have only a limited idea of your company's full data inventory and virtually no perception of what portion of your data assets are being fully utilized today. We will cover this in more detail in Chapter 2 as we talk through the incumbent's advantage, and in Chapter 6 where we show you how to both safeguard your data from the digital disruptors and put it to work for yourself.

Rule 4: Accelerate through Innovation Networks

Overcome the curse of "not invented here."

As you saw in the GM example, achieving Goliath's Revenge is going to require a more rapid pace of innovation than you or your company are likely capable of today. You need a second gear—one that can translate your current level of investment and effort into innovative offers that deliver step-change customer outcomes.

This second gear requires your company to develop and leverage broad external innovation networks that augment what you and your peers can deliver internally. This means reorienting from "not invented here" and "we know everything" mindsets to one that is welcoming and attractive to external innovators and ventures. It requires the right ecosystem, tools, structure, and funding mechanisms to quickly identify, validate, and spin-in new innovations from outside your company or even outside your industry. Established companies need to couple a venture capital (VC) mindset with their privileged domain knowledge around customer needs and operational systems to drive these early-stage ventures to commercial impact without crushing the butterfly. We will show you how other companies have upshifted to this second gear of innovation in Chapter 7.

Rule 5: Value Talent over Technology

Preemptive skill development pays off.

In the typical company, only 2% of today's workforce fits the emerging needs of digital businesses. If you've made it to Rule 5, then you likely have this sinking feeling that the demand for new skills in areas such as user-experience design, data science, machine learning, robotics, and artificial intelligence (AI) is going to grow much faster than you and your company are ready for. The core technologies of digital transformation are available to every company with a bank account.

The speed at which you integrate your industry domain knowledge with the capabilities of these new digital technologies will be the greatest determinant of your future success. Realizing this, aspiring Goliaths are investing heavily in preemptive skill development and resource recycling. They are valuing new competencies in the areas highlighted above as leading indicators of their companies' future industry power, revenue growth, and margin expansion.

They also realize that what gets measured gets done, so they are resetting the metrics for how they recognize and reward their employees to accelerate the organizational focus on digital innovation. Too much focus on near-term financial metrics is a sure way to discourage the medium- to long-term investments needed in building your company's digital talent base. For some companies, an intermediate step is needed that we call a two-speed organization design. We will cover that in detail in Chapter 8.

Rule 6: Reframe Your Purpose

Have the guts to stay focused on what really matters.

The paralyzing fear of cannibalizing their current profitable businesses is the single greatest concern of established companies in the digital age. Kodak invented the digital camera but chose not to commercialize it in order to protect its film profit margins. Blockbuster lost out to Netflix by protecting the excess margins it garnered from the late fees its customers hated. The examples are endless.

Established companies turning the tables on digital disruptors are embracing smart cannibalization. They are setting up competing businesses to fully participate in both the old wave and the next one. They are allocating human and financial capital from separate pools to avoid stealing from the future to pay for the present. Doing all this requires these aspiring Goliaths to reframe their mission and to redefine the businesses they are in. They are setting their sights on a broader, more compelling mission that aligns employees, customers, and shareholders while refocusing on the triple bottom line (profits, people, planet).

Without this fundamental reframing of your mission, too many of your peers will simply wait out the digital transformation your company requires, clinging to a mindset of this too shall pass. We will cover this "nothing risked, nothing gained" aspect of Goliath's Revenge in Chapter 9.

How Much Time Have You Got?

It is gut-check time. None of these new rules provides a quick fix independently of the others. For most established companies, achieving Goliath's Revenge is a three-to-five-year journey. Even the most aggressive aspiring Goliaths are typically acting on only a subset of these six rules today. Being honest about where you and your company are relative to these new rules should not feel harsh or critical. It is not a time to round up or to sugar coat the realities of the tectonic shifts impacting your career, company, and industry.

The hard truth is that digital disruptors are waking up every day trying to reset the pecking order of your industry and gain mind share with your most important customers, employees, and shareholders. Only you can answer the question of how much time you and your company have to align with the six rules before your industry's digital disruptors are too powerful to overcome. You are in a foot race whether you realize it or not.

The first step in deciding how much time you have to turn the tables on these digital disruptors is accurately understanding your starting point. Are you and your company ready to achieve long-term success and profitable growth in spite of the digital gyrations impacting your industry? One thing is clear—just working harder to defend the status quo is not a path to success.

While we've only given you a basic introduction to the six rules, it is time for some homework to determine how much time you have and the level of urgency you should feel. Take out two blank sheets of paper and write the six rules down the left side of each one. On the first sheet, grade yourself with an A, B, C, or D based on how well you think you're positioned professionally against the new rules relative to your peer group. On the second sheet repeat the grading exercise, but with your company in mind relative to the emerging competitors in your industry.

Be a tough grader. That is, grade on a C curve, as your best university professors did. If you are average relative to your peer group/industry competitors on a given rule, then assign a mark of C. If you believe you or your company is below average, then assign a D. We will not be giving out any F grades—consider this your midterm assessment, when it is just too early to declare failure. On the other hand, if you think that you are already at the head of the class by all means give yourself an A. A grade of B means that you are above average compared with your peer group but not yet the reference standard.

We will get a lot more scientific with this grading when we get to the detailed discussion of each rule in the chapters ahead. You can then assign your final grades with full knowledge of what the final exam covers. For now, this is your opportunity for a subjective self-assessment. It will provide a baseline for the exercises to come as you work through the remainder of the book.

To help you complete this self-assessment, we have included two examples. Figure 1.2 shows one that individuals can use to assess their careers, using a hypothetical employee of GM named Grace. As with the final credits in movies, any similarity between this Grace and other Graces you may know is purely coincidental.

CAREER SIX RULES MID-TERM REPORT CARD "GRACE" EXAMPLE

Rule #1 Deliver Step-Change Customer Outcomes	**A**	+ Degree in studio art highly valued in new user experience role + Tapped into motivations, preferences of millennial car buyers
Rule #2 Pursue Big I and Little I Innovation	**A**	+ New digital rotation program allowed for rapid skill development + Helped launch car sharing offer and drove internal productivity efforts
Rule #3 Use Your Data as Currency	**D**	− Limited math background may delay promotion potential + Taking online statistics courses through Udacity and Kahn Academy
Rule #4 Accelerate Through Innovation Networks	**B**	+ Denver emerging as a thriving high-tech ecosystem + Proactively building professional relationships beyond automotive
Rule #5 Value Talent Over Technology	**B**	+ Taking online stats course on personal time at Kahn Academy − Had to delay Coding Basics course at Udemy due to travel schedule
Rule #6 Reframe Your Purpose	**C**	− Have been "heads down" working hard to master current role − Still working on balance between professional and personal goals

FIGURE 1.2 Sample Six Rules Career Midterm Report Card

As you can see, Grace has found a way to leverage her background in an entirely new way. It turns out that studying studio art in college positioned her incredibly well as established companies realized how important user experience design is in delivering step-change customer outcomes. On the flip side, Grace is having to address gaps in her skill set by investing personal time in online training courses for the basic statistics and coding capabilities needed to translate her creativity into a work product that her employer, GM, cannot live without. Grace realizes that lifetime employment for her generation is a little like running up a down escalator. It requires a mindset of continual and preemptive skill development.

In Figure 1.3, we have included a sample of how our fictional Grace might assess her employer, GM, against the six rules. Of course, other employees of GM may well assign grades different from our fictional Grace. That is almost certain to happen within your company and is the real point of this part of the exercise. These midterm company-level report cards are meant to spur frank, open discussions between you and your peers on where your company is well positioned to achieve Goliath's Revenge and where there is still work to do.

We have highlighted GM as a case example throughout this chapter because we believe that it is strongly positioned to disrupt the disruptors in the automotive industry over the long term. As you can see in Figure 1.3, that does not mean that GM is above average on all six of our rules. On the contrary, Grace's midterm assessment is that her company has made substantial progress on Rules 2, 4, and 6 but still has significant improvement opportunities for Rules 1, 3, and 5.

It is hard to imagine any established individual or company getting straight As on these assessments at this stage of digital disruption. Take the time now to look back at how you and your company scored on each rule and come up with a rough average across the six rules on each sheet. If your average is a B+ or higher, then you are ahead of your peers

COMPANY SIX RULES MID-TERM REPORT CARD
GENERAL MOTORS EXAMPLE

Rule	Grade	Notes
Rule #1 Deliver Step-Change Customer Outcomes	**C**	+ Delivering no compromises electric cars for the masses − Overall customer experience not yet a breakthrough
Rule #2 Pursue Big I and Little I Innovation	**A**	+ Cumulative experience with electrification allows big bets + Playing both product and business model innovation in parallel
Rule #3 Use Your Data as Currency	**C**	− Fragmented approach to data rights, aggregation, analytics − No machine learning program on full fleet driver telemetry
Rule #4 Accelerate Through Innovation Networks	**A**	+ Many innovation paths: R&D, partnerships, investments, acquisitions + Agile approach to business creation firmly established
Rule #5 Value Talent Over Technology	**B**	+ Used M&A to gain critical mass in autonomous driving skill sets − Still more focused on hardware than software and analytics
Rule #6 Reframe Your Purpose	**A**	+ Bold, clear description of industry evolution and new mission + Putting future customer outcomes at the center of the mission

FIGURE 1.3 Sample Six Rules Company Midterm Report Card

and can take the long-term view in applying the lessons in this book for profitable growth in adjacent markets. Congratulations—you and your company are ready to be the disruptor, not the disrupted.

If your average is a B or B−, then it is time to reallocate your resources in a way that balances the near-term protection of your current business with the medium-term goal of going on the digital offense. You need to put on your strategic bifocals in terms of your professional development and your company execution.

If you averaged a C+ or below, then it is time to ring the alarm bell. You need to immediately develop a clean-sheet action plan and act with urgency to make up for lost time. Your current core business is likely already under threat and your peers are already ahead of you on at least some important dimensions of Goliath's Revenge.

Time to Jump In

Goliath's Revenge is structured around three major questions you need to answer:

1. How will my industry, company, and career be impacted by digital disruption?
2. What steps can I take to position myself and my company for long-term success?
3. How should I prioritize my efforts to get the maximum return with the minimum risk?

Chapter 2 will help you inventory the unique advantages that your company is starting the journey to Goliath's Revenge with. Chapter 3 will help you calibrate the pace of transformation required, given the winner-takes-most dynamics of digital disruption. Each chapter provides real-life examples of other companies across industry sectors that are having success turning the tables on the digital disruptors.

As you think about the future strategy for both your career and your company, a sophisticated understanding of how the digital disruptions are playing out will be essential. In particular, we distinguish digital disruption from other forms of competition and explain why turning the tables on these new attackers should be your number-one priority. That said, if you are the impatient type and already have a thorough grasp of your company's incumbent advantages and digital-related industry shifts then feel free to jump directly to Chapter 4.

Achieving Goliath's Revenge requires coordinated action against each of the six rules we've outlined above. You've completed the first step through the self-assessment of your professional capabilities and experience against each rule. That exercise is like the high school aptitude tests that helped prioritize your college studies and focused your early career aspirations. The next step is for you and your colleagues to have a frank discussion about which of the new rules your company is acting on effectively, which you've collectively swept under the rug, and what needs to be done to better position your organization for Goliath's Revenge.

Chapters 4 through 9 provide the frameworks and models needed for these dispassionate, objective discussions. They prescribe how to apply each new rule in service to accelerating your career trajectory and growing your company through this era of digital disruption. We mentioned that the subjective midterm report card exercise above would get a lot more specific. In each of Chapters 4 through 9, you will find two detailed assessment grids—one for your career and one for your company strategy. Those grids provide an objective calibration of what the grades A, B, C, and D mean within the context of each rule. You will use the grids in two ways—first to level set where you are today and then to prioritize which actions are required to improve your final grade. Both are important as you develop the plan for your career and your company.

The discussion of each new rule also includes detailed case studies to bring the rule to life. Each of the companies featured is emerging as a leader in the race to achieve Goliath's Revenge within its industry. Each is positioned to have the last laugh in the digital-disruption game and is using this period of rapid change to grow their importance, revenues, and profits. These real-world case studies cover a wide range of industries and regions to give you practical examples as you plan your path forward.

We wrap up the book with the structured approach you'll need to align your vision, strategy, and execution for the future. In Chapter 10 we introduce the disruptor's playbook, a framework for the structured execution plan your company will follow in pursuit of Goliath's Revenge. You cannot change everything at once or you risk breaking the business you have. A realistic, pragmatic sequencing of actions will be required. On the other hand, a head fake of broad announcements and top-down initiatives without a cross-functional transformation plan is sure to waste the little time you have before the winners take most in your industry. We include lessons from companies executing disruptor's playbooks so that you can learn from their successes and mistakes.

In Chapter 11 you will build your professional execution plan that prioritizes the new skills, capabilities, and experiences you should invest in now to ensure your long-term career success. Regardless of whether you are a board member, senior executive, middle manager, front-line team leader, or individual contributor, you have an important role to play. It is likely different from the role that has made you successful so far—it may very well feel as if you need to disrupt yourself now for an upside career trajectory later. Industries that have already been disrupted, such as retail and financial services, have demonstrated that waiting for the reskilling plan to come top-down just puts your professional satisfaction and career health at risk.

One particular area of focus in this final part of the book is a recommendation that you and your colleagues embrace what we call smart cannibalization. Sometimes the medicine you need to stay healthy does not taste very good as you swallow it. Smart cannibalization is going to be like that. In any important business decision, risk and reward are inextricably linked. The actions required to achieve Goliath's Revenge and disrupt the disruptors in your industry are no exception. We will arm you with a model of smart cannibalization that will help you reach the efficient frontier of risk versus return. This model will force you to make explicit trade-offs between the risk that your digital transformation will prove to be too slow and the risk that going fast will negatively impact the near-term profitability of your core business.

So pause the social media for a bit, learn the lessons in the chapters ahead, invest time in the exercises that help you apply the new rules to your unique situation, and plot your path for long-term professional and company success. If this seems a little daunting, let us share some good news: you might be better positioned for Goliath's Revenge than you think. It is time to understand the incumbent's advantage.

Chapter 2

The Incumbent's Advantage

"Play to your strengths."

"I haven't got any," said Harry, before he could stop himself.

"Excuse me," growled Moody, "you've got strengths if I say you've got them. Think now. What are you best at?"

—*J. K. Rowling*, Harry Potter and the Goblet of Fire

S pend any time at an industry conference in Silicon Valley and you will be startled by the palpable, sometimes offensive, hubris of the startup culture. You'll hear a lot of "Big companies just don't get it" and "The fast eat the slow for breakfast," backed up with "When one of our people left to go to a big company, the average IQ of both companies went up." Experienced sages will actively be counselling startup CEOs in the hallways to be careful about partnering with big, established industry leaders lest their companies be dumbed down, slowed down, or both.

On the face of it, this can be written off as part fake-it-until-you-make-it bravado and part irrational youthful exuberance. Dig deeper, though, and you can sense the remarkable fragility that is the venture-funded startup. Startups survive one funding round to the next based on what are often subjective assessments made by their investors using metrics such as "eyeballs"—or the even more vague "market traction." Early-stage startup CEOs often spend one-third to one-half of their time raising capital for the next funding round instead of running their businesses.

Your Crown Jewels

As the wizard Alastor Moody implores Harry Potter, it is time to pause and think hard about what you are uniquely good at. Specifically, what are your crown jewels? These are not just any random advantages that are available to you. Crown jewels are assets or capabilities that form the starting point for your company achieving Goliath's Revenge. They are the source of your incumbent's advantage and the foundation for how you and your company are going to shift from defense to offense as the first step in disrupting your industry's digital disruptors. To qualify as a crown jewel, each of these assets or capabilities must pass three tests:

1. **Essential to customer value.** If you asked 10 of your customers whether a given asset or capability is an important part of the reason that they spend their money on your products or services, would eight or more of them say yes?
2. **Uniquely controlled by you.** Are the given assets or capabilities ones that your industry's digital disruptors also possess, or do they differentiate your company from those emerging competitors?
3. **Hard to replicate by others.** Would it take your industry's digital disruptors at least a year to copy those assets or capabilities, thereby providing you with enough runway to put them to work?

Defining your specific crown jewels is going to require an honest self-assessment. You need to go beyond "What are we good at?" and get to "Why those things matter" to your customers as digital competition reshapes your industry. While any asset or capability is a candidate for your crown jewel inventory, we thought it helpful to give you a starting point.

The established companies that are effectively turning the tables on digital disruptors tend to have crown jewels across multiple areas of their businesses. There are seven areas that we would encourage you to explore as you follow Moody's advice: self-funding innovation, brand reach, existing customer relationships, installed base, data sets, blocking patents, and standards influence.

Now before we jump into a discussion of each of these seven areas, let us highlight one asset that established companies talk a lot about, but which is not inherently valuable on its own: domain knowledge. The problem with domain knowledge is that it hardly ever passes the second test above. If a startup wants some, they can hire a representative set of people from that domain who will gladly bring them an understanding of an industry's value chain, core processes, profit levers, and so forth. Or even cheaper, startups can hire retired experts as consultants to bring this level of understanding. As you will see below, it is the manifestation of domain knowledge as actionable assets or capabilities that creates the incumbent's advantage.

Self-Funding Innovation

Established companies almost always enter the fray of digital disruption with an existing core business that is capable of self-funding at least some of their required innovation investments. The most fortunate companies have multiple core businesses that may be experiencing decelerating growth but are still healthy enough to deliver prodigious free cash flow. This capability of self-funding innovation can be a powerful crown jewel in dealing with digital disruption.

Some examples might help. Microsoft has the massive Office and Windows businesses that have provided the multibillion-dollar cash flow needed to compete in the high-growth IaaS (infrastructure-as-a-service) market globally. In fact, Microsoft has made big enough bets early enough to establish itself as a clear market leader alongside Amazon Web Services. Over the past several years, Azure has actually been growing faster than AWS, which is a remarkable feat. Microsoft's self-funding innovation capability has been particularly effective against pure-play attackers such as Rackspace, Equinix, and others that have to rely on the good graces of the capital markets to raise the substantial funding needed to compete in IaaS.

This self-funding innovation crown jewel is demonstrating its power across many other industries. In financial services, Schwab's massive-scale mutual fund business provides the discretionary investment dollars needed to build its own robo-advisor, which is competing effectively against digital disruptors Betterment and Wealthfront. Many customers already view Schwab's automated wealth management offering as comparable to those of the pure-play attackers, even though those disruptors had a multiyear head start.

Internationally, Japan-based Hitachi benefits from a broad portfolio of global businesses across diverse sectors of the economy. Hitachi's market leadership across elevators, escalators, water treatment, trains, power generation, grid management solutions, and heavy construction machinery produces over 700 billion yen ($6.3 billion US dollars) in operating income and over 250 billion yen ($2.3 billion US dollars) in free cash flow. This financial strength is enabling Hitachi to accelerate development of its horizontal Internet of Things applications to turn the tables on the dozens of vertical IoT software companies attacking the various industries that Hitachi competes in.

The list goes on. This ability to decouple long-payoff investments that position a company for digital success from a startup's reliance on the next funding round is an underappreciated asset that almost every established company has at its disposal.

Brand Reach

After having the financial strength to self-fund innovation, brand reach comes second in terms of its potency. Brand value is remarkably effective and unexpectedly flexible as a tool for established companies seeking to defend against, and eventually outflank, their industries' digital disruptors.

The key principle is that brand value is much more than just name recognition. The intrinsic value of a company's brand is rooted in that organization's cumulative history of customer promises kept. In an analysis by consultancy Brand Finance, brand value was estimated to be worth $61 billion at Walmart and $82 billion at AT&T. International brand-value leaders include oil and gas company Pemex (valued at $8 billion in Latin America), telecom company Etisalat (worth $8 billion in the Middle East), and consumer electronics player Samsung (valued at $92 billion in Asia).

While startups might garner effusive media mentions as well as high volumes of clicks, follows, and likes related to their latest press releases, few enjoy the persistent brand value that forms part of the incumbent's advantage. Startup brands often suffer from their relatively short operating histories and inconsistent delivery on their customer promises. Some even accumulate negative brand value over time through a growing track record of overpromising and underdelivering.

You may be asking yourself what the difference is between "brand value" and the "brand reach" that we have highlighted as a potential crown jewel for your company. The answer lies in how elastic your brand value is. Do you believe that your cumulative history of customer promises kept will translate into customers giving you the benefit of the doubt as you compete in adjacent markets or launch digital offerings alongside your core business?

Only you can answer that question. If your answer is yes, then you can convert your existing brand value into the incumbent's advantage of brand reach. Your brand value will become a means to that end. Your brand reach will effectively underwrite a new customer promise—an innovation insurance policy, if you will. You will enable your industry's mass market, pragmatist customers to adopt new and innovative solutions without risking the potentially career-limiting mistake of relying on a startup that overpromises and underdelivers.

GE has made great strides in translating its global brand value into brand reach for its digital offerings. GE's services business, in particular, which keeps the world's aircraft engines, MRI machines, power plants, and oil and gas rigs running in some of the harshest environments on the planet, has a multidecade history of delivering on customer promises. As GE sought to grow beyond its traditional remote monitoring and diagnostics offering, its GE Digital branding provided the opportunity to extend its digital footprint within its customer base to new areas like asset performance management and field service automation. It is important to note that this translation of GE brand value into the GE Digital brand reach did not come for free. Starting in 2012, GE made substantial investments across traditional and digital media, in parallel with the launch of its annual Mind + Machines customer conference, to stretch its reputation for promises met to the digital realm.

Existing Customer Relationships

Existing customer relationships are the third potential crown jewel in the incumbent's arsenal. These customer relationships have market-shaping power beyond the brand reach that we have discussed above. In nearly every industry, the cost of acquiring a new customer is three to five times the cost of selling a new offering to an existing customer. This simple math can gradually but irreversibly tip the scales in favor of established companies.

For most digital disruptors, nearly every dollar of revenue growth is coming from selling to new customers, while in established companies of all sizes, new deals within long-established customer relationships account for the majority of revenue growth. From a return-on-sales perspective, the impact of this is profound. The race for long-term industry leadership is more of a marathon than a sprint.

It is relatively easy to sell to the first three-to-five visionary customers in any market. Every industry has a set of known early adopters that implement disruptive innovations before their peers in search of a lasting competitive advantage. Think Goldman Sachs in financial services, Tesco in retail, Disney in entertainment, and Virgin Atlantic in aviation. They may be demanding, but they are also an easy sale for innovative solutions.

The hard part comes when an innovation needs to get past time to market and on to the tougher challenge of time to scale. The first-mover status enjoyed by digital disruptors often fades during the market transition from pre-chasm visionary customers to post-chasm pragmatist ones. The buying criteria and process of these mass-market customers heavily favor established companies.

Mass-market customers simply do not like starting from scratch with companies they do not know. People buy from people. The multiyear, sometimes multidecade, professional relationships between your company's sales representatives and your customers' buyers are much stronger than you give them credit for. You are probably on customers' approved supplier lists with preset payment terms and conditions already in place. Your people that are on-site with customers have likely already cleared whatever background checks and security audits that those customers have in place. They may even have badges that afford them access to customer premises alongside the customer's own employees.

Beyond those more administrative aspects of your existing customer relationships, your people almost certainly have insider knowledge about the unique needs and expectations of your customers. This will be invaluable as your company, organically and through acquisitions, broadens the range of innovative solutions that you can sell back to these long-term customers.

Consumer companies, such as GM, and industrial companies, such as GE, have demonstrated how successful this innovation cross-selling approach can be. GM fully leverages the footprint of its dealer network and the long-standing sales and service relationships it represents to compete with digital disruptors, such as Tesla. GE overlays its industry-specific sales professionals with digital sellers recruited from the technology industry to execute four-legged sales calls as the most effective way to cross-sell digital solutions to existing customers. Even if you are more fast follower than first mover in terms of innovation, don't underestimate the incumbent's advantage of your existing customer relationships.

Installed Base

A powerful derivative of your existing customer relationships is your company's installed base: that is, the total number of assets or services that are in use by your customers. Think of this as the cumulative impact of multiple generations of past product and service innovations. The best candidates for Goliath's Revenge have sophisticated systems to track this installed base and a strong orientation in their innovation programs to bringing more value to it, for both themselves and their customers.

To assess how well you've activated your installed base as a crown jewel, you need to calculate what we call your "digital yield"—that is, your annual digital revenues divided by the cumulative installed base value of your products operating within your customer base. A back-of-the-envelope approximation of your company's installed base value is to multiply your average annual product revenue over the past 5–10 years by your estimate of how long an average customer operates your products before they dispose of them.

So if you are an HVAC contractor with an average annual product revenue of, say, $1 million, and your customers refresh the types of products you sell every 10 years on average, then your estimated installed base value would be $10 million. If you are Apple selling an average of, say, $100 billion worth of iPhones a year and your customers swap out their phones every third year on average, then your estimated installed base value would be $300 billion. You get the point.

Your digital yield is the annual revenue of your digital innovations this year divided by that estimated installed base value. If you are the HVAC contractor offering a remote monitoring and predictive maintenance service to your customers with an annual subscription revenue of $500,000, then your digital yield is 5%. If you are Apple, you could think of your digital yield for the iPhone business as the $12 billion you keep from customers' App Store purchases plus the $30 billion from annual services revenues (including iTunes and iCloud) divided by your $300 billion estimated installed base value, or 14%.

Cisco has long appreciated the incumbent's advantage of its installed base and does an excellent job activating this crown jewel to both defend against digital disruption in its core switching and routing markets and to grow into higher-growth market adjacencies. A decade ago Cisco made substantial investments in developing sophisticated customer installed base management tools, such as Smart Net Total Care. In parallel, Cisco digitized both its customer support and network optimization service offerings. In its core business, Cisco has driven up its digital yield by shifting customer support from break-fix reactive services to fix-before-break proactive ones. To drive customer adoption in adjacent markets, such as TelePresence remote collaboration and Internet of Everything applications, Cisco has innovated new optimization solutions that ready customers' networks for these new workloads based on increasingly granular configuration parameters that are adjusted by Cisco algorithms instead of customers' IT teams.

Whatever your starting point, viewing your installed base as a crown jewel will focus your energy on driving up your digital yield over time. That incumbent's advantage protects your core business today and serves as a springboard for growth into new markets tomorrow.

Data Sets

Data sets might be the least understood but most valuable source of the incumbent's advantage over the long term. Digital disruptors would kill for the chance to gain access to years of granular data about business processes, operations metrics, customer buying patterns, industry return on investment (ROI) models, and the like. In fact, some established companies are unknowingly squandering their potential advantage by openly sharing their data sets with startups for what will prove to be pennies on the dollar.

As AI, machine learning, and bigger data analytics continue to expand their pivotal roles in the operation of entire industries, we will start to think in terms of algorithmic advantage: that is, which company in any given industry has most effectively translated domain knowledge of their markets into computer-based insights that go beyond what a human expert can deliver. Nearly every core business process is fair game for this better-than-expert optimization based on sophisticated algorithms.

In the first wave of digital disruption, a company's algorithmic advantage tended to rely on the efforts of a small, expensive team of data scientists. These water walkers would gather fragmented data from various operational and IT systems, cleanse and normalize that data to make it useful for analytics, and apply statistical, visualization, and analytic approaches to glean insight needles from the data haystack. Early pilots and proofs of concept were promising but, as we will touch on in Chapter 6, scaling this human-driven data science approach has proven challenging.

Future algorithmic advantage will increasingly be developed by machine learning. Computers can aggregate, normalize, and identify patterns in data sets at rates that human data scientists will never match. Preparing for this second wave of algorithmic advantage requires established companies to do a much better job of understanding the inventory of data that they control, putting in place data governance policies and tools to safeguard it, and investing in or partnering for the machine learning capability needed to translate that data from a potential incumbent's advantage into a powerful crown jewel.

The dirty secret of data science is that most established companies have a minimal understanding of the data sets that their businesses produce on a daily basis. Data is likely fragmented across your legacy "systems of record" applications from the likes of SAP, Oracle, or Intuit; your proprietary customer service systems that might be running inside third-party service firms; various spreadsheets that your finance team uses to understand trends in your operations; and emerging "systems of engagement" applications, such as the social media platforms millennial customers favor when engaging with your company.

Companies such as Splunk have grown from relatively small businesses to billion-dollar service providers helping established companies of all sizes aggregate and index their data assets. If you believe that digital solutions will be critical to your future revenue growth and profitability, then you are probably not spending enough today to inventory, harness, and activate the data sets you already control.

Blocking Patents

Another potential area of incumbent's advantage you should consider is intellectual property (IP): specifically, whether your years of past innovation, research, and development have produced what are called "blocking patents," which can buy you the time needed to achieve Goliath's Revenge. Blocking patents provide a time-limited exclusive opportunity for your company to market a given product or execute a specialized business process. The most powerful blocking patents, in terms of their potential for incumbent's advantage, have both few viable workarounds and a significant time period remaining until the protections they afford expire.

We have put this later in the list for a reason—IP protection is often the hardest source of incumbent's advantage to activate. Patents first need to be filed in all of the countries and regions that you compete in. Those patent filings then need to be adjudicated by the respective patent-granting authorities and issued. Finally, the issued patents must be asserted against those who might be infringing on your IP.

This final step almost always requires the threat, and often the reality, of legal action to enforce your blocking patent rights on aggressive competitors seeking to disrupt your core business. Digital attackers, in particular, have tended to take an ask-for-forgiveness-not-permission approach when it comes to IP. Uber's $245 million settlement of Google's lawsuit claiming that Uber infringed on its Waymo self-driving car IP comes to mind.

Blocking patents are not for the faint of heart. They can be highly effective, though. One of this book's authors ran the products businesses for enterprise mobility leader Symbol Technologies (now part of Zebra Technologies) earlier in his career. Symbol's years of R&D on moving laser beams to read barcodes and making rugged mobile computers work in challenging industrial environments resulted in a powerful portfolio of blocking patents. The digital disruption Symbol faced at the time was the transition from printed barcodes to the talking barcodes called RFID tags. Symbol's blocking patents in barcode scanning and enterprise Wi-Fi power management provided the competitive protections, high-margin licensing revenues, and extended time period required for the company to acquire RFID leader Matrics, integrate that team into Symbol's operations, and come to market with next-generation rugged mobile computers that could read both printed barcodes and RFID tags. At least in Symbol's case, blocking patents proved to be the most important source of incumbent's advantage.

Standards Influence

This seventh and final potential source of incumbent's advantage is related to the blocking patent protection we just discussed. Society as a whole is ill prepared for the transition to a digital future. Some skills are being devalued while others are in short supply. Some companies are capturing massive industry power, revenues, and market capitalization, while others are being torn apart after century-long periods of success. With gyrations like these, governments are flexing their muscles to ensure that country-level imperatives are realized, worker safety and financial security are prioritized alongside corporate profits, and consumer privacy is protected in a world where data really is king.

Digital disruptors are rookies at the standards game. At least when they are small, their venture capitalist backers want to spend money only on engineers (people who make things) and sales staff (people who sell things). All other expenses are good candidates for elimination from proposed budgets. This can work to the advantage of the established companies that aspire to Goliath's Revenge. In almost every country, there are both government and industry standards bodies that define and enforce the rules of competition for a given industry.

At a minimum, these rules directly impact the pace at which digital disruption is likely to unfold. Established companies can therefore buy time for their own innovation program to succeed through their direct influence on both emerging government regulations and the self-enforcing rules defined within industry associations. Taken further, these regulations and rules can tip the scales in favor of one innovation or business model over another. That impacts the eventual winners and losers in the race for industry leadership as digital disruption unfolds.

Companies such as Broadcom and Qualcomm are particularly effective at influencing standards for the wireless industry in ways that favor their chips and innovations. In every transition—from 3G to 4G, and now, from 4G to 5G—industry trade groups, such as the Cellular Telecommunications and Internet Association (CTIA), exert a direct influence on which technical capabilities are embedded in the standard and which are left out. CTIA actively lobbies government regulatory bodies, such as the Federal Communications Commission (FCC) in the United States and the Body of European Regulators for Electronic

Communications (BEREC) in the European Union. Both the FCC and BEREC govern critical aspects of success in the wireless industry, including access to spectrum, rules on net neutrality, and various universal service obligations.

Beyond the wireless industry, examples abound of established companies buying time for their innovations to bear fruit through standards influence. Monsanto and DuPont have been adept at securing positive government regulation and fending off negative rules regarding their innovations in genetically modified seeds and foods. Amgen and Genentech have invested vast sums to influence how genetic therapies are approved by the US Food and Drug Administration as well as by other national health regulatory bodies. American cable companies went so far as to create a shared, not-for-profit innovation organization called CableLabs that helped them get DOCSIS—Data Over Cable Service Interface Specification, if you are really interested—accepted as the carrier network standard that gave them a competitive advantage over traditional telecommunications companies.

Regardless of the industry you compete in, don't underestimate the powerful potential of your existing standards influence to sway regulations, rules, conventions, and technical standards in your favor as you turn the tables on digital disruptors.

What Are Your Crown Jewels?

In Chapter 1 we covered the remarkable comeback story of GM. GM is activating multiple crown jewels to utilize its most important sources of incumbent's advantage. First, GM sells over 10 million gas-powered cars annually, providing the financial fuel to self-fund much of the multiyear innovation investment required across electrification, autonomy, and car/ride sharing. In comparison, Tesla sold just 100,000 cars in 2017. That is a 100-to-1 advantage for GM. Second, GM has invested for decades in a global portfolio of brands that are widely recognized in each country where GM competes. Just one of those brands—Chevrolet—is estimated to be worth $12 billion. GM has activated that brand value into brand reach through the Chevy Volt and Chevy Bolt.

Third, GM enjoys significant cost-of-sales leverage due to its extensive dealer network and the ability to cross-sell new electric cars to existing loyal customers. Fourth, GM has a history of investing for digital yield: OnStar dates back to 1996. That is two years before Google even existed. Fifth, in recent years GM has focused more heavily on integrating its data across brands, regions, and operating companies as the basis for both internal productivity and launching new high-growth businesses.

Sixth, in 2016 GM joined with Ford, Honda, Hyundai, and other automotive leaders to pool IP in a way that prevents companies called patent trolls from inhibiting their rapid commercialization of innovation. Finally, GM has been deeply involved in the pacesetting of automotive standards all the way back to when a California government mandate was the catalyst for GM's launch of the EV1. More recently, GM has invested heavily in environmental testing facilities at its Warren Technical Center to demonstrate to regulators that battery-powered vehicles are both safe and reliable in any weather.

Now, we don't expect your company to have an incumbent's advantage in each of the areas we've outlined here. GM is a fairly unique case in that regard. However, you may have additional assets or capabilities with crown jewel potential beyond these seven categories that we have highlighted. Your homework is to identify your potential crown jewels within each area, then score them against the tests above (essential to customer value, uniquely controlled by you, and hard to replicate by others). The ones that pass all three tests represent your basis for incumbent's advantage and your starting point in applying the six rules of Goliath's Revenge.

Chapter 3

Winner Takes Most

Yesterday's home runs don't win today's games.

—*Babe Ruth, baseball player*

W e've now moved on to what you might consider the "bad news" part of "I've got good news and bad news for you." We did not even ask you which one you would prefer first. With your inventory of crown jewels that confer your incumbent's advantage in hand, we feel that you are ready for the tough medicine. The hard reality is that we are heading into an era in which the spoils of innovation are not being distributed evenly, democratically, or (what some might consider) fairly.

The competitive moats that have protected companies, large and small, for decades are being drained month by month, quarter by quarter, and year by year. In parallel, some companies aspiring to Goliath's Revenge are stealing a page from the digital attackers to put in place even stronger and more durable sources of competitive differentiation.

The End of Average

Back in high school we were taught that the most important concept in statistics was the normal distribution. It was a comfortable idea: that the random observations for a given variable tend to be tightly clustered around the average observation, with relatively few outliers below and above that average. As individuals, if we were of average intelligence then we were about as smart as the vast majority of the people we knew. We were "normal" and part of the group. While we might very well have aspired for more, ending up as average was not a particularly uncomfortable place to be. We were living within the nicely symmetrical predigital curve of Figure 3.1.

The uncomfortable part of Figure 3.1 is the right-hand curve—the postdigital one. It is called a skewed barbell distribution—one in which more observations are at the extremes than in the middle and where one hump—the left-hand one in this case—is higher than the other. No matter if you're living in a developed or developing country, that right-hand curve is troubling. You almost certainly know people

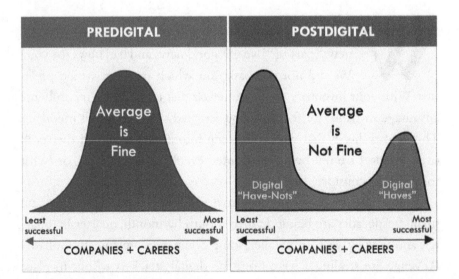

FIGURE 3.1   The End of Average.

who attended good schools, worked hard, and applied themselves, yet still find that the promotions they expected did not come or unemployment snuck up on them in the middle of their careers like a bad cold.

The term "digital divide" has been used to describe the vastly different career trajectories of the digitally savvy employees in the right-hand hump versus the digitally disadvantaged ones in the left-hand hump. The tough math is that only a minority of employees within an industry are on a path to see their career prospects brighten dramatically and their incomes rise rapidly. For every one of those digitally advantaged employees, there are likely to be many of their peers who see their careers prematurely plateau or worse. Many of you are reading this book to figure out what skills to develop now to ensure your long-term position on the right-hand side of that curve.

The digital divide applies to companies as much as to the people that work for them. A few established companies are taking the necessary proactive steps to claim their spot on the right-hand side of that postdigital curve. We will share their stories as we work through the six rules that define the route to that long-term success. The aspiring Goliaths featured in the case studies are already growing their market power and revenues, even if their planned margin expansion is somewhat delayed due to the substantial innovation investments required in the near term.

Unfortunately, most companies are clinging to the hope that "average" will remain a comfortable competitive position going forward. They are hoping that digital disruption will blow over like a summer storm and everyone can just go back to "normal." The hard news is that whole industries are being divided into digital haves and have-nots, with few companies left in the middle. Yesterday's average company is facing the prospect of seeing its industry standing, revenues, and margins diminish over the coming three to five years. Let's look at one industry in which "average" is getting less comfortable every month—retail.

The Retail Industry: A Cautionary Tale

In basketball, there is something called a shot clock. The team with the ball has a maximum of 24 seconds to shoot, or it loses the chance to do so. If you are not the confident type, then it might actually feel good just holding the ball, as that means that the opposing team is not scoring either. However, if you don't shoot, you cannot score. If just holding the ball is your go-to strategy in basketball, then you are not going to be playing for very long.

Online retail is starting to feel like a basketball game in which one team is taking all the shots. Regardless of which industry your company competes in, you should be looking at retail as a cautionary tale. Waiting too long to translate your incumbent's advantage into digital leadership is the sure path to failure. This is the list of major retailers that have gone bankrupt in just the United States between 2015 and 2018: The Limited, American Apparel, Nine West, Quicksilver, Alfred Angelo, PacSun, Payless Shoes, Rockport, Linens 'n Things, A&P, Sports Authority, City Sports, Brookstone, RadioShack, Borders, Gymboree, Toys 'R' Us, Good Time Stores, Vitamin World, and, most recently, Sears. They cover nearly every segment of the retail industry—food, apparel, shoes, electronics, books, toys, entertainment, and sporting equipment.

Globally, venerable retailers such as Eaton's department stores in Canada, Carven in France, and BrightHouse Group, Aquascutum, and Jaeger in the United Kingdom have suffered a similar fate. This gravitational pull toward the left-hand hump of the postdigital barbell distribution in Figure 3.1 is strong. Store-based retailers' collective hesitation to reinvent themselves for a digital future has destroyed substantial shareholder value and dramatically shortened thousands of careers.

So where have all the shoppers gone? That right-hand hump in the postdigital barbell distribution is remarkably concentrated. Read the next sentence slowly. Amazon's e-commerce revenues are almost equal to the total e-commerce revenues of all of the other retailers in the United States put together. Based on data from eMarketer, Amazon represented 49% of all US e-commerce in 2018, up from just 38% two years ago.

Things look even worse in terms of the head-to-head competition that the basketball analogy brings to mind. As shown in Figure 3.2, Amazon is dominating e-commerce Davids and established Goliath retailers alike. The number of logos on the right represents how many of that company you would need to put together in terms of e-commerce revenues to match Amazon.

Amazon is the wake-up call for established companies aspiring for Goliath's Revenge. The retail industry shows what can happen when you and your company are in denial about your core business being under threat or simply hoping to postpone the unpleasant changes required to position your organization for success in a digital future.

This natural reaction to the challenges of digital disruption leads to the dynamic we call "winner takes most." Understanding the forces that concentrate power in the hands of just a few companies is critical as you seek to disrupt your industry's version of Amazon while you still have time.

Don't just hold the ball—run your play and take your shot. If you get behind the curve of innovation and skill development, you will face challenges ad nauseam. Get ahead of it and you will enjoy rewards ad infinitum. Those are the consequences of winner takes most. Let's turn our attention to the most important driver of this winner-takes-most dynamic: the customer expectation ratchet.

The Customer Expectation Ratchet

If you have ever tightened the nut on a bolt, you likely know what a ratchet is—that tool that looks like a wrench but allows motion in only one direction. When you use a ratchet, you hear it click as the hidden

DAVID BECAME GOLIATH IN ONLINE RETAIL

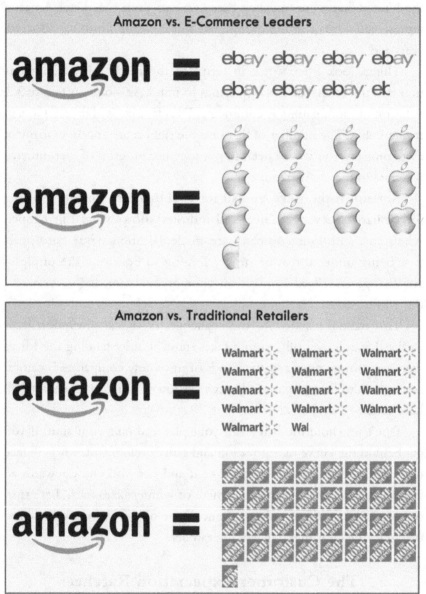

FIGURE 3.2 Winner Takes Most, Retail Edition.

SOURCE: EMARKETER, AMAZON PRIME DAY REPORT, JUNE 2018.

pawl passes from one tooth to another on the gear inside. When the ratchet is moving forward, it is unrestricted and rotates easily. When you twist it backward, the pawl locks into the teeth and prevents motion in that direction.

Customer expectations work the same way. Once you or one of your competitors deliver a step-change customer outcome (which we will talk about in Chapter 4), there is no going back. That click you hear is the start of a race in which all competitors seek to match that new outcome before they lose significant market share.

Now, you might say, "Isn't that just how capitalism works?" Well, yes and no. As long as companies have existed they have played a game of leapfrog, in which competitor A attempts to one-up competitor B and steal that laggard's customers. However, those skirmishes have almost always been fought feature by feature, using the limited arsenal of continual improvement and product innovation. Competitor B could be nicked or bruised but was hardly ever mortally wounded in this corporate equivalent of hand-to-hand combat.

With digital disruption, that polite and honorable competition is giving way to one with much more lethal consequences. The frequency of hard-to-replicate, game-changing customer outcomes being deployed in almost every industry is increasing. Those disruptive customer outcomes are often based as much on business model innovation—redefining the fundamental gives and gets of an industry—as on product innovation.

Blockbuster thought it was in the business of renting DVDs (and collecting late fees), while Netflix reframed the industry purpose as anytime, anywhere entertainment. Kodak got stuck selling high-margin film, while Sony and Samsung were 100% focused on enabling immediate gratification for parents taking digital pictures of their kids. The opening salvo is almost always fired by a digital-from-birth attacker, but the response from your traditional competitors can be just as disruptive to the status quo. As we discussed in Chapter 1, GM has innovated its way into the right-hand hump of the curve and is leading the disruption of the automotive industry alongside companies such as Tesla and Google.

This acceleration of breakthrough innovation has produced a generation of customers with incredibly short attention spans. We all have an innovation version of attention deficit disorder. Customer expectations around price, performance, quality, service, and value are being locked in just like the pawl in the ratchet described above.

Yesterday's continual improvement is today's standard feature. Today's step-change innovation is tomorrow's must-have capability. This customer expectation ratchet is driving the winner-takes-most dynamic in both the consumer and industrial sectors of the economy. Let's focus on one example from each sector.

My Car Gets Better with Age

A car has historically been one of the few products in our lives to age gracefully. In fact, the average car on the road in the United States today is approaching 12 years old. The minor feature improvements introduced by traditional automakers over the past decade have not been sufficiently compelling to get us to trade in our older vehicles. That is about to change.

Tesla is clicking the customer expectation ratchet with dramatic implications for the rest of the automotive industry. Tesla has engineered its technology platform, prioritized the skill set of its team, and aligned its business model with improving the value its cars deliver after you own them. Tesla does this by adding new capabilities to every car it sells through a lifetime of over-the-air software upgrades. These are not just minor bug fixes or modest updates. They are entirely new features you did not think you paid for when you bought the car.

Examples of these new capabilities include hillside brake hold, rain-sensing wipers, automatic emergency braking, home Wi-Fi connectivity, and the "summon" command that allows you to back your empty car out of the garage or a tight parking space using just your phone. All of these new features were delivered as free software updates to cars that did not ship from the factory with those capabilities. Even more impressively, Tesla has made its cars accelerate (from zero to 60 MPH) and decelerate (from 60 to zero MPH) faster solely through software-based acceleration and braking performance upgrades. It is like buying a car with a four-cylinder engine and waking up one morning to it performing like an eight-cylinder one. Talk about business-model innovation! Tesla has rewritten the playbook for what the gives and gets are between car manufacturers and buyers.

This is a revolutionary idea. Seemingly overnight, every three-year-old car that's not a Tesla feels out-of-date—and a five-year-old one seems downright antiquated. Traditional cars miss out on the free performance upgrades and innovative new features that Tesla is delivering every month or two. Even worse, the existing capabilities of traditional cars get a little less wonderful with every day of ownership. The outdated maps and early Windows user interface in the navigation system of your car might be a good example.

"My car gets better with age" is a great example of a step-change customer outcome. Tesla is fundamentally redefining the buying criteria of the automotive industry and every other car company is hearing the click of the customer expectation ratchet. The impact is amplified by the fact that Tesla drivers are a vocal, evangelical bunch. They enjoy sharing their love of that six to eight times per year Christmas morning surprise of new features and performance magically appearing in their cars.

Within five years it will be hard to sell a car that does not have this over-the-air software update capability. Every traditional automaker is facing massive talent gaps in responding to this click in the customer expectation ratchet. As recently as 2015, an estimated 60% of Tesla's technical talent consisted of software engineers, versus just 2% at a traditional car company.[1] That mismatch between skill demand and supply has every established automotive manufacturer playing catch-up. The ones that react fast enough can become the winner in winner takes most.

Our Trains Have Zero Unplanned Downtime

The customer expectation ratchet is impacting the industrial and commercial sectors of the economy in many of the same ways that Tesla is impacting the automotive industry. The ability for equipment to "phone home" through a remote telemetry capability has been quietly built into products as diverse as building HVAC systems, aircraft engines, locomotives, MRI machines, and power-generating gas turbines over the last two decades.

Originally this remote telemetry enabled a one-way flow of data and was used to pull machine configuration parameters, operating status, performance metrics, and sensor data back to a centralized server for tracking and analysis. These systems were traditionally called "remote monitoring and diagnostics," or just RM&D. RM&D solutions tended to focus on just the highest-value machines and often came included with the extended service agreements that customers signed with the manufacturers of their equipment.

More recently, the customer expectation ratchet within these industrial and commercial sectors has clicked twice. First, as the cost of advanced sensors, edge storage, remote networks, and data transmission have come down, industrial and commercial customers have extended this remote machine visibility to their mid- and low-value machines. These include assets such as pumps, valves, controllers, forklifts, and conveyers. This broad proliferation of sensor networks is now bringing end-to-end digital visibility to entire industrial and commercial operating processes instead of just a few expensive machines within them.

With the second click, the one-way data flow has become two-way. The most advanced industrial and commercial equipment manufacturers now enable remote preemptive adjustments to the operating parameters of their machines to help customers avoid unplanned downtime and maximize operating performance. RM&D systems are giving way to sophisticated asset performance management and operations optimization based on massive data analytics and machine learning. These solutions use algorithms to remotely act on customers' enhanced digital visibility instead of just displaying their operations on showy dashboards that don't really do anything.

Both of these clicks in the customer expectation ratchet are happening now in the rail industry. The granularity, frequency, and volume of sensor data on a modern locomotive is remarkable, with over 250 separate sensors producing up to 150,000 data points per minute. Just pause and think about that. A train engineer can work up to a 12-hour shift, meaning that a single train journey can produce up to 108,000,000 data points.

This digital visibility covers everything from weather, location, acceleration, and speed to vibration, temperature, fluid levels, configuration parameters, and operator actions. It is not just the train, or even the locomotive, being monitored. Sensor data is now being captured down to the level of each major subsystem within the locomotive, including systems such as the high-pressure fuel pump, the turbocharger, the brakes, the compressor, and the controller.

All of this data is being constantly incorporated into what GE calls a "digital twin" and Hitachi calls a "digital avatar"—a real-time simulation of the machine within a computer. Some of these data sets are so large that they are stored onboard and are only visible to the railroad operator's remote monitoring systems once the train arrives at a station or service depot with access to Wi-Fi. However, the most important data is now available in real time, via cellular or satellite data transmission.

The second click has radically enhanced customers' ability to manage their trains remotely in real time. The algorithms embedded in their digital twins or avatars are constantly looking for patterns that represent leading indicators of failure. In fact, those algorithms are calculating what is called the "remaining useful life" of every subsystem every day for every locomotive. Historically, these calculations were just used to prioritize the railroad's maintenance activities—when a given locomotive should be serviced, the best depot for that service to be completed at, the additional preventative maintenance that should be completed while the locomotive is in the depot, and the parts that should be prepositioned at the depot to minimize downtime.

The step-change customer outcome in the rail industry is the ability to remotely extend that remaining useful life, at least in the short term. For example, GE's most advanced locomotives can now be de-rated from, say, 4,800 horsepower to a "limp home" mode of, say, 2,400 horsepower when the sensor network identifies an impending maintenance issue that could disable the train. By operating at lower power, the locomotive can buy time to get back to the service depot and avoid blocking a track, which can cost a railroad many thousands of dollars in lost productivity. Trains don't have the luxury of going around obstacles as ships, trucks, and planes can.

Again, we see that one company—GE in this case—is changing the buying criteria of the long-established market for locomotives. These digital solutions that remotely optimize railroad performance are pushing the industry toward a future where trains no longer suffer unplanned downtime. Nearly every industrial and commercial sector has its own GE—a company clicking the customer expectation ratchet in a way that puts its competitors on the defensive and positions itself for the right-hand hump of the winner-takes-most curve.

Why Time Is of the Essence

Let's come back to the competitive shot clock and the discussion of why the wait-and-see approach to dealing with step-change shifts in customer expectations no longer works. Two dynamics favor early movers and penalize complacency: parabolic customer adoption and perpetual algorithmic advantage.

Parabolic Customer Adoption

With incremental innovation, if customer A implements one of your new-and-improved offers this year and customer B implements it next year, there has historically been little difference in the overall financial performance of the two customers. In essence, customer

B got a free option to watch customer A's adoption of the innovation and assess whether it delivered the promised benefits or not. If it did, then customer B could adopt the innovation a year later without any material penalty. If it didn't, then customer B could save the time and investment required to put the innovation to work.

Those incremental innovations tended to gradually seep out through your current and prospective customer base over a long period of time, as depicted by the two lower lines in Figure 3.3.

You might ask, "Why would customer A agree to serve as the industry's guinea pig?" Good question. Remember the concept of visionary customers from Chapter 2? Well, these customers are more than happy to try out unproven innovations on the leading—or even the bleeding—edge. Those three-to-five visionary customers per industry are almost always led by executives who thrive on giving the keynote at their industry's annual conference. Their professional motivation is to claim the glory of having implemented the latest innovation—the corporate

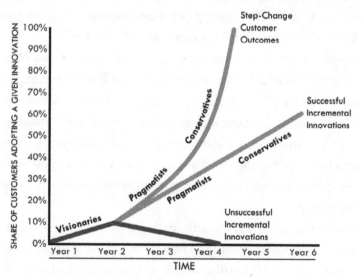

FIGURE 3.3 Incremental Innovation versus Step-Change Customer Outcomes.

version of being the first on your block to get an electric car. Their go-ahead-of-the-herd instinct is as much personal as it is institutional.

An example might help here. Linda Dillman typifies the profile of a powerful, effective, visionary leader within an established company. She was the chief information officer (CIO) at Walmart back in 2004 when the company went big with RFID—the talking barcodes—for case and pallet supply-chain management. Every other retailer did a small pilot, or proof-of-concept, project while carefully studying Walmart's broad production deployment of the then-new innovation. Over a period of 18 to 24 months, it became clear that the financial return to Walmart of the talking barcode, as compared to a paper-based one, was quite modest relative to the cost and risk inherent in the technology at that point.

Sensing this, retailers such as Tesco, Albertsons, Sainsbury's, and Safeway could afford to deploy the new RFID-based systems through a measured approach over a lower-risk timeline. The adoption curve followed the gradual-up-and-to-the-right shaped line of a successful but incremental innovation (the middle line in Figure 3.3). Even a decade later, most packaged consumer goods are still being moved from manufacturers to retailers using paper-based barcodes. It may be another decade or more before RFID systems are fully deployed.

Step-change customer outcomes have a very different adoption profile—one represented by the upper, parabolic line in Figure 3.3. The disruptive impact of combining product and business-model innovation, coupled with the potential to reshape industry profitability, alters the adoption behavior of these pragmatist and conservative customers. Delaying the implementation of a step-change customer outcome is too risky, so these customers shortcut the watch-the-visionary phase and adopt en masse.

Robo-advisors in the wealth management industry are a good example of this rapid, industry-wide adoption of a step-change customer outcome. Traditionally, wealth management had two primary components: a financial advisor who managed an investor's asset allocation (bonds versus stocks versus cash) and a set of investment managers who actually invested the money. A financial advisor for the high-net-worth crowd might alternatively be called a private wealth manager, private banker, or estate planner, but for the rest of us, is more likely to go by the title independent financial advisor or financial planner. An investment manager goes by different titles depending on which types of investments are being managed. The most common is a mutual fund manager, but other titles include venture capitalist, hedge fund manager, private equity general partner, and even the old-school stockbroker.

The investment manager role has been under disruption for two decades because of the ongoing shift from active to passive investing. Passive investments, such as index funds, hold all of the stocks in a given sector—say the S&P 500—and seek to deliver just the market return. Active investments, such as traditional mutual funds, attempt to outperform the overall market by preferring some stocks and not others.

Over the 15 years from 2001 to 2016, 92% of large-capitalization active mutual funds failed to outperform the S&P 500. That means that 9 out of 10 investors that put their money into a large-cap active fund would have made more money if they had just accepted the market return. Over the past decade, even unsophisticated investors have gotten wise to this heads-I-win, tails-you-lose math. Almost one-third of all assets in the United States are now being invested passively through index mutual funds or ETFs (exchange-traded funds). In 2017 alone, US investors pulled nearly $200 billion out of actively-managed US equity funds and added a similar amount to passive stock funds. So the disruption of the investment manager role has generally been following the same path as supply chain RFID—the gradual-up-and-to-the-right shaped (middle) line in Figure 3.3.

It is the financial advisor role that is being disrupted now, and the disruption is following Figure 3.3's top, parabolic line, which represents a step-change customer outcome. A key aspect of success in passive investing is to periodically rebalance your overall portfolio across the various asset classes available—for example, domestic versus international, stocks versus bonds versus cash, and so on. The rebalancing seeks to maintain a fixed percentage of your assets in each of those investment types over time. It has the positive effect of selling small quantities of investments that have increased in value at a high price and buying small quantities of investments that have decreased in value since the last rebalancing at a low one. Financial advisors have traditionally charged retail investors a wrap fee of anywhere from 1.0% to 1.5% of the total value of their investments per year to undertake this systematic rebalancing.

Robo-advisors came into the mainstream with the rise of digital disruptors Betterment and Wealthfront, both founded in 2008 and launched in 2010 and 2012, respectively. These companies systematized this periodic rebalancing activity into algorithms and charge just 0.25% of assets per year to do the work. This savings versus typical financial advisors' fees of about 1% of assets per year might not seem like a step-change customer outcome at first glance. However, the typical long-term returns on a well-balanced retail investment portfolio are 5–6% per year. So, avoiding that extra 1% in financial advisory fees represents about 20% in extra return. That additional 1% in annual return also represents 100–200% of the interest that investors have been getting from their savings accounts these past years.

The response of established financial services industry leaders has been swift. It has followed that (top) parabolic line in Figure 3.3. Within just five years, robo-advisors had been launched by over 100 companies and recently were managing in excess of $220 billion in assets. Together, Betterment and Wealthfront now have an estimated $16 billion of that total, so they have continued to grow. However, the market leaders in robo-advisors are now industry stalwarts Vanguard (with $83 billion in assets under robo-management) and Schwab (with $20 billion). Other established financial services companies have followed their lead. Fidelity now has its digital advisor, Morgan Stanley has its digital investing platform, and TD Ameritrade has its essential portfolios offering.

The financial services industry's fast reaction time in the face of what was clearly a step-change customer outcome eliminated the opportunity for the industry's version of Amazon to achieve a scale that established companies could not compete with. Vanguard, Schwab, Fidelity, and others saw the parabolic customer adoption coming and realized that, left to digital disruptors such as Betterment and Wealthfront, it would produce a winner-takes-most outcome and relegate their wealth management businesses to the digital-have-nots part of the industry.

These established industry leaders took a different approach. They invested heavily in their own product and business-model innovations, delivered competitive robo-advisor offerings quickly, and redeployed headcount from their retail brokerages to capital-market business units. Their willingness to cannibalize their existing asset and wealth management businesses to protect their long-term customer relationships moderated the winner-takes-most dynamic and positioned them for Goliath's Revenge.

Perpetual Algorithmic Advantage

The second major driver of winner-takes-most outcomes is what we call perpetual algorithmic advantage. A mouthful, we know. The short description is that the company in any industry that captures, manages, analyzes, and systematizes the most data today has a substantial and lasting advantage in terms of AI and machine learning tomorrow.

At an extreme, such a scenario can become winner takes almost all, with a duopoly position forming at the hub of an industry. Some would argue that Bloomberg and Reuters enjoy that privileged position in the financial services industry's trader workstation market. Together they collect over $15 billion a year in revenue from financial markets. You would struggle to find a trader on Wall Street, or its equivalent in London, Frankfurt, or Hong Kong, that does not use two, three, or four Bloomberg or Reuters terminals. Many have them both at home and at their desk on their bank's trading floor. A single terminal subscription can cost up to $24,000 a year and there is not really a third-best option.

This same dynamic is playing out in the advertising industry. The predigital version of the industry had a diverse set of companies competing for the advertising dollars of all those potato chips, beer brands, cars, movies, and so forth. Each country had its own three or four major TV networks (ABC, CBS, NBC, and Fox here in the United States) as well as two or three national newspapers (the *Globe and Mail* and the *National Post* in Canada). Advertisers liked it that way. They could play off one form of media against another, and the hungry competitors within each, to lower their cost per impression over time. That has changed in the postdigital era. Google and Facebook now control an estimated 73% of all online ad revenue and are capturing an estimated 83% of the growth in online ad spending. Online advertising has started to look a lot like market data subscriptions on Wall Street: winner takes almost all.

You see this same dynamic playing out across industries. IRI and Nielsen have positioned themselves as the only real game in town for consumer behavior analytics in the packaged goods and retail industries. Equifax, TransUnion, and Experian have their credit scores so deeply embedded in the lending processes of every major US bank that it is highly unlikely a fourth company can compete.

Driving each of these extreme examples of winner takes most is a perpetual algorithmic advantage. That advantage is based on companies in the right-hand hump of the postdigital curve in Figure 3.1 taking three self-reinforcing actions ahead of their industry peers, as illustrated in Figure 3.4.

Preemptively Capture Data

Each company that has secured a perpetual algorithmic advantage made a bold, preemptive move. It invested heavily to capture the maximum volume of data from the broadest set of sources, even if that meant sustaining losses in the near-term.

Back in 1981 Michael Bloomberg founded the company that now bears his name with a reported $10 million severance payment received

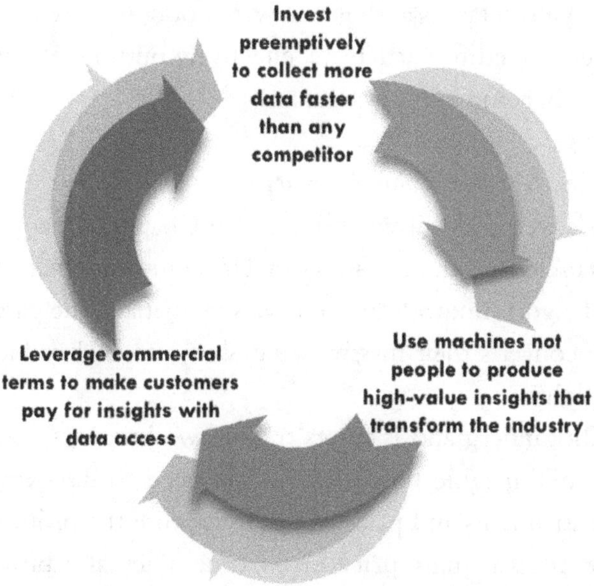

FIGURE 3.4   The Three Steps in Perpetual Algorithmic Advantage.

when his previous employer, Salomon Brothers, was acquired. He used that money to develop a computer-based system for capturing all of the data about stock and bond transactions at a time that no other company had aggregated it all in digital form. That bold bet paid off handsomely, making him a billionaire over time, and eventually, the mayor of New York City.

Similarly, back in the late 1990s Google took on the audacious (and expensive) task of crawling the entire World Wide Web. In fact, the brand "Google" is an altered spelling of the term "googol," which means a 1 followed by 100 zeros. That was the scale of the data that Google sought to capture, analyze, and manage.

Finally, both IRI and Nielsen took an interesting path in their attempt to capture the maximum amount of data possible on consumer purchase patterns. They went to the major retailers with a proposition— a barter of sorts. They asked for access to the raw transaction data from the retailers' point-of-sale machines with a promise that those retailers would get "free" or discounted insights back from the data if they agreed to participate. Most retailers at the time were not doing anything with that data, so they agreed to participate, effectively putting IRI and Nielsen on a path to become industry data hubs.

Use Machines, Not People, for Analytics

As we will cover in detail when we get to Chapter 6, people just can't scale in data science, but machines can. The companies that have secured a perpetual algorithmic advantage have systematized the pattern recognition that converts their massive data assets into high-value, industry-altering insights.

Both Bloomberg and Reuters trading workstations come with all of the prebuilt analytic tools that traders need to discover mispriced financial instruments and place trades to capture the profit that comes from those assets being repriced over time. They also provide a flexible environment in which advanced traders can develop their own computer-based models for the algorithmic trading that seeks to capture even minuscule mispricings that may exist for only milliseconds at a time.

Google was not the first search engine, but it was the first one with two world-beating algorithms. First, PageRank organized the world's information in a unique way. It counted how many other websites linked to a given website. The more links there were, the more valuable that PageRank thought that website might be, and the higher it featured in search results. Google's search results were simply better than those of Infoseek, Yahoo!, AltaVista, and others that were the status quo at that time. Second, AdWords contained an algorithm that effectively auctioned attention online to the highest bidder. The price of your paid link showing up on the right-hand side of the search window was set dynamically based on supply and demand. This AdWords algorithm enabled the business model that is already in the Silicon Valley Hall of Fame—it simply prints money.

Finally, IRI and Nielsen used early data-science tools to develop algorithms such as store catchment analytics and price-elasticity tools.

The former helped retailers answer the question, "How far do shoppers travel to buy at each of my retail locations?" The latter was even more valuable for food and beverage companies in that it answered, "How much volume will my sales of a given product fall if I raise the price by 10%?" Most of those price-elasticity tools were built by human data analysts, but recent ones are increasingly being developed through machine learning tools.

Leverage Commercial Terms to Get Even More Data
The third step is what puts the "perpetual" in perpetual algorithmic advantage and creates the massive returns to scale that these postdigital leaders enjoy today. Unseen in the contracts between these industry-altering companies and their customers are clauses that, at a minimum, reserve the right for the digital disruptor to use details about customers' actions to improve their offerings over time. More broadly, these terms and conditions sometimes allow the disruptor to tap into entirely new pools of data that make the algorithm in question fundamentally more powerful.

As discussed above, this "data for insight barter" was and is a major driver of the success of IRI and Nielsen. While each has additional sources of consumer purchasing data, such as end-customer panels, these cover only a small sample of the overall customer set in any given country. The rights to use the raw purchase data from point-of-sale systems is the basis for both their existing algorithms getting better with time and the development of entirely new algorithms that allow them to charge their packaged goods and retail customers more.

Facebook has done a remarkable, or some would say scary, job of engaging its two-billion-plus social media users in this data barter over time. It has rewritten its terms and conditions dozens of times, defaulted new services to Facebook-friendly user-data permissions, launched new services (such as Messenger) that provide broad new data sources, and acquired companies such as Instagram and WhatsApp to tap into their prodigious stores of granular consumer data. We all know that Facebook is using our data to more finely target the ads it sells to companies that want to sell us products and services. We are generally fine with that given the value Facebook's other algorithms deliver to us as individuals. We see news we might otherwise have missed and connect with long-lost friends we might otherwise have forgotten.

Taken together, these three actions—preemptively capture data; use machines, not people, for analytics; and leverage commercial terms to get even more data—confer the perpetual algorithmic advantage.

This winner-takes-most outcome, driven by parabolic customer adoption and perpetual algorithmic advantage, is why you and your company need to act immediately on the six rules of Goliath's Revenge. Without further ado, let's dig into Rule 1: Deliver step-change customer outcomes.

Note

1. Adam Jonas, *Why Tesla Motors Might Be the World's Most Important Car Company* (Morgan Stanley Research video, 2015).

Chapter 4

Rule 1: Deliver Step-Change Customer Outcomes

I'm actually as proud of many of the things we haven't done as the things we have done. Innovation is saying no to a thousand things.

—Steve Jobs, Apple CEO

We now shift from the descriptive to the prescriptive— from "What is going on?" to "What should I do about it?" If you have done the homework from the first few chapters, then you should have three things in hand: your career and company midterm report card grades for the six rules of Goliath's Revenge (Chapter 1) and the inventory of crown jewels that give your company the incumbent's advantage (Chapter 2). We now turn our attention to what each of these six rules means for how you and your company will navigate digital disruption and carve out your place in that right hump of Figure 3.1's winner-takes-most curve.

The knee-jerk reaction of most established companies when faced with aggressive digital disruptors is "We need to get more innovative." While that is certainly better than being less innovative, it is not very helpful in choosing what areas to focus your career's and your company's innovation strategy on. Every organization, no matter how large, has a fixed amount of energy, talent, and capital to spend on innovation. You must concentrate your efforts on the step-change customer outcome that is most likely to deliver profitable growth for your company and an upward career trajectory for you.

As Steve Jobs so succinctly put it in the quote that opens this chapter, innovation-driven growth is as much about choosing what not to do as it is about going all in on the specific innovations that you ultimately decide to pursue. Under his leadership, Apple evolved from its roots as a niche personal computing innovator to a company that digitally reinvented industry after industry, with its iPod in music, its iPhone in smartphones, and its iPad in tablets. What few appreciate is that the engineering for both the iPhone and iPad was largely completed at the same time in 2007.

Apple had the intestinal fortitude to hold back the iPad for two full years. Jobs had decided that delivering a single step-change customer outcome—transforming your mobile phone from a communications device into the command center of your life—was enough in any two-year period. Apple focused 100% of its innovation energy on building out the applications ecosystem required for the iPhone to deliver on that disruptive customer promise. It eventually launched the iPad in 2010 to much success. Pause and imagine the discipline and confidence that decision to hold the iPad back required. It is a major part of what has made Apple one of the world's most valuable companies.

So, how do you make these pivotal innovation prioritization decisions for your company? What factors should you consider and how can you ensure that others in your organization are aligned with the answers? This chapter will guide you through the three steps needed to have your Apple moment:

1. **Pick a destination.** Define the step-change outcome that has the potential to deliver 10X value for your customers and uniquely leverages your company's incumbent's advantage.
2. **Plan your journey.** Sequence the more near-term, achievable goals in that step-change customer outcome and map them to the four unique buyer personas that occupy the steps in the stairway to value (Figure 4.2).
3. **Get going.** Specify the whole offers at each step of your stairway to value that deliver an important aspect of your step-change customer outcome but at a scale that your current and prospective customers know how to consume.

We will conclude the chapter by finishing the self-assessment that you started in Chapter 1, when you gave yourself midterm grades on how ready your career and company are for each of the six rules. We will give you the answer key for the final exam, at least for Rule 1.

Pick a Destination: Thinking Customer-In

Jim Collins and Jerry Porras introduced the notion of a BHAG—a big, hairy, audacious goal—in their 1994 book called *Built to Last*. Most companies defined their BHAG from an inside-out perspective: that is, an internal financial objective, or worse, a boast about what they were good at. Examples include "We will build a billion-dollar business in stem cell therapies" and "We will enter India and China to double our profitability over the coming five years." Mission statements became all the rage. Some companies even had little plastic cards printed with them to remind employees of the "big purpose" that their employer had chosen for them.

Microsoft's early BHAG was focused on the democratization of computing: "a PC on every desktop and in every home." That step-change customer outcome enabled Microsoft to become the Robin Hood of the tech industry. It aligned all of its innovation efforts with taking an expensive product that was available only to a privileged few and making computing available to nearly everyone.

Google's early BHAG was to "organize the world's information"— a customer outcome that harnessed the Internet's ability to dissemi-nate massive amounts of information with a search engine that could help humans make sense of it all. Tesla's BHAG has always been much broader than any other car company's: "accelerate the world's transition to sustainable energy." This drove Tesla to innovate across cost-effective battery storage systems and rooftop solar arrays, as well as electric cars and supercharger stations. These goals all seemed impossible when Microsoft, Google, and Tesla set their sights on them. However, all were at least partially achieved within the first 7 to 10 years after they were committed to.

While the examples above focus on step-change outcomes for con-sumers, other companies are using the same approach to put their organi-zations in service to the problems faced by entire industries. Japan-based Hitachi is a great example, with a step-change outcome centered on "digital solutions for social innovation." Hitachi is putting in place a big-data and AI capability to allow a global network of thinkers and doers to collaborate on novel solutions to persistent social problems. These social problems span areas as broad as accelerating renewable energy produc-tion, ensuring product quality and safety across increasingly fragmented global supply chains, and delivering on the promise of socially respon-sible urban development.

Whether your company sells to consumers or to other companies, it is time to set aside your dusty inside-out mission statement about the new revenues and profits you want to capture. Think customer-in and define in 10 words or less what your BHAG should be. This first step in your journey to Goliath's Revenge will likely guide your innovation investments for a decade or more, so take some time to get it right. You need to answer two fundamental questions:

1. What big, hairy, audacious customer problem is your company in service to?
2. Why are you uniquely qualified to solve that problem?

It would be reasonable to ask, "Just how big, hairy, and audacious should you be?" Well, you are searching for a customer outcome that has 10X potential. By this we mean an outcome in which customers perceive 10 dollars in value for every one dollar they spend on your product, service, or solution. In business-to-business markets, measuring customer value is straightforward, as nearly every B2B industry ultimately prioritizes just three value metrics: higher revenues, lower costs, and reduced risk. Your 10X outcome may focus on just one of those metrics—Google's AdWords comes to mind, with its focus on higher revenues through fine-grained targeting of advertisements—or a combination of the three.

In business-to-consumer markets, the definition of customer value varies by industry. In healthcare, it might be measured in terms of patient outcomes, such as lower mortality, fewer side effects, and healthier lives. In media, value may be assessed indirectly in terms of likes, follows, and shares by demographic segment. In the automotive industry, customer value would more likely be determined by subjective consumer perceptions of performance, reliability, quality, and satisfaction.

The key point is that you are aiming for the opposite of "slightly better than last year" or "new and improved." You are raising your sights to define your industry's version of the game-changing customer outcomes that digital disruptors are already investing in. Amazon entered the cloud computing business with the step-change customer outcome of infinitely elastic computing and storage at a time when IBM, HP, Dell, EMC, NetApp, and others were all selling fixed-capacity boxes to corporate data centers. Uber entered the transportation business with the outcome of no longer needing to own a car to get where you want to go. Netflix turned both the network television and movie industries upside down with remarkable entertainment anytime, anywhere, on any device for far less money.

These Davids know how to do 10X. It is embedded in the Silicon Valley culture that many of them were nurtured in. Digital disruptors have the mindset that "If we aim for the moon and end up among the stars, we are still going to be successful." By setting 10X as a goal, they are confident of delivering a step-change outcome in the eyes of their customers and a higher valuation for their shareholders.

Assuming you have three-to-five good candidates for your 10-words-or-fewer step-change customer outcome, it is time to rank them using your crown jewels inventory from Chapter 2. You are not picking a step-change customer outcome for just any company. You are selecting one that your organization is uniquely positioned to deliver. This is the hardest part in applying Rule 1 of Goliath's Revenge—connecting your inside-out sources of incumbent's advantage with an outcome that has the potential for 10X customer value. To help, we have included an assessment grid in Figure 4.1.

Put your top candidates for your step-change customer outcome in the columns on the right. In the first set of rows, assess each outcome against the customer value metrics common to your industry. We have built this grid with the metrics applicable to B2B markets, but if your industry's customers use different metrics, then feel free to change them. Rate each potential step-change customer outcome on a scale of 0 (empty circle) to 4 (fully shaded circle) and calculate an average across the various metrics to get an overall customer value score.

Repeat this exercise for the rows that contain the seven categories of potential crown jewels that you inventoried in Chapter 2. Again, you may only have an incumbent's advantage in three or four of those seven categories. Just eliminate the rows you are not using. Calculate an average again to arrive at an overall score for your crown jewel leverage in each of your potential step-change customer outcomes. The highest ranked step-change outcome is the one that scores highest on both the customer value metrics and the crown jewels leverage (option 2 in Figure 4.1).

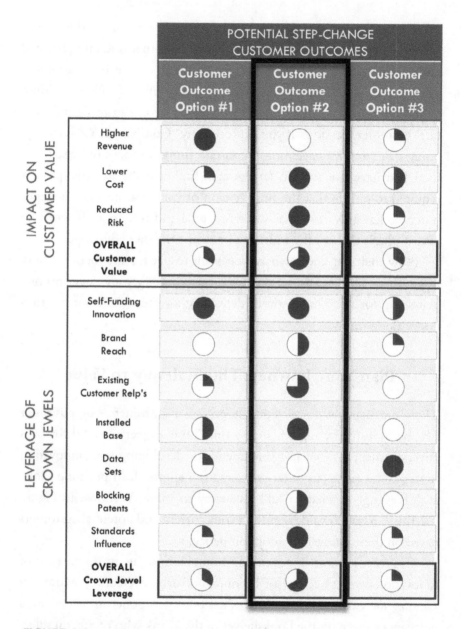

FIGURE 4.1 Step-Change Outcome Ranking Grid.

The final step is to talk to your best customers and get their frank and unfiltered reactions to the step-change customer outcome that you ranked the highest. If you've aimed high enough on the 10X customer-value aspect, then you should get a fifty-fifty mix of "That outcome would be world changing" and "Are you sure you can really pull that off?" customer reactions. If you get too many "Company XYZ is already doing that" or "We have more important things to focus on" reactions, then you have not pushed far enough. Embrace the iterative process required to ensure that the final version of your step-change customer outcome has 10X customer value potential and is a good fit with the crown jewels that are the source of your incumbent's advantage.

Now that you know where you want to get to, let's focus on how to get there. Specifically, we don't want you betting your career on one giant leap for mankind without delivering a series of measurable successes along the way.

Plan Your Journey: The Stairway to Value

There are many ways to segment potential customers—by customer size, by industry, by region, and so on. Those are very helpful for sales coverage mapping, but not very useful for developing your innovation strategy. The right customer segmentation approach in pursuing Goliath's Revenge is what we call a stairway to value. As shown in Figure 4.2, the stairway to value segments your current and potential customers based on their innovation adoption behavior.

One of the most important and durable insights in the history of innovation was conceived of by our good friend Geoffrey Moore in *Crossing the Chasm* back in 1991. That book has gone on to occupy a permanent space on the bookshelves of the who's who of Silicon Valley leaders and is still required reading for anyone trying to understand how customers acquire, deploy, and consume disruptive innovation.

Geoffrey laid out the four unique customer personas that any successful innovation strategy must address. We have summarized those

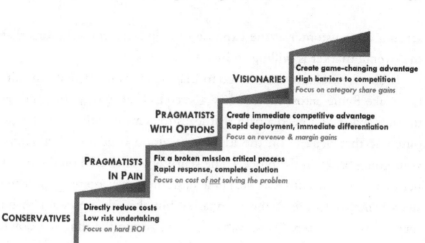

VISIONARIES · Create game-changing advantage
High barriers to competition
Focus on category share gains

PRAGMATISTS
WITH OPTIONS · Create immediate competitive advantage
Rapid deployment, immediate differentiation
Focus on revenue & margin gains

PRAGMATISTS
IN PAIN · Fix a broken mission critical process
Rapid response, complete solution
Focus on cost of not solving the problem

CONSERVATIVES · Directly reduce costs
Low risk undertaking
Focus on hard ROI

FIGURE 4.2 The Stairway to Value.

personas and the related implications for step-change customer out-comes as steps in Figure 4.2's stairway to value.

Visionaries versus Conservatives

Let's start with the top step, where the customer persona that your CEO may have been onstage with at a major industry event resides: the visionary.

As was introduced in the Walmart RFID example, visionar-ies want to adopt a disruptive innovation far ahead of others and have a single purpose in mind—game-changing competitive advan-tage. They are very helpful in uncovering the step-change customer outcome that your organization should aspire to over a three-to-five-year period. They represent the finish line in the winner-takes-most competition. Visionaries can, however, be a remarkable distraction in the near term. At one point, one of your authors had half of his RFID engineering team in Bentonville handhold-ing the deployment of the then-new disruptive innovation in Walmart's labs, distribution centers, and stores. Not a lot of prod-uct development is getting done if you commit to everything a visionary wants years before it can really be delivered. You end up serving one customer at the expense of delivering the solutions that the overall market is willing to invest in.

In short, visionaries want to go to Mars when your current capabilities make flying across the country a stretch. That is why the stairway to value exists. You need a path that leads to achieving the step-change outcome that delivers on the long-term vision over time, but avoids your going broke in the process. The stairway is anchored on the buyer persona called the conservative. These customers may aspire to the same step-change outcome as the visionaries, but they do not want to go there in one big step. Conservatives say, "Give me the slimmed-down version of the disruptive innovation that mere mortals can implement today, delivers a hard-dollar ROI, and gets us ready to step up the stairway over time as the innovation matures."

Pragmatists in Pain versus Pragmatists with Options

Delivering for the buyer personas represented by the middle two steps of the stairway is where you are going to make the most money for your company and gain the most momentum in your career. They are really two flavors of the same persona—the pragmatist. This persona is on the fence—aspiring to the benefits of disruptive innovation but preferring the safety of implementing market-proven innovations. The pragmatist actively seeks out other pragmatists to ask them, "Are you already implementing this innovation?"

On step 2 of the stairway, you'll find the pragmatist in pain. These customers have an immediate need to address a broken, mission-critical process. You do not have to convince them that they are sick, you just have to supply the cure for what ails them. Their fundamental motivation for adopting your disruptive innovation is the avoidance of pain.

The buyer persona on step 3—the pragmatist with options—is primarily motivated by the capture of gain. This persona is similar to the visionary but with a tighter time frame, which is focused on investments that pay off within two to three years. Pragmatists with options want to have their cake and eat it too—they demand rapid deployments and the path to a sustained competitive advantage.

Applying the Stairway to Value: Examples

A couple of examples might help. GE Transportation is using the stairway to value to sequence its digital innovation investments. GE is helping rail industry customers to "connect, digitize, and optimize your entire supply chain." While previous waves of technology investments have addressed point problems, they have resulted in fragmented data sets and islands of automation in the midst of a supply chain that reaches from rail yards to shipping ports to intermodal trucking. GE's step-change customer outcome is audacious in that it seeks to bridge across the end-to-end supply chain in order to optimize the whole path that shipments take. As shown in Figure 4.3, GE has broken this long-term step-change customer outcome down into four sub-outcomes that address each of the buyer personas on the stairway to value.

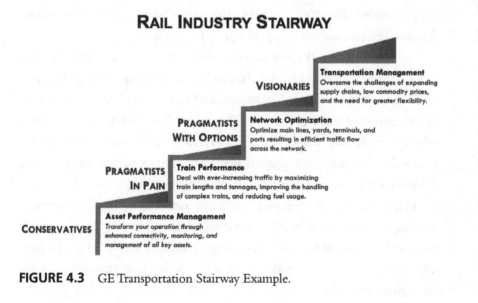

RAIL INDUSTRY STAIRWAY

VISIONARIES
Transportation Management
Overcome the challenges of expanding supply chains, low commodity prices, and the need for greater flexibility.

PRAGMATISTS WITH OPTIONS
Network Optimization
Optimize main lines, yards, terminals, and ports resulting in efficient traffic flow across the network.

PRAGMATISTS IN PAIN
Train Performance
Deal with ever-increasing traffic by maximizing train lengths and tonnages, improving the handling of complex trains, and reducing fuel usage.

CONSERVATIVES
Asset Performance Management
Transform your operation through enhanced connectivity, monitoring, and management of all key assets.

FIGURE 4.3 GE Transportation Stairway Example.

This approach to sequencing the sub-outcomes that lead to delivering a longer-term audacious goal can be applied to a function as much as to an industry. Almost five years ago, a major technology company used the stairway to value to sequence its innovation efforts around the modernization of the IT function for its enterprise customers. The step-change customer outcome that company developed was to help the IT function deliver infinitely elastic computing to its internal, line-of-business customers while fully leveraging corporate data center infrastructure.

At the time, very few IT organizations within established companies had the necessary skills to shift their computing workloads to a public cloud-computing model. These IT teams also knew that most of their data center assets were bought and paid for. This meant that, on a cash basis, an internal data-center-as-a-service offering could actually be cost competitive with even the most aggressive IaaS offering from public cloud vendors such as Amazon, Microsoft, and Google.

These IT organizations wanted to ensure full utilization of their existing data centers while capturing the flexibility, scalability, and financial advantages of cloud computing. This particular technology company committed itself to delivering that step-change customer outcome through the stairway to value shown in Figure 4.4.

As you can see, the visionary customers on the top step wanted the outcome of the dynamic balancing of computing workloads across internal (private) and third-party (public) clouds. With the innovations of the time that was not possible. This technology company prioritized sub-outcomes that could drive near-term success with conservatives, pragmatists in pain, and pragmatists with options as the steps toward delivering the longer-term step-change customer outcome.

Five years later, the top-step customer outcome on that data-center-as-a-service stairway is finally becoming a reality. Through both acquisitions and internal R&D, that technology company has developed a new high-margin, multibillion-dollar business by helping customers climb the stairway to value.

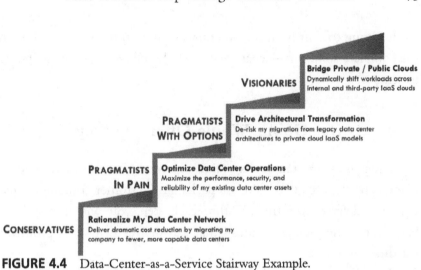

FIGURE 4.4   Data-Center-as-a-Service Stairway Example.

Fit Your BHAG to the Stairway to Value

It is time to break down that BHAG you developed, validated, and refined earlier into the sub-outcomes that fit on the stairway to value. Think hard about the adoption motivation specific to each of the four buyer personas as shown in Figure 4.2. Define a mini version of your overall step-change customer outcome that fits perfectly with each of those motivations, yet still provides a clear path to the top step once your innovations are ready to deliver it.

One important note. On any good stairway, you could almost certainly walk up the steps without focusing your attention on each one. In fact, you could almost walk up with your eyes closed because the treads are all the same height. Your stairway to value should work the same way. Don't build a stairway where one step is tiny and the next one is a giant leap. That will just make your customers stumble—as you yourself might have experienced in the physical world if you've ever walked up mismatched steps. You want your customers to achieve a similar jump in value for each step they take. That will encourage the maximum number of customers to come along on the journey to your promised step-change outcome in the minimum period of time.

It is time to shift from the outcomes your customers want to buy to the complete solutions—what we call whole offers—that you are going to sell.

Get Going: Whole Offers by Step

Each step in your stairway to value represents an intermediate outcome on the road to the step-change customer outcome that you will deliver over time. Within each step, you will now prioritize a set of repeatable solutions that can deliver that step's promised customer outcome.

We call these repeatable solutions "whole offers." The difference between a whole offer and just an offer is that you have thought through every capability the customer requires to secure the outcome the customer wants, whether you provide that capability or not. For the capabilities that you are unable to deliver in the near term, you are going to orchestrate the actions of partners that can fill gaps in your whole offers.

As your Big I and Little I innovation investments that we will cover in Chapter 5 start to bear fruit, you can gradually reduce the role that some of your partners are playing. For now, don't focus too much on which capabilities will be internally delivered through your products, services, innovations, and acquisitions versus which ones will be delivered by a partner through the ecosystem of third parties that you will cultivate.

Let's use the example of Uber. Uber's go-to whole offer is an inexpensive spontaneous private trip from point A to point B—what it calls "uberX." Of course, Uber has many other whole offers—scheduled rides, fancy black cars, multistop rides, UberCHOPPER helicopter trips, and even cheaper rides with strangers called UberPOOL—but uberX is its most frequently purchased one. The critical capabilities that Uber delivers to enable its go-to uberX whole offer include a mobile app that knows where you are, a cloud-based optimization algorithm that matches riders and drivers, and a payment processing system that moves money from you to the driver with a little off the top for Uber itself.

To complete the whole offer, Uber orchestrates a massive ecosystem of drivers who provide the labor to get you from point A to point B along with providers of funding who deliver the capital some drivers need to afford the late-model car that will be your temporary mode of transportation. We are simplifying here, but you get the point. The brilliance of Uber is the whole offer that completely delivers the promised customer outcome—an inexpensive spontaneous private trip from point A to point B—and not just the relatively small portion of the required capabilities that Uber delivers internally.

In the same way that going up the steps is a gradual shift from less to more sophisticated buyer personas, moving left to right within a step is a staged progression from relatively simple to increasingly complex whole offers. As shown in Figure 4.5, you should number the whole offers as "step number dot whole offer number" to keep them straight. For example, whole offer 3.2 will be the second whole offer on step 3 of your stairway.

Start with step 1 and think about the simplest whole offer that your company could deliver now or in a short period of time—six months at

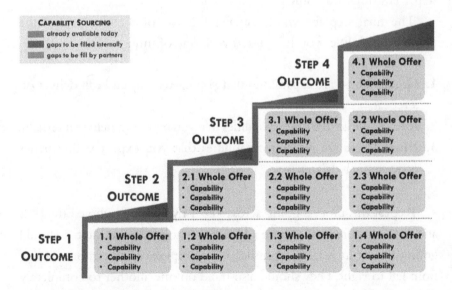

FIGURE 4.5 Whole Offers By Step.

the latest. That will become whole offer 1.1 and will serve two important roles in your Goliath's Revenge strategy. First, it will be the go-to whole offer for customers that are ready to at least go to step 1 now in your stairway to value. That is, it will be your equivalent of Uber's inexpensive spontaneous private trip from point A to point B. It will also demonstrate a quick win to your executives and shareholders as evidence that you've started to turn the tables on your industry's digital disruptors.

For whole offer 1.1, take the time to define the most important capabilities required for customers to obtain an important aspect of that step's promised outcome. Use the Uber example above as a guide. At this stage, you are not trying to define every aspect of the product, service, and business model that your whole offer will include. You are just trying to identify the polestar, or most important capabilities.

On the other hand, make sure you put the "whole" in whole offer. Don't just take whatever product or service you have on the shelf and call that a complete solution. Push yourself and your peers to work customer-in. Identify the most important capabilities that a customer with the conservative buyer persona requires to obtain the promised step 1 customer outcome.

The final step for whole offer 1.1 is to color code each of the polestar capabilities you have listed with one of three colors:

1. **Green.** These are capabilities that you have today and can deliver on a repeatable basis.
2. **Red.** These are missing capabilities that you expect to deliver internally.
3. **Blue.** These are missing capabilities that you expect your partner ecosystem to deliver.

Repeat this process going across step 1 by defining whole offers 1.2 and 1.3, at a minimum. Those additional whole offers on step 1 should go in order of increasing sophistication, complexity, and customer value from left to right. They should also build on one another to completely deliver the customer outcome you defined for that step. Taken together, your step 1 whole offers represent a gradual way for customers with the conservative buyer persona to consume your innovation over time.

Undertake the same work for steps 2, 3, and 4 to specify the whole offers that will deliver promised customer outcomes for the pragmatists in pain, pragmatists with options, and visionary buyer personas, respectively. If you get stuck, go back to Figure 4.2, which lays out the motivations of each of those personas.

You can expect that the number of whole offers per step is likely to decrease as you climb the stairway to value. That is a consequence of the buyer personas represented by steps 3 and 4 being more aspirational than the more immediately actionable ones located on steps 1 and 2. It is also likely that you are going to have a lot more red and blue color-coded capabilities for the whole offers you specify near the top of the stairway. That is just a reflection of your internal readiness to deliver on the more advanced customer outcomes that those higher steps represent.

Once you have a draft of your version of Figure 4.5, it is time for your second round of customer validation. Reach out again to your most trusted customers who have a vested interest in your company's success and will give you unvarnished feedback on your draft set of whole offers by step. Use these interactions to identify the additional whole offers that customers will require to achieve the step-specific outcomes. Also, spend some time to understand the additional capabilities needed within each whole offer that you might have missed.

Once you have completed this second wave of customer validation, you are ready to move on to Rule 2: Pursue Big I and Little I Innovation. All of those red-colored capabilities are candidates for your near-term innovation investments.

Rule 1: Company and Career Readiness

Before you jump to Rule 2, let's pause to complete the more objective version of the report cards you worked on at the start of the book. Remember that we said that those report cards represented just midterm assessments of your company and career grades against the six rules? Well, it is time to see how ready you really are for Rule 1. Figure 4.6 shows an example of what output from the Rule 1 self-assessment effort detailed below might look like.

As you can see, we've gone from the simple midterm grading of A, B, C, and D to something more sophisticated. Each new rule chapter will end with two calibration grids that will help you fill in the bars shown on Figure 4.6 accurately.

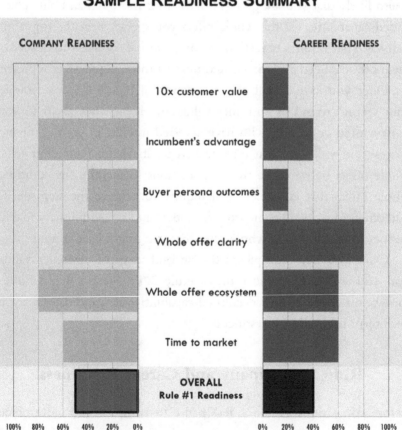

RULE #1: STEP-CHANGE CUSTOMER OUTCOMES SAMPLE READINESS SUMMARY

COMPANY READINESS   **CAREER READINESS**

10x customer value

Incumbent's advantage

Buyer persona outcomes

Whole offer clarity

Whole offer ecosystem

Time to market

OVERALL
Rule #1 Readiness

100% 80% 60% 40% 20% 0%   0% 20% 40% 60% 80% 100%

FIGURE 4.6 Sample Rule 1 Readiness Summary.

Company Readiness Self-Assessment

Let's start with your company's readiness for Rule 1. Read through the options within each row of the Rule 1 company self-assessment grid shown in Figure 4.7.

As you can see, the cells across each row describe the capabilities a company would have at minimal, limited, moderate, advanced, and world-class performance levels within each of the assessment areas. These

RULE #1: STEP-CHANGE CUSTOMER OUTCOMES COMPANY SELF-ASSESSMENT GRID

	0-20% Minimal Capability	20-40% Limited Capability	40-60% Moderate Capability	60-80% Advanced Capability	80-100% World Class Capability
10X customer value	Outcome value not yet validated with customers	Traditional customer value model with a 3-5 year payback	Differentiated value on two of: higher revenue, lower cost, reduced risk	Differentiated value on three of: higher revenue, lower cost, reduced risk	Customer-validated ROI model showing 10X cash-on-cash returns
Incumbent's advantage	Outcome does not leverage any existing crown jewels	Outcome builds on crown jewels in 1-2 categories	Outcome builds on crown jewels in 3-4 categories	Outcome builds on crown jewels in 5-6 categories	Outcome builds on crown jewels in all 7 categories
Buyer persona outcomes	Overall step-change customer outcome not yet broken down by buyer persona	Outcomes developed for only a subset of the 4 step-specific buyer personas	All 4 step-specific customer outcomes developed but not yet validated	Step-specific outcomes validated with < 10 customers in each of 4 personas	Step-specific outcomes validated with 10+ customers in each of 4 personas
Whole offer clarity	Whole offers specified by step but without detailed capability definitions	Capability definitions in place for 2+ whole offers on each of steps 1 and 2	Capability definitions in place for 2+ whole offers on each of the 4 steps	Build vs. Partner decisions made for capabilities in step 1 and 2 whole offers	Build vs. Partner sourcing clear for every whole offer on every step
Whole offer ecosystem	Whole offer capabilities partners not yet sourced and signed	At least 1 validated partner sourced and signed for Step 1 and 2 whole offers	Multiple validated partners sourced and signed for Step 1 and 2 whole offers	At least 1 validated partner sourced, signed, and trained for all whole offers	Multiple validated partners sourced, signed, and trained for all whole offers
Time to market	1+ whole offer(s) can be in market within 12 months on each of steps 1 and 2	1+ whole offer(s) can be in market within 6 months on each of steps 1 and 2	1+ whole offer(s) already in market on stairway step 1	1+ whole offer(s) already in market on each of steps 1 and 2	1+ whole offer(s) already in market on each of steps 1, 2, 3

| 0% | 20% | 40% | 60% | 80% | 100% |

FIGURE 4.7   Rule 1 Company Self-Assessment Grid.

descriptions will help you complete the self-assessment in an objective way to ensure that your ratings can be compared with those of your peers.

Think through which cell on each row best reflects your company today. There are two ways to complete this exercise. If you prefer an offline approach, use the blank self-assessment grid in Figure 4.7 and circle the one cell in each row that is most representative of your company's current capabilities.

If you would rather work online, go to www.goliathsrevenge.com to complete the interactive self-assessment and receive a complete readiness summary once you get through all six rules. Either way, these self-assessments will form the most important input to your company's disruptor's playbook in Chapter 10.

Career Readiness Self-Assessment

Enough about your company; let's focus on you and your career. Now, these career self-assessment grades are just for your benefit. It is not as if we are naming a valedictorian here and you are under no obligation to share your ratings with others.

These career self-assessments are built to help you plan your professional development. That might include supplemental training courses, lateral job moves, career mentorship programs, and external networking opportunities. Your goal is to close your capability gaps as quickly as possible so that you can reach the world-class performance level shown on the right side of Figure 4.8. We will give you a structured way to think about this professional development plan in Chapter 11.

For now, repeat the exercise you just went through, but with your career in mind. Read through the full grid shown in Figure 4.8 to make sure that you understand the career capability calibration within each of the cells.

As always, resist the urge to round up. Being honest with yourself is the only way to know what your capability gaps are. Again, you can use the blank Rule 1 career grid in Figure 4.8 if you are

RULE #1: STEP-CHANGE CUSTOMER OUTCOMES CAREER SELF-ASSESSMENT GRID

	0-20% Minimal Capability	20-40% Limited Capability	40-60% Moderate Capability	60-80% Advanced Capability	80-100% World Class Capability
10X customer value	Current role and past experience not related to customer value delivery	Indirect role in the company's customer value delivery process	Recognized experience delivering substantial customer value	A past role was an essential part of 10X customer value delivery	Current role is central to delivering the validated 10X customer outcome
Incumbent's advantage	Not involved with any of the crown jewels that support the step-change outcome	On the team related to a crown jewel that supports the step-change outcome	A major contributor to a crown jewel that supports the step-change outcome	The go-to person for a crown jewel that supports the step-change outcome	Played a leadership role on teams related to 2+ crown jewels over time
Buyer persona outcomes	Role does not entail any professional interactions with customers	Support teams that interact with customers but do not do so personally	Could independently qualify a customer as one of the 4 buyer personas	Have professional relationships with customers to enable co-innovation efforts	Have professional relationships with customers in each of the 4 buyer personas
Whole offer clarity	Can add minimal value to the creation of whole offer specifications	Up-to-date with market research on customer needs and current competition	Recognized expert on the unmet needs of customers in each buyer persona	Go-to leader who can specify capability requirements for multiple whole offers	Recognized expert for Build vs. Partner decisions within multiple whole offers
Whole offer ecosystem	Can add minimal value to whole offer partner selection and contracting	Up-to-date with the capabilities of potential whole offer partners	Past experience validating and contracting with whole offer partners	Recognized expert within an important category of whole offer partners	Recognized expert across multiple categories of whole offer partners
Time to market	Minimal training and experience in past time-to-market initiatives	Trained in Agile methodology and co-innovation initiatives	In-demand team member for urgent projects and strategic initiatives	Experienced team leader for urgent projects and strategic initiatives	Recognized companywide for excellence in urgent strategic initiatives

0%   20%   40%   60%   80%   100%

FIGURE 4.8   Rule 1 Career Self-Assessment Grid.

working offline or complete your Rule 1 career self-assessment online at www.goliathsrevenge.com.

One caveat here. Given that some of the concepts introduced in this chapter may be new to you, you may not have had a chance to demonstrate capability in certain rows. If your company executes an innovation strategy that is similar to what we've described in this chapter but uses different terms, feel free to substitute your company's terminology for ours.

Rule 1 Readiness Summary

Now that you've completed both your company and career self-assessments for Rule 1, you can enter your results in the Rule 1 readiness summary shown in Figure 4.9. If you are working online, this readiness summary will be created for you automatically.

It is now time to focus on building those innovative whole offers that will deliver your company's step-change customer outcome. Let's shift our attention to Rule 2: Pursue Big I and Little I Innovation.

FIGURE 4.9   Rule 1 Readiness Summary.

Chapter 5

Rule 2: Pursue Big I and Little I Innovation

Failure is not the opposite of success; it's part of success.

—*Arianna Huffington,* Huffington Post *cofounder*

I f you've put Rule 1 into practice, you now have a clear idea of your step-change customer outcome, stairway to value, and whole offers by step. Now is the time to start delivering on the innovations required for that BHAG while buying time for it to pay off through the continual improvement of your core business.

No company aspiring for Goliath's Revenge gets a free pass. It would be easier if you and your team could focus exclusively on either the future or the present. Unfortunately, that is not the world you live in. Your shareholders, who might be just you in a small company, demand both near-term performance from your core business and long-term, profitable growth in markets beyond it.

Achieving both requires a balanced diet of Big I disruptive innovations and Little I continual improvement—terms we picked up from

Wharton's George Day. Big I changes the game while Little I plays the current game better. Big I and Little I are the two food groups of corporate longevity. To keep your business healthy, ensure that your company takes in a sufficient quantity of each.

This requires focusing on six priorities: differentiate Big I from Little I, nurture a company-wide innovation culture, act fast on Little I ideas, unlock the power of and, launch your venture investment board, and run the Big I relay race.

Differentiate Big I from Little I

Whether you are part of a small, medium, or large company, turning the tables on digital disruptors requires a structured process for putting good ideas to work. As you can see in Figure 5.1, this process starts with a wide funnel that is open to ideas from all sources and that doesn't presuppose the role each might play in your innovation portfolio.

The ideas coming in from the top of your innovation funnel might be from your employees, executives, board members, shareholders,

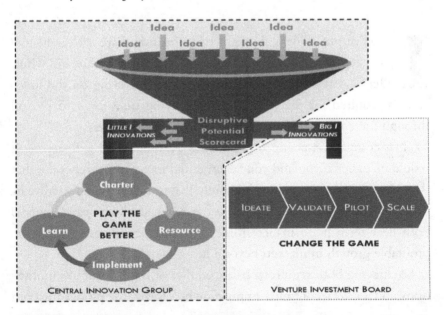

FIGURE 5.1   Channeling Big I and Little I Innovation.

strategic partners, customers, consultants, or startups. It is a mistake to filter ideas in advance. No one in your organization, including your CEO, is smart enough to anticipate every aspect of how your industry is going to evolve, what innovations your competitors may unleash, what new customer segments may emerge, and what unmet needs your customers will value most highly.

While the mouth of your innovation funnel must be wide, it should narrow quickly to concentrate your resources on the ideas with the greatest likelihood of success. The disruptive potential scorecard, shown in Figure 5.2, initiates this choke point.

Think of this scorecard as a repeatable way to separate ideas with Big I disruptive innovation potential from ones that represent continual improvement Little I opportunities. Give each idea in your funnel a yes or no on the five criteria. An idea that gets zero or one yes is pushed to the Little I side of the funnel for evaluation as an incremental improvement by core business stakeholders.

On the other end of the spectrum, an idea that gets two or more yes answers has Big I potential and gets routed through the skinny pipe at the bottom-right of Figure 5.1.

Could the innovation . . .	YES	NO	
Be critical in delivering your step-change customer outcome?	✖		
Produce a crown jewel that adds to your Incumbent's Advantage?	✖		SCORING KEY
Fundamentally redefine the cost structure of your industry?		✖	Zero/One "YES" = Potential Little I
Be a direct threat to your current business model?		✖	Two+ "Yes" = Actionable Big I
Act as your springboard to grow into an adjacent market?	✖		

FIGURE 5.2 Disruptive Potential Scorecard Example.

Don't assume that Big I ideas are more important than Little I ideas. They are equally important components of your balanced innovation portfolio—kind of like having both equities and bonds in your personal investment portfolio. In a bull market, when everything is going right, you would make more money if all of your retirement savings were in equities. However, you will appreciate the inclusion of bonds when the inevitable bear market comes, as they serve to diversify your investments and diminish the overall risk in your portfolio.

Big I is essential for your long-term success but faces two major challenges. First, Big I ideas have a higher risk of failure than Little I ones. That is just the price of being disruptive. In a typical early-stage VC portfolio, seven out of 10 investments are strikeouts wiping out the VC investment, two are base hits that return their invested capital, and one is a home run returning at least 10 times its capital.

Second, there are only a few genuine change-the-game Big I opportunities in a given industry at a time. That is true whether you are a small company or a large one. Current examples include blockchain-based transactions in financial services and the shift from episodic, provider-centric to continuous, patient-centric care in healthcare. The Big I part of your innovation portfolio must overcome both the low hit rate and relative scarcity of Big I ideas.

Little I innovations seek to play the current game better. This may sound as if you've embarrassed yourself with a low goal. You haven't. For every Big I opportunity, there are likely a dozen actionable Little I ideas in your innovation funnel. Each one may have only a modest impact on your business, but it enjoys a high likelihood of success. This combination of large quantity and higher hit rate makes Little I an important balancing aspect of your Goliath's Revenge strategy.

Digital disruptors and startups can afford to be maniacally focused on Big I. However, those startups enjoy none of the incumbent's advantages that you identified in Chapter 2. Channeling both Big I and Little I plays to your strength.

Nurture a Company-wide Innovation Culture

So how can you ensure your innovation funnel is always full of actionable Big I and Little I ideas? The key is making innovation a fundamental part of your company culture, not just a slogan printed on the wall near the employee entrance. We will focus on the "who," then the "how."

Your Central Innovation Group

As you can see from the area inside the dashed line in Figure 5.1, your central innovation group is the driver of your end-to-end innovation process. In a large company, this is often a well-funded, global team led by the chief innovation officer, chief digital officer, or head of new ventures. In a midsized company, this may fall under your chief strategy officer or head of corporate development. In the smallest company, this "group" might be how your CEO spends his or her Saturday mornings.

Your central innovation group is charged with empowering every employee to think creatively about how to make your company better. For example, The Weather Channel is constantly testing out new capabilities in its flagship app to increase user engagement and drive click-throughs for IBM's advertising partners. GM is constantly squeezing more fuel efficiency, acceleration, and reliability from their existing vehicle designs. Hitachi is dual-sourcing key components in their equipment to de-risk manufacturing execution and improve margins.

Ideas like these should be streaming in from the front lines of your company daily. They are critical to sustaining the competitiveness of your current business and delivering the profits and talent required to fuel your Big I initiatives.

Expanding Your Innovation Funnel

Think through how to solicit innovative ideas in a way that fits the style and tempo of your organization. You need to implement a formal program, not an ad hoc contest or campaign.

As you will see in Chapter 10, our research shows that large companies are better at this than small ones. Our survey results show that 81% of large companies have a formal innovation program in place, versus just 55% of smaller companies. Steal a page from industry leaders such as Pfizer, General Mills, and Adobe to design a program that works for your company.

Pfizer's program, called Dare to Try, is sponsored by its CEO, Ian Read. That top-down commitment makes idea generation a priority for every employee. Dare to Try encourages employees to think big about new product and service offerings. Employees are given access to facilitation, design, and prototyping resources to shape their ideas into investable opportunities.

General Mills uses what it calls "lemonade stands" in its program, which provides market acceleration for new offers through an expedited test-market process. Early exposure to real customers helps kill bad ideas fast, so that substantial marketing can be concentrated on products with market-moving potential. General Mills has seen its average product-development cycle time cut in half.

Adobe's Kickbox program allows employees to run their own experiments and take ideas from concept to reality. Every employee is given an Adobe Kickbox kit with a prepaid credit card, innovation framework, and direct access to senior management. Prioritizing the specific focus areas is left up to the front-line employees closest to the market.

An internal program at a major industrial company generated 187 ideas from 114 individual participants within a single business unit. Twenty-nine of those innovation ideas got to the planning stage, with 12 receiving seed funding. The breadth of that business unit's innovation funnel provided a remarkable diversity of actionable ideas for potential investment.

These examples demonstrate the broad range of systematic innovation programs that can improve the quantity and quality of ideas entering your innovation funnel. Pick the attributes that will work best within your organization, launch your own program, and unlock the idea generation potential of your team, division, or company. Once you get started, reinforce your company-wide innovation culture by acting on ideas, not just identifying them.

Act Fast on Little I Opportunities

Nike has it right—just do it. That should be your mantra when it comes to Little I. These high-volume, incremental-improvement ideas should each have an obvious ROI and rapid financial payback. If these attributes are not immediately clear, then send them back to your innovation funnel for additional refinement.

Put your team's energy into acting on ideas instead of building Excel models or PowerPoint slides about them. Distill each Little I proposal down to the main idea that is most actionable and has the greatest potential business impact—the minimum viable idea, if you will.

Now, just do it. Follow a four-step process to put your Little I ideas to work: charter, resource, implement, and learn.

Step 1: Charter

A charter structures each Little I opportunity around a one-page innovation contract. The innovation contract should include five sections: expected business impact, critical learning objectives, key success metrics, committed talent and capital, and important milestone dates. That's it.

The innovation contract defines the "what" but leaves the "how" open-ended to allow for maximum flexibility and pace. Entrepreneurial leaders do not want to be told how to achieve their goals, so let them figure out the details along the way.

Step 2: Resource

The people best positioned to rethink your current business are the employees closest to the processes and experiences that most need improvement. This means backing up your innovation contracts with some difficult resourcing decisions.

You see, the people who are on the bench and easiest to deploy for a new Little I team are seldom the ones you need. Free up your best and brightest for Little I duty, even if that means additional work from having to backfill them temporarily.

Use your Little I initiatives as an audition of sorts. Identify hidden entrepreneurial leaders and latent technical, financial, process redesign, change management, and project coordination talent.

The right Little I team members work late on exciting ideas, unlock energy in other employees with their vision, and align internal and external resources to get their concept implemented. They are scrappy. They really do more with less.

Step 3: Implement

To implement Little I ideas, maintain a bias for yes. Anyone can find holes in the thinking of scrappy Little I teams. Don't expect them to have an answer for every question or corner-case scenario that you can dream up.

Stay focused on the goal of generating rapid, parallel improvements from the Little I part of the innovation portfolio. Install a monthly checkpoint to ensure your team is on track with the goals laid out in its innovation contract. Adjust the scope, resourcing, and execution as needed to maximize the probability of success.

Step 4: Learn

Every Little I innovation contract will include explicit learning goals. While your initiative leaders should be single-mindedly focused on achieving their objectives, your Little I portfolio serves a broader purpose: building the organizational capacity to turn the tables on your industry's digital disruptors.

This step is the company equivalent of doing yoga to get more flexible. Past success often limits future flexibility. Humans are naturally afraid to mess up what is already working. They are more comfortable doing nothing than trying something new and having it fail.

Including learning goals in every Little I initiative makes it impossible for a team to completely fail. Every team can get partial credit for adding to your company's innovation IQ. Share the lessons learned from every Little I team broadly in order to improve the odds of future teams having success.

With a steady stream of Little I ideas helping your company play the current game better, you have earned the right to change the game. That requires you to embrace the power of and.

Unlock the Power of And

In established companies, the weight of the current business is like the gravity of a large planet. It prevents disruptive innovations from achieving escape velocity. It locks your company into its comfort zone, making you a prime target for digital disruption.

To act on John Chambers' "power of and" that we introduced back in Chapter 1, winning Goliaths must run a two-speed organization model. They must fearlessly pursue Big I innovation independently from their core business at the same time that they are acting on multiple Little I ideas closer to home.

Big I success requires courageous, beyond-the-orbit-of-our-core-business bets. Examples include GM's Maven ride-sharing business, Cisco's TelePresence remote collaboration product, Hitachi's Lumada IoT platform, and BBVA's digital banking suite. However, many otherwise-experienced leaders shy away from these bets.

Our research indicates that there are seven key indicators that define companies with this Big I avoidance syndrome. Which of the following fits your organization?

- Limited market intelligence capacity to anticipate customer needs
- Focused exclusively on incremental operational improvements
- Short-term financial focus prevents longer-term bets

- Minimal executive support for innovation
- Underwhelming incentives for employee innovation
- No centralized innovation team or process in place
- Overly concerned with legal, regulatory, and IP risks

Overcoming Big I avoidance syndrome requires a new decision-making team, called the venture investment board (VIB), and a new innovation process, called the Big I relay race.

Launch Your Venture Investment Board

Compared with the just-do-it bias of Little I ideas, Big I initiatives are highly likely to create tension in the leaders running your core business. To thrive, Big I bets need to be protected from the rest of your company until they are big enough to stand on their own.

Why Big I Initiatives Need Protection

Big I pushes the boundaries with clean-sheet offers, experiences, and business models. It requires investments in unfamiliar technologies, talent, and partnerships. It demands significant human and financial capital up front, with the potential for a substantial but uncertain return later.

As a result, the seasoned operators running your core business are the least likely to support it. At best, they will fight hard to avoid "their" headcount and budget being reallocated to the Big I initiative. One of our partners has a saying: "Cash cows like to drink their own milk." Graphic, we know, but anyone who has spent time inside a medium- to large-sized company understands the analogy.

At worst, insecure leaders in your core business may actively undermine the Big I initiative to preserve their standing in the company. They will hate to see the limelight shift to someone charged with building the future.

What Decisions Can Your VIB Make?

To overcome these organizational antibodies, decision-making, funding, resourcing, coaching, tracking, and portfolio management for your Big I initiatives must be removed from your line-of-business organizational structure. Those responsibilities should be shifted to your new VIB.

The VIB structure replicates the decision-making process of the best VC firms. A diverse group of leaders without core business responsibility makes decisions on which Big I initiatives to undertake, how much human and financial capital to allocate to each, and which venture general manager should lead a given initiative.

On an ongoing basis, your VIB provides air cover to undertake disruptive innovation unfettered by your core business. This could mean allowing a Big I initiative to run in stealth mode until that initiative has made a real breakthrough. It could also mean allowing a Big I initiative to compete directly with your existing businesses.

This smart cannibalization is critical to avoiding the *real* Kodak moment: that is, the point in Kodak's history at which Steven Sasson invented the world's first self-contained digital camera and the company chose not to aggressively commercialize it for fear of hurting its lucrative film business.

Netflix is the example you should follow. Netflix's original business model entailed sending millions of customers DVDs in the mail. To achieve this feat, Netflix built advanced robotic automation into its distribution centers. Soon thereafter, a step-change in the capacity of home Internet service enabled streaming and put Netflix's growing franchise at risk.

Reed Hastings went all in on smart cannibalization. He created an entirely new division of Netflix for streaming that could compete head-on with its current core business. That courageous decision has made Netflix one of the few companies to outcompete Amazon in one of its priority markets.

Who Should Lead Your VIB?

So, who should lead your VIB? Cisco provides a good model. During its most successful period of Big I innovation, Cisco's version of the VIB was called the Emerging Solutions Council. It was led by three extraordinarily talented executives: Chris White, Marthin De Beer, and Bill Ruh.

At the time, Chris White was the head of a dedicated salesforce focused on Cisco's Big I initiatives. Marthin De Beer was the executive in charge of Cisco's in-house incubator—the Emerging Technology Group—in which Big I innovations such as TelePresence, Smart Grid, and Digital Media Systems were developed into businesses. Bill Ruh led Cisco's advanced services business and brought the perspective of how visionary customers were actually putting Big I solutions to work. (Yes, this is the same Bill Ruh who went on to become CEO of GE Digital and invent the Industrial Internet.)

White, De Beer, and Ruh made a formidable team. Together they made decisions that would rival those of many top Silicon Valley venture capitalists and protected Cisco's Big I initiatives from the organizational antibodies that would seek to kill them. If you do not have similar venture-minded leaders available, augment your VIB with outside advisors who can provide a market-in perspective and balance the gravitational pull of your core business.

How Do I Know Our VIB Is Working?

VIBs should be rewarded for beating the odds of failure for disruptive innovation. It is a sobering fact that only 1% of the startups founded in the United States ever make it to $10 million in revenue. Even the best external incubators, such as Y Combinator, get less than 25% of their Big I startups beyond the validation phase to actually scaling up.

The only way for your VIB to consistently beat those long odds is to fully leverage the crown jewels that confer an incumbent's advantage on your Big I initiatives. This is where your VIB must diverge from an external VC firm.

Now that you have a protective decision-making and management structure in place, let's focus on the new process you need to execute: the Big I relay race.

Run the Big I Relay Race

In Olympic relay races, individual runners synchronize their talents to compete as one team. Winning is not only dependent on the performance for each leg, but how well the legs are orchestrated and build toward the final outcome. In the 2012 Summer games, Usain Bolt shattered the 100-meter Olympic record with a time of 9.63 seconds. More amazingly, Bolt's Jamaican team for the 4×100 Relay ran a time of 36.84 seconds. That is about 1.7 seconds faster than if Bolt, the world's fastest man, ran each of the four legs in the relay personally. Athletic synergy at work.

The Big I relay race is much the same. Individual team members might be world class at one of the ideate, validate, pilot, and scale steps shown at the bottom-right corner of Figure 5.1. However, the Big I relay race integrates your entire team to deliver results far greater than the sum of the parts.

Step 1: Ideate

The Big I ideas that make it through your innovation funnel are almost always too high level to be investable opportunities. Refining them to an actionable level of detail is the focus of Step 1. Your relay race team should examine the Big I idea through three lenses: external disruptors, future user experiences, and business model innovation.

For the external disruptor lens, appoint a small team to role play the executive leadership in each of your most-feared competitors or potential new entrants. Have each team build a pro forma crown jewels inventory for its assigned competitor. Now the hard part—develop a high-level strategy for how each competitor could pursue your Big I idea. Use this as input to shape your own Big I plan in a way that out-flanks your competition.

In future user experiences, envision how your disruptive innova-tion could solve the most important customer pain points in your target market. For example, a future banking user experience may not include a branch or even cash and be based solely on cryptocurrencies. Again, adjust your Big I plan to front-load delivery of these breakthrough user experiences.

In business model innovation, identify how your Big I idea could reshape your industry's value chain and economic model. Analyze the baseline economic model of your markets to isolate how and where profits are made today. Identify potential business model shifts that could weaken your competitors, ward off digital disruptors, and favor your company. Build these conclusions into your Big I plan to make sure that your relay race team is actively thinking about how to put the most money into your company's pocket.

Step 2: Validate

Now the real work begins. It is time to direct, de-risk, design, and down-select. For "direct": identify a venture general manager to lead your Big I relay team. We will describe the venture general manager role in detail when we get to Chapter 8. For now, just think "intra-preneur" in residence. Surround this venture general manager with a small Big I founding team whose members are pulled from design, engineering, product management, services, operations, and busi-ness development.

For "de-risk," build a reverse P&L—a powerful tool for surfacing the underlying assumptions and risks of your Big I venture. Start with a standard pro forma P&L that assumes your Big I business achieves success over the coming three to five years. Work backward in each

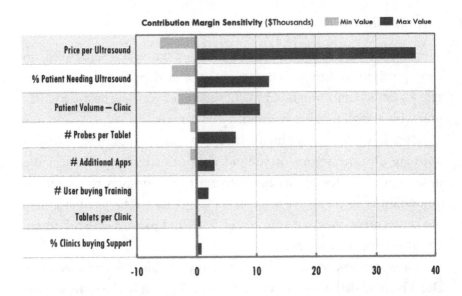

FIGURE 5.3   Reverse P&L Healthcare Example.

area of the P&L to surface the key assumptions around the operating metrics your business needs to demonstrate to deliver the planned financial outcome. See Figure 5.3 for an example of the sensitivity analysis output from a reverse P&L exercise for a breakthrough hand-held medical imaging device.

For "design," conceptualize how your Big I idea is going to work in the real world. Your relay race team should leverage a diverse mix of strategy, user experience, technology, and data science skills to build V0.1 (version 1) of the final innovation. That V0.1 could be a hardware or software mock-up, simulation, video, or basic prototype. In fact, your team should develop five to eight options, if possible, to ensure it is pushing the envelope far enough.

For "down-select," execute your version of the popular TV show *Shark Tank*. It is pitch day. Individual members of your relay race team will present conceptual designs and prototypes to your VIB. By the end of that day, your VIB will have decided on one or two final designs to take forward to step 3.

Step 3: Pilot

They say that no battle plan survives contact with the enemy. Well, no conceptual design survives contact with the market. There is no substitute for launching a rough but useful version of your disruptive innovation with a small number of visionary customers.

Back in Chapter 2 we highlighted how existing customer relationships are a prime source of your incumbent's advantage. Now is the time to pull in a few favors and ask your best customers to try out an innovation at its formative stage. If the Big I idea is targeted at a new market segment, then use your brand reach and partner network to tap into these new customers.

These customers will find big holes in your thinking and execution. Don't be offended or defensive. That data is invaluable if you are to beat the long odds that Big I disruption entails. The earlier you know where your concept is wrong, the easier and cheaper it is to fix it.

Sometimes, using an alternative brand can provide a low-risk piloting opportunity. When Walmart acquired Asda in the United Kingdom, it was able to incubate a disruptive solution for automated click-and-collect stores in Europe. Walmart worked out the kinks there before launching a refined offering in the United States.

Step 4: Scale

It is put-up or shut-up time. Your VIB is going to need to make a go/no-go decision about rolling out your Big I disruption based on incomplete information. This is exactly the situation that the best Silicon Valley venture capitalists face every Monday at their weekly partner meeting.

Your VIB is going to commit substantial human and financial capital on the back of a preproduction solution and some preliminary customer validation. If that worries you, you should not be a member of a VIB.

This is no time for half measures. Either fully fund the Big I relay team with the resources it has requested for scaling up, or shut it down and move on to the next opportunity in your innovation funnel. Too many established companies dilute their scale-up dollars across too many Big I ideas. Don't. Just don't.

Play the game as Steve Jobs did at Apple when he held back the iPad to put all of the company's weight behind launching the iPhone. Act with conviction. All of those Little I incremental innovation successes have bought you the right to make a big play. Don't shortchange yourself and steal defeat from the jaws of victory.

You are now ready to differentiate Big I versus Little I, nurture your company-wide innovative culture, act fast on your best Little I ideas, unlock the power of and, launch your VIB, and run the Big I relay race. That can seem like a lot. Mastercard provides an example showing how to put this methodology into practice.

Mastercard Pursues Both Big I and Little I[1]

Given that commerce and payments are at the forefront of digital disruption, Mastercard knows it can't sit still. Under its Mastercard Labs Group, Mastercard fuels both Big I and Little I opportunities. Its Innovation Management Team runs the company-wide programs that generate, qualify, shape, and develop innovative opportunities.

Employee-led innovation starts with the "Take Initiative" program. During a 48-hour hackathon, employees from around the world take time out of their day jobs to ideate game-changing solutions. The top-scoring teams take part in Idea Box, Mastercard's ongoing innovation program inspired by CEO Ajay Banga's challenge to break down barriers and think out of the box.

Stealing a page from Adobe Kickbox, each selected team gets an Orange Box including a modest prepaid card and 60 days to build their pitch. If it hits the mark with a panel of innovation executives, the team moves to Red Box with a heftier prepaid card to fund development of their prototype over a 90-day timeline.

These teams then pitch their proposed venture to Banga himself for a chance to be selected for a Green Box. This is a "full go," where a selected Big I team becomes a virtual startup within Mastercard Labs and is funded for six months to achieve initial commercial success. The program has already hatched a wide range of new product innovations, and, as importantly, is creating a culture of innovation and an army of innovators across the company.

Stress-Test Your Innovation Program

You may already have a defined innovation program in your company. Take the time to stress test your current program against the following eight best practices that make companies such as Pfizer, General Mills, Adobe, Cisco, and Mastercard so successful:

1. **Talent.** Use nontraditional filters to identify potential intrapreneurs.
2. **Training.** Teach how to turn good ideas into great businesses.
3. **Time.** Allow participants to focus on innovation, even if they are key employees.
4. **Coaching.** Help participants create a solid plan and communicate it clearly.
5. **Friction Free.** Break down organizational silos to maximize the pace of execution.
6. **Transparency.** Share both successes and hard-earned lessons broadly.
7. **Sponsorship.** Ensure executive sponsorship is clear to all.
8. **Advisors.** Bring an outside-in perspective to bear on key decisions.

Few Big I and Little I programs meet all eight of these criteria. For now, just identify where yours is well positioned versus where it needs to be improved.

Rule 2: Company and Career Readiness

So, how do you and your company size up in the pursuit of Big I and Little I innovation? It is time to complete your self-assessments for Rule 2. As with Rule 1, you can complete this exercise using the templates here or go to www.goliathsrevenge.com to use the interactive version.

Company Readiness Self-Assessment

To complete the company readiness self-assessment, read the grid in Figure 5.4 carefully, then place your company in one of the columns for each row.

Try to think of specific examples from your experience about how your company executes on Big I and Little I opportunities today. There are no right or wrong answers, just your honest assessment of how well

RULE #2: PURSUE BIG I AND LITTLE I COMPANY SELF-ASSESSMENT GRID

	0-20% Minimal Capability	20-40% Limited Capability	40-60% Moderate Capability	60-80% Advanced Capability	80-100% World Class Capability
Both Big I and Little I	Innovation, what innovation?	100% focused on Little I incremental improvements	Last Big I idea did not work so we never tried again	80% Little I and 20% Big I innovation portfolio today	50%/50% perfect balance between Little I and Big I
Innovation culture	We are solely focused on running today's business	A dedicated innovation team is in place – that's enough	25%+ of our employees feel engaged in innovation	50%+ of our employees feel engaged in innovation	Every employee is empowered to deliver innovation
Fast action on Little I	Little I initiatives struggle for access to human and financial capital	Little I initiatives are often late in delivering their promised results	Well-honed process in place to expedite execution of Little I improvements	Success across many Little I initiatives has built deep bench of entrepreneurial talent	Taking market and profit share through impact of Little I improvements
Power of And	We do not seem able to balance competing priorities well	Central Innovation Group is in place but has no power to control resourcing	Central Innovation Group manages portfolio effectively across initiatives	Sophisticated risk vs. return metrics used to pursue competing initiatives in parallel	We operate at the "efficient frontier" of innovation portfolio management
Venture Investment Board	No Venture Investment Board in place today	VIB is in place but plays a coordinating role, not a decision making one	VIB prioritizes ideas but relies on BUs for headcount and budget	VIB has internal and external experts plus its own headcount and budget authority	VIB is empowered to compete with our core business as required to grow
Big I Relay Race	Big I ideas follow the same process as any other project in our company	Big I initiatives are allowed to run in "stealth mode" away from core business	Big I initiatives follow a well-defined, test-and-learn methodology	Big I ideas have special rules to allow for rapid execution and risk taking	Big I has CEO-level prerogative to move at Silicon Valley velocity

| 0% | 20% | 40% | 60% | 80% | 100% |

FIGURE 5.4 Rule 2 Company Self-Assessment Grid.

developed your company's capabilities are relative to the benchmarks in each of the cells.

Career Readiness Self-Assessment

Now switch your focus to your own career. Read the grid in Figure 5.5 carefully to understand what each gradient of capability means within each of the six assessment areas.

RULE #2: PURSUE BIG I AND LITTLE I CAREER SELF-ASSESSMENT GRID

	0-20% Minimal Capability	20-40% Limited Capability	40-60% Moderate Capability	60-80% Advanced Capability	80-100% World Class Capability
Both Big I and Little I	Have not been part of any innovation initiative	Was on a continuous improvement team a long time ago	Recognized as a valued Little I initiative team member	Have been a key member of both Little I and Big I teams over time	Have led multiple Little I and Big I initiatives to achieve their goals
Innovation culture	If we have an idea generation program, I am not familiar with it	I know the email alias to send suggestions to but have never done so	Am a regular contributor of improvement and new business ideas	Have received executive recognition as source of successful innovative ideas	Have been asked to lead part of our companywide innovation program
Fast action on Little I	I need to focus on delivering the core commitments of my current role	I am willing to put in extra effort to be part of rapid improvement teams	I am the "go to" person for teams that need to get things done	I have a network across the company that can help push through innovations	I am the benchmark for how to execute innovation with limited resources
Power of And	I focus on one thing at a time and often lose track of other priorities	I am working hard on my time management skills to be able to do more in parallel	I can handle two initiatives in parallel but adding a third one is too much	I am highly productive acting on multiple competing priorities	Have a high tolerance for ambiguity; willing to act in the face of limited information
Venture Investment Board	I did not realize that we had a Venture Investment Board	Was part of a team that made an unsuccessful proposal to our VIB	Was part of a team that gained "GO" approval from our VIB	Have led multiple successful teams that gained "GO" approval from our VIB	Have been asked to be a board-observer on our VIB to represent my group
Big I Relay Race	Have never expressed interest in being part of a Big I initiative team	Am trained in our Big I methodology but have not yet been on a Big I team	Have been a core member of at least one successful Big I team	Have been a team leader on at least one successful Big I team	Have acted as a faculty member within our company's Big I training program

| 0% | 20% | 40% | 60% | 80% | 100% |

FIGURE 5.5 Rule 2 Career Self-Assessment Grid.

Pick the cell in each row that best fits your current career progress toward becoming a powerful Big I and Little I leader. Put your completed Figure 5.5 grid somewhere safe. You will be coming back to it when you get to Chapter 11, which covers how to disrupt yourself for long-term career success.

Rule 2 Readiness Summary

Now that you've completed your company and career self-assessments for Rule 2, you can fill in your readiness summary in Figure 5.6. As with Rule 1, if you are doing the self-assessments online at

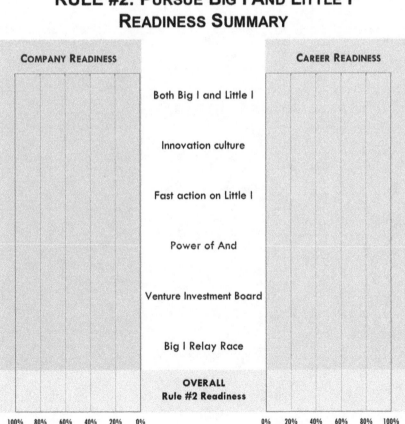

RULE #2: PURSUE BIG I AND LITTLE I READINESS SUMMARY

COMPANY READINESS

CAREER READINESS

Both Big I and Little I

Innovation culture

Fast action on Little I

Power of And

Venture Investment Board

Big I Relay Race

OVERALL
Rule #2 Readiness

100% 80% 60% 40% 20% 0%   0% 20% 40% 60% 80% 100%

FIGURE 5.6 Rule 2 Readiness Summary.

www.goliathsrevenge.com, this readiness summary will be produced for you automatically.

With your self-assessments complete, let's move on to Rule 3: Use your data as currency. This rule covers how analytics, data science, and machine learning can accelerate both Big I and Little I innovations.

Note

1. Deborah Barta (SVP innovation channel management and startup engagement, Mastercard), in an interview with the authors, August 2018.

Chapter 6

Rule 3: Use Your Data as Currency

Data is the new oil. Companies that will win are using math.

—*Kevin Plank, Under Armour CEO*

As the world moves from analog to digital, data is the new currency. Data-rich companies are tapping into vast new revenue streams and profit pools. Data-poor ones are facing diminished market power, industry relevance, and profitability.

Back in Chapter 3 we showed you how securing a perpetual algorithmic advantage drives these winner-takes-most dynamics. Claiming a spot on the right-hand hump (Figure 3.1) of your industry's future profit distribution requires focus across three areas: building your data balance sheet, valuing data optionality, and maximizing return on data.

Those three actions will add a new crown jewel to your arsenal. They will position your company to deliver the step-change customer outcomes you committed to under Rule 1 and accelerate the Big I and Little I innovations you prioritized under Rule 2.

Some Historical Context

Before we jump into how you can treat your data as currency, some historical context is in order. The lasting value of data is what makes the digital age fundamentally different from the industrial age and the agricultural age that preceded it.

During the agricultural age, control over arable land determined economic wealth as hunter-gatherer labor was gradually replaced with mechanized farming. While the Earth has a surface area of about 200 million square miles, just 57 million square miles consist of land and only 12 million square miles are suitable for growing crops. In medieval Europe, control of arable land was the basis of economic power, with lords controlling vast swaths of farmland (fiefs) and serfs exchanging their labor for a lifetime of basic sustenance.

In the industrial age, control of the means of production formed the basis of economic success, with human manufacturing labor gradually being replaced with mechanized assembly lines. Mechanization, automation, and steam power delivered a step-change improvement in the cost of production. Economies of scale and scope, combined with ready sources of investment capital, pulled manufacturing activity into larger and larger plants. The big got much bigger and many smaller manufacturers just went away.

In the digital age, computers, algorithms, and AI use data to augment human effort across virtually every sector of the economy. Let's take two industries you likely know well as examples: entertainment and sports.

Entertainment Goes Left Brain

It used to be that new TV shows were developed by creative people spitballing, or throwing ideas against the wall, then using small test screenings to determine how audiences might respond. The process was long and nondeterministic, with most ideas being discarded along the way.

In the United States, NBC, CBS, ABC, and Fox were happy to have Netflix as a distributor of their content. "We get to reach whole new audiences, what is not to like?", said many a network TV executive. But seemingly overnight, Netflix has become a top-five content producer in direct competition with those established TV networks.

You see, Netflix viewed data as currency, and not just as an asset for its IT organization to manage. Netflix builds shows through a proprietary mix of right-brain creative talent and left-brain machine learning insights. It constantly taps granular data from over 100 million subscribers consuming 250 million hours of video per day to anticipate what content viewers will respond best to. That massive data advantage enables Netflix to produce shows that outperform those from other networks by a factor of two to one.

Moneyball Wins Games

As detailed in Michael Lewis's popular book *Moneyball*, the Oakland Athletics made the Major League Baseball playoffs in the fall of 2003 with an annual payroll of $44 million. For context, the New York Yankees spent $125 million that same year.

Oakland discovered that letting the data speak determined which players should play better than the gut feel of experienced coaches and managers. For baseball purists this was heresy, but the A's came out of nowhere to go from laughingstock to pennant contender.

The Oakland A's organization literally viewed its data as currency. The organization understood that the more games played in the playoffs, the more ticket, merchandise, concession, and TV revenue the team would receive. Once its data showed that on-base and slugging percentages were far better predictors of offensive success than the batting-average and runs-batted-in metrics other teams were using, the A's were not shy about changing how they made lineup and in-game decisions.

Oakland's disruptive innovation altered how every team in Major League Baseball is run. The impact has even been felt in other sports, such as basketball and football, where data science teams are growing in funding, size, and importance.

Just as mechanization substituted for physical labor in the agricultural and industrial ages, data is being substituted for mental labor in the digital age. This is causing every industry to fragment into the data rich and the data poor. Which are you going to be?

Build Your Data Balance Sheet

The core management tenet "What gets measured gets done" makes this first area of focus a critical one. Unless you measure the quantity and quality of data that your company owns outright or has contractual rights to, then you are almost certain to be outflanked by the Davids of Silicon Valley. Those digital disruptors are building their businesses with a data-as-currency mindset.

If your goal is becoming data rich, then the first order of business is building your company's data balance sheet. What data assets does your company control that will allow you to apply data science and machine learning for industry-shaping insights? What data liabilities do you have such that you "owe" data or payments associated with data to third parties? See Figure 6.1 for the data balance sheet that you and your team need to complete.

Let's start with the easy one: the data assets side of the ledger. That is, how much of each type of digital data does your company have at its disposal? You'd think that would be an easy question to answer—just call up your CIO and ask.

Think Broadly about Your Data Assets

In our experience, it is not nearly that simple. Even in a small or mid-sized company, the data sets you're looking to inventory are scattered

DATA ASSETS			
DATA SET	**KEY ATTRIBUTES**	**DATA RIGHTS**	**POTENTIAL VALUE GAINED**
Name	• Source • Size • Location • Owner	• Exclusivity • Limits • Permissions • Regulatory	• Outcome enabler • Big I enabler • Little I enabler
Name	• Source • Size • Location • Owner	• Exclusivity • Limits • Permissions • Regulatory	• Outcome enabler • Big I enabler • Little I enabler
Name	• Source • Size • Location • Owner	• Exclusivity • Limits • Permissions • Regulatory	• Outcome enabler • Big I enabler • Little I enabler

DATA LIABILITIES			
DATA SET	**KEY ATTRIBUTES**	**DATA OBLIGATIONS**	**POTENTIAL VALUE LOST**
Name	• Source • Size • Location • Owner	• To whom? • For what? • By when?	• In data • In insights • In dollars
Name	• Source • Size • Location • Owner	• To whom? • For what? • By when?	• In data • In insights • In dollars
Name	• Source • Size • Location • Owner	• To whom? • For what? • By when?	• In data • In insights • In dollars

FIGURE 6.1 Your Data Balance Sheet.

across disconnected pockets of your business. Beyond the typical data residing in your IT systems, look for data sets that are:

- Known only to some industrial automation guru in one of your manufacturing plants, where the data is "owned" by production operations, not IT
- Buried in a past acquisition that was sponsored by one of your business units and no one talks about anymore
- Part of an RM&D solution within your services business that is monitoring equipment operation at customer sites
- Hidden in the installed base data management tool in your repair depots as part of service entitlement management
- Aggregated in someone else's cloud as part of a SaaS (software as a service) application, such as Salesforce for customer information or Workday for employee data
- On a storage-as-a-service platform, such as Amazon S3 or Microsoft Azure Data Lake, that your marketing team chose for a major customer trial program

- Embedded within the indecipherable log files on your servers that track user behavior across enterprise and Web applications
- Available through your channel, marketing, service, or manufacturing partners as part of your contractual arrangements with them
- Located within the instrumentation of your products themselves, but not yet cataloged, backhauled, and aggregated into a usable form

The list could go on, but you get the picture. You have access to more data assets than you think but have fewer under management than you hoped.

Aspiring Goliaths are increasing their focus on one particular area: data from their customers. For example, Waze enhances its own data sets through granular visibility to the activity of every user of its navigation app. This provides Waze with a cheap way to know the real-time speed of traffic in any market in which it has a critical mass of customers.

John Deere has integrated data from sensors in farmers' fields and equipment to deliver cost-effective predictive maintenance and unlock the potential of precision farming to increase crop yields. The average farm is on its way from generating 190,000 data points per day in 2014 to a projected 4.1 million data points by 2020.

For companies such as Waze and Deere, access to granular customer data presents an enormous opportunity for cocreating new products and services. Ensure that your data asset inventory has sufficient focus on this rich source of potential data rights.

Understand Your Data Liabilities

On the right side of your data balance sheet, you probably have many more data liabilities than you'd expect. For example, you may be licensing data from third parties and incurring either in-cash or in-kind costs. Also, new data security, governance, privacy, and sovereignty regulations, such as GDPR in the European Union, make managing personally identifiable data more expensive and higher risk. In addition to Europe, governments in California, China, and India are becoming increasingly aggressive in this area.

Beyond data licensing and regulatory compliance, you almost certainly have data liabilities to your customers and suppliers in terms of what you can and cannot do with data that comes from your interactions with them. Just as with data assets, it is likely that your management of these data liabilities is far too fragmented today. That is becoming a high-risk approach.

Privacy breaches at brand-name companies, such as Equifax, Target, Saks Fifth Avenue, Panera Bread, Under Armour, and Facebook, have put data privacy front and center in the minds of customers. Companies like these are building high-value, hyperpersonalized experiences around granular, customer-identified data.

If you're estimating the liability side of your data balance sheet, be clear about the true costs of acquiring and protecting that data. Catalog your obligations to be transparent about how data is used and secure the necessary data rights as you undertake your digital transformation. Aspiring Goliaths are pursuing new models of data anonymization and even providing customers with simple self-service portals that allow them to opt in or out at multiple levels of data sharing.

Rate the Quality of Each Data Asset

Now that you have your data balance sheet in place, it is time to rate each data asset in terms of quality. Company after company boasts about how big its big data is. "Our airplane produces multiple terabytes of sensor data per flight." "We can see the condition of every bolt on our oil rigs." "We have information on a hundred million customer purchases."

While size does matter, it is just part of the story. The dirty little secret is that most of that data is unused—what we call "dark data." It is sitting idle for a reason. Most of it is low quality. It lacks the attributes that make it useful in improving your core business and winning in adjacent markets.

Aspiring Goliaths are more sophisticated. They rate the assets on their data balance sheet against seven indicators of data quality:

1. **Freshness.** How recent is the data, and therefore, how predictive is it likely to be when applied to your current products, services, and operations?
2. **Duration.** Does the data cover an extended time period that reflects the normal seasonality and business cycle variations inherent in your business?
3. **Context.** Is the data tagged with metadata that makes the data valuable in understanding an end-to-end business process or customer interaction?
4. **Consistency.** Is each data item collected in a consistent way over time to allow trending and correlation analyses to be run with high statistical validity?
5. **Attributability.** Can the data in question be attributed to specific customers or machines, or has it been de-identified for data privacy reasons?
6. **Reach.** Does your data reach beyond the installed base of your current customers, products, and services to be reflective of your industry as a whole?
7. **Exclusivity.** Do you enjoy exclusive data rights, or is that data available to your current and potential competitors as well?

Pay Special Attention to the Edge

Domo's Data Never Sleeps analysis shows that 2.5 quintillion bytes of data are being produced each day. That is 2,500,000,000,000,000,000 bytes. *Forbes* reports that 90% of the data in the world today was produced in just the past two years. Gartner predicts that by 2022, 75% of enterprise-generated data will be created and processed outside of traditional data centers or cloud infrastructure. That is up from just 10% today.

Most of this data is being produced at the edge—machines, cars, phones, and sensor networks. Little of it is backhauled to traditional

IT systems today. It dwarfs much of the structured data that you've inventoried in your data balance sheet.

A few examples. Self-driving cars harvest massive amounts of sonar, radar, and video sensor data to learn about their environments and make real-time decisions about how to drive safely. Nike has made significant investments to extend its Nike+ platform of connected sneakers and wearables to collect granular data on over seven million runners. Under Armour spent nearly $560 million to acquire MapMyFitness, MyFitnessPal, and Endomondo to access data on 150 million digital fitness users, then launched Healthbox to extend its data collection into health and wellness. In industrial markets, platforms such as GE's Predix and Hitachi's Lumada collect and bring context to massive stores of machine and operational data.

As you finalize your data balance sheet, make sure that you have fully considered the future value of your equivalents of these edge data stores. In a digital future, you may find them more important than the ones you've traditionally run your business on.

Value Data Optionality

The "perpetual" in perpetual algorithmic advantage is based on the fact that more data today means better algorithms tomorrow resulting in more data the day after that. It is a self-reinforcing cycle. The challenge is, how do you get that cycle jump-started?

How can your company gain access to enough data fast enough to secure an algorithmic advantage? It means spending heavily now for a hard-to-model future return and at least some improvement in corporate longevity. It requires your organization to value the second- and third-order effects of assets in your data balance sheet, not just the first-order ones.

Few companies are good at valuing real options when it comes to allocating scarce human and financial capital. CFOs are notorious for bringing a show-me-the-money discipline in the annual planning and budgeting exercises that midsized and larger companies run. They expect a direct linkage between investment decisions today and near-term improvements in orders, revenue, costs, and margins.

This is the antithesis of a future defined by machine learning prowess. Artificial intelligence systems learn by being fed a large quantity of high-quality data over an extended period of time. Anyone who has driven a Tesla on autopilot can attest to this. There are no overnight successes in machine learning.

Aspiring Goliaths value the optionality of data and are willing to invest substantial capital today to secure data assets that will pay off over years or decades. A few saw this opportunity long ago.

As discussed in Chapter 3, in the 1990s, IRI and Nielsen offered sophisticated analytics and reporting to retailers for "free" so that they could aggregate the SKU-level point-of-sale data produced by the retailers' normal checkout process. They each built billion-dollar businesses selling insights based on that data to consumer packaged-goods companies.

In the early 2000s, Microsoft's Hotmail and Google's Gmail both offered "free" email in return for the right to analyze every word you wrote. They sold insights based on those analytics back to advertisers in the form of highly tailored marketing campaigns. Facebook is the modern equivalent.

In the 2010s, Progressive Insurance "paid" for data on individual driver behavior by offering auto insurance discounts and "free" monitoring devices that customers inserted into their cars' diagnostic ports. More recently, Monsanto acquired Precision Planting for $210 million and The Climate Corporation for $930 million to aggregate data on customer use of Monsanto products.

As you will see in Chapter 10, our survey shows that only 12% of large companies and 5% of small ones believe that they are using data extensively to power their innovations. Learning how to value the optionality of data is a critical step in joining that elite group.

Maximize Return on Data

When IBM's Watson beat Ken Jennings on *Jeopardy!* in 2011 and Google's AlphaGo beat Lee Sedol in Go in 2016, it might have seemed trivial at the time. Both are games, after all. However, for those who are part of the AI community, the events were watersheds. They demonstrated that machine learning had made the leap from rapid retrieval of the right information to creating entirely new insights that even the world's best human in those domains could not master.

Your company needs to master machine learning before it masters your industry. A robust data balance sheet and the willingness to grow it by valuing the optionality of data are useless if you cannot turn data into insights and insights into actions. The digital value stack, shown in Figure 6.2, is how you are going to maximize your return on data.

We've already covered the bottom row, so let's focus on the top two: understanding the customers of your digital value stack and the machine learning capability that can turn data into gold.

Digital Customer Segments

Your efforts to maximize your return on data need to focus on four customer segments: internal make-it and sell-it teams, as well as external

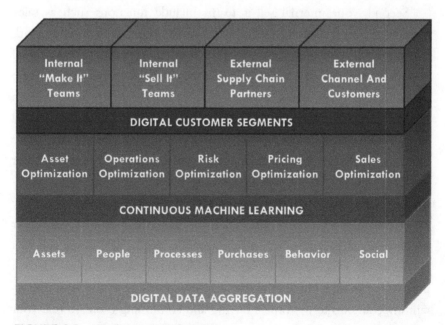

FIGURE 6.2   The Digital Value Stack.

supply chain partners and customers. Just like Watson or AlphaGo, your goal is to augment the expertise of the people in that segment in order to make better decisions faster and more often. You will be shifting your company from fact-free to fact-based operations.

First up are your internal make-it teams, which might work in functions such as product management, design, business incubation, R&D, engineering, manufacturing, and service delivery. They invent, design, develop, produce, and deliver the products and services that your customers purchase. Those teams have the potential to act as both suppliers of new data—by designing additional digital instrumentation into their offers—and consumers of algorithmic insights. Show them which capabilities customers most value and they can stop designing ones that customers do not use. Help them understand the real-life way that customers use your products and they can manufacture them to fail less often and require less service. Identify the unexpected ways that customers want to use your products and services and your make-it teams can dream up entirely new solutions to grow your business.

Second, your internal sell-it teams include functions such as sales, marketing, lead generation, pricing, and distribution channels. They work to extract the maximum gross margin from the maximum number of customers every week, month, and quarter. Show them how to calculate prices that optimize across gross margin percentage and revenue growth rate for maximum gross profit dollars. Help them optimize their digital and traditional marketing spend for lowest cost per converted lead. Enable them to see future demand through the scoring of prospective customer activities—reading white papers, watching videos, subscribing to newsletters, attending webinars—that represent expressions of interest. Give every sales representative the next button that tells them the most likely customer in their assigned accounts to buy and the offer most likely to convert to a profitable sale. Propose get-well actions for end customers that have made a purchase of an offer but have not yet consumed it. Identify the most important impediments to customers buying and consuming more, so that your sell-it teams can design out the commercial friction.

Third, make sure your external supply chain partners can be reached via your procurement and supply chain planning teams. You might ask, "Why would I commit scarce algorithmic resources to help my suppliers?" Well, you are not doing it for free. Companies such as Walmart have become remarkably sophisticated at using data as currency in a literal way with their suppliers. Give them more granular visibility to demand so that they can avoid both excess inventories and out-of-stocks while balancing production in their factories efficiently. Provide them with detailed benchmarks about how their on-time, on-quality, on-quantity performance varies from their peers and what they can do to improve. Help them see through to end customer usage of their products so that they can design them for higher value, reliability, and performance.

Finally, external channel partners and end customers are increasingly dependent on your algorithmic insights. Help your channel partners see the most valuable ways to combine your products and services for maximum commercial velocity. Give your B2B customers visibility to the installed base of your products in their operations at a level of detail their own IT teams cannot match. Enable your best customers to evolve from time-based to condition-based maintenance for both higher uptime and lower overall maintenance costs. Provide your end customers with anonymized benchmarks for how other customers get more value from your offers more quickly and help your channel partners target complementary products and in those areas.

This is by no means an exhaustive list. It is merely a starting point in your efforts to prioritize the highest-value algorithmic insights within each of these four digital customer segments.

Master Machine Learning

Let's turn our attention to the middle row of Figure 6.2—the algorithms that realize the value of your data for each of those four digital customer segments. It would not be hyperbole to say there has been an explosion of activity in this middle layer.

In year 2000, there were just 570 patent applications that mentioned "algorithm" in their title or description. By 2015, there were 17,000 such patent applications, a number estimated to reach 500,000 by 2020. If you are not already focused on acquiring or building an algorithmic advantage, then you are falling behind.

Some of these algorithms are horizontal in nature and can often be sourced from third parties. Examples include remote asset monitoring solutions for services, propensity to buy models for sales, cyber intrusion detection for IT, and spam filtering for all of us.

However, many algorithms are industry specific and likely to require internal development. Examples include fraud detection for financial services, price elasticity models for packaged consumer goods, object identification for self-driving cars, predictive maintenance models for sophisticated industrial equipment, and emergency room throughput optimization in hospitals. New algorithms in healthcare are even out-performing certified radiologists in diagnosing acute conditions, such as pneumonia and stroke.

The range of algorithms is broad, but most companies focus on five algorithm categories: asset optimization, operations optimization, risk optimization, pricing optimization, and sales optimization. Note that the internal and external customer segments on the top row of Figure 6.2 seek algorithmic advantage from many of these categories.

These algorithms can be built in two different ways—data science teams and continuous machine learning. Both are still important, but many aspiring Goliaths are in the midst of shifting their focus from the first to the second one.

Traditionally, companies seeking an algorithmic advantage have made a sizable investment in hiring a chief digital officer or chief data officer and staffing up a data science team. These highly trained (and compensated) statisticians, modelers, and programmers specialize in each of the five categories of algorithms in the middle row of Figure 6.2.

In fact, for the past five years data scientist has been one of the hottest jobs in Silicon Valley. Parents have stopped telling their kids to become doctors and lawyers so that they can focus their studies on math and statistics. As shown in data from McKinsey in Figure 6.3, demand for data scientists is dramatically exceeding supply.

For context, there were just 150,000 people employed in data science 10 years ago. Now the gap between supply and demand is almost that big. These individuals require a unique combination of a masters- or PhD-level math background, advanced data modeling and programming skills, and domain knowledge of the business problem that the algorithm seeks to solve. While data science is not going away anytime soon, basing your future algorithmic advantage on the hiring of a big-data science team is going to take too long and cost too much.

The second approach has greater potential for long-term success. Continuous machine learning is, in many ways, the great equalizer. Given the broad availability of both on-premise and cloud-based

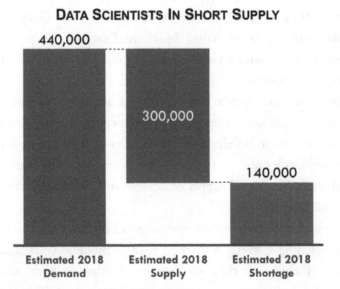

DATA SCIENTISTS IN SHORT SUPPLY

440,000

300,000

140,000

| Estimated 2018 Demand | Estimated 2018 Supply | Estimated 2018 Shortage |

FIGURE 6.3 Shortage of Data Scientists.

Sources: McKinsey; US Census Bureau; Dun & Bradstreet; Bureau of Labor Statistics.

machine learning tools, it is becoming possible for every small, midsized, and large company to let its data speak.

At the most simple level, continuous machine learning is an automated way to find actionable patterns in large data sets. You might hear terms such as deep learning, neural networks, and cognitive models as specific approaches to how computers find nonintuitive patterns on their own.

While the basic math has been around for decades, an arms race is underway between Amazon, Microsoft, Google, Baidu, and Tencent to provide your company with a ready-to-deploy platform for continuous machine learning. These tech titans are taking advantage of step-function advances in computing horsepower through AI-optimized GPUs, the availability of massive integrated data sets to train new models, and ready access to AI development platforms, such as Google TensorFlow and Amazon AI.

This is great news for you and your company. The pace of innovation is rapid and accelerating. The cost of entry is coming down. If you are just starting out, self-directed platforms such as Google Cloud's AutoML and Microsoft Azure Machine Learning allow your core developers to use your existing data to build algorithms without an army of data scientists.

As new methods such as reinforcement learning—machines training machines—continue to advance, you can expect this reduced reliance on data scientists to accelerate. The ultimate goal is to allow business people to ask the right questions of continuous machine learning platforms directly. Maybe the supply of doctors and lawyers in Silicon Valley will be safe after all.

For most aspiring Goliaths, investing in both data science and continuous machine learning is the best path to building your algorithmic advantage. Focus your data scientists on developing high-value algorithms, where their unique combination of math skills and domain knowledge is essential. In parallel, unleash continuous machine learning on those same areas, as well as the next tier of use cases for your four digital customer segments.

In the overlap areas, play king of the hill. That is, let the best approach win through ongoing A–B testing between data scientist–developed and continuous machine learning–derived algorithms. In the next tier use cases, let time be your friend as continuous machine learning solutions tend to get better with more time and bigger data.

Now that you've built your data balance sheet, learned to value data optionality, and used the digital value stack to maximize your return on data, let's turn to a case example of a company that is certainly using its data as currency.

The Weather Channel

New CEO David Kenny and CTO Bryson Koehler faced an enormous task—transforming The Weather Channel from a declining media business into a high-growth weather insights company. By 2013, it was too late to just build a mobile weather app that could help TWC grow beyond its cable TV roots. There were already 1,000 of those.

Kenny and Koehler settled on a bigger, hairier, more audacious goal—helping people around the world make better weather-related decisions. It would require TWC to forward integrate into industries with the most to lose when the real weather is different from what was forecasted.

TWC put a three-phase plan into action. Phase one focused on the bottom row of the digital value stack shown in Figure 6.2. TWC doubled down on its unique combination of data sets and scientific experts to create the most accurate weather forecasting engine on the planet. TWC's army of 200 meteorologists classified 108 different forecastable weather patterns. To extend its data balance sheet, TWC acquired Weather Underground for its vast pool of crowdsourced microclimate data. Extending TWC's forecasting prowess required rearchitecting its IT infrastructure, consolidating from 13 disparate data centers to a single cloud and big-data infrastructure. The hard work paid off with the cost of a million application programming interface (API) calls falling from $70 to just $1.

In phase two, TWC shifted its focus to the digital customer segments layer of the stack. Instead of internal and external user groups, Kenny and Koehler prioritized vertical industries based on the business risk those industries faced in getting weather predictions wrong. Aviation is a good example of one of the industries targeted, as predicting turbulence keeps passengers safe and minimizes the litigation risk that airlines face. To drive this, TWC brought in creative thinkers such as Chris Huff, who added deep domain knowledge about the retail and packaged consumer goods industries. Together the team installed a culture of experimentation and innovation through employee-led hackathons and special incentive programs. This extended TWC's algorithmic advantage into areas such as the integration of weather into health and fitness platforms.

In phase three, TWC opened up the data-rich platform it had created to a broad ecosystem of people interested in building algorithms and apps around the weather. Getting innovators excited was not very hard. Most people think working with weather is cool and the ability to touch the lives of a billion or more people around the globe is highly motivating. The success was remarkable. With over 25,000 partners making 26 billion daily calls to its APIs, TWC is one of the largest API platforms in the world. By experimenting with the highest-potential innovations inside its flagship weather app, TWC was able to test new concepts quickly with minimal up-front investment. One example was linking the app more tightly with the Apple Watch. This delivered value to Apple users but also added a new data asset to TWC's data balance sheet—access to hundreds of millions of barometric pressure sensors within the Apple devices.

Bryson admits that it was an intense three-year journey: any faster and TWC would not have been able to see its Big I and Little I innovations achieve their promise; any slower and the new leadership team might have lost momentum and the necessary support from employees and shareholders.

TWC showed how using data as currency pays off. The business is now a growing and vibrant unit in IBM's Watson division and is recognized as the leading weather-insights company, powering over 150,000 airline flights a day, providing energy-demand forecasts to utility providers, delivering important insights to global insurance companies, and helping billions of people plan their lives around the weather.[1]

Others are following in TWC's footsteps. For example, Walmart's Data Café has made the company's 40 petabytes of retail sales data available to innovators across its business. Data Café leverages 200 internal and external data streams to cut the cycle time for data-driven solutions from three weeks to 20 minutes. Innovations incubated through Data Café include the Social Genome project, which predicts sales based on conversations on social media; Shopycat, which analyzes how shopping habits are influenced by friends; and Polaris, which analyzes search terms on websites.

Rule 3: Company and Career Readiness

With this case example of TWC in mind, it is time to assess your readiness to use data as currency.

Company Readiness Self-Assessment

To complete your company readiness self-assessment, thoroughly read the grid in Figure 6.4, then identify the level of capability that your company has demonstrated within each row.

RULE #3: USE YOUR DATA AS CURRENCY
COMPANY SELF-ASSESSMENT GRID

	0-20% Minimal Capability	20-40% Limited Capability	40-60% Moderate Capability	60-80% Advanced Capability	80-100% World Class Capability
High quality big data assets	No large data sets are within our control today	A few large data sets that meet at least 4 quality criteria	Many large data sets that meet at least 4 quality criteria	A few large data sets that meet all 7 quality criteria	Many large data sets that meet all 7 quality criteria
Manageable data liabilities	Have not even started to assess our exposure here	Inventory of our data governance issues in place	Just starting to act on our data governance obligations	Compliant in most countries but work to do in a few	No outstanding data liabilities as we are in full compliance
Place value on data optionality	Do not value future profit streams from data in any systematic way	Treat second-order value of data as "upside" with no explicit value	Willing to make big up-front investments to acquire new data assets	Can calculate the future value of new data sets on a one-off project basis	Sophisticated financial model in place to value second- and third-order effects
Broad customer segment focus	We have no systematic approach to prioritizing digital use cases	Just starting to classify use cases into digital customer segments	Solely focused on the needs of internal digital customers today	Delivering high-value solutions to at least three of the digital customer segments	Delivering high-value digital solutions to each of the four customer segments
Building data science team	Do not yet have any data scientists on the payroll	Have generalist data scientists today without any specialization	Have data scientists focused within at least 1 of the algorithmic optimization areas	Have data scientists focused within at least 3 of the algorithmic optimization areas	Have data scientists focused within each of the 5 algorithmic optimization areas
Mastering machine learning	No platform or capability in place to embark on machine learning yet	Heavily reliant on human data scientists with machine learning just getting started	Data science and machine learning having an equal impact today	Our algorithmic advantage is now delivered by machine learning	Machine learning breakthroughs have made us the industry benchmark

0%   20%   40%   60%   80%   100%

FIGURE 6.4 Rule 3 Company Self-Assessment Grid.

Career Readiness Self-Assessment

Repeat the exercise above with your career in mind. What roles are you playing in helping your company use its data as currency? Mark your self-assessments on the grid shown in Figure 6.5.

RULE #3: USE YOUR DATA AS CURRENCY
CAREER SELF-ASSESSMENT GRID

	0-20% Minimal Capability	20-40% Limited Capability	40-60% Moderate Capability	60-80% Advanced Capability	80-100% World Class Capability
High quality big data assets	Have not been part of my company's push into big data and analytics	Appreciate the value of high-quality data but do not have skills in this area	Invested personal time to learn data science basics but on-the-job experience is limited	Deep experience in making data valuable for data science and machine learning	Go-to leader for assessing the quality and business potential of new data sets
Manageable data liabilities	Not involved with commitments around data rights and obligations	Have negotiated commercial contracts that include explicit data rights	Up-to-speed on the trend toward more complex data governance laws	Substantial expertise in implementing data privacy and security safeguards	Recognized expert on regional data sovereignty and governance
Place value on data optionality	Do not see any intrinsic value in data – it is just a means to an end	I am only able to place a value on the direct, near-term impact of data	Willing to include future data value as we make prioritization decisions	Attribute explicit value to second-order effects of acquiring new data assets	I built our company's model for valuing second- and third-order effects
Broad customer segment focus	No material experience yet delivering on digital use cases	Direct experience in the use cases within at least 1 digital customer segment	Direct experience in use cases within at least 2 digital customer segments	Direct experience in use cases within at least 3 digital customer segments	Direct experience in use cases for all 4 of the digital customer segments
Building data science team	Few data science skills and minimal big data analytics experience yet	Built data science skills through online and company training programs	Demonstrated success across multiple data science projects	Go-to leader within multiple stages of the analytics value chain from data to insights	Expert in all facets of turning big data into actionable, high-value business insights
Mastering machine learning	No experience or skill yet in machine learning tools and projects	Building my skills as part of my first machine learning project	Experienced with multiple successful machine learning efforts	Viewed as the go-to expert to deliver continuous machine learning	Teach machine learning at our local college in my spare time

0%	20%	40%	60%	80%	100%

FIGURE 6.5 Rule 3 Career Self-Assessment Grid.

Rule 3 Readiness Summary

Now that you've completed your company and career self-assessments for Rule 3, fill in your readiness summary in Figure 6.6. Again, if you are doing these self-assessments online at

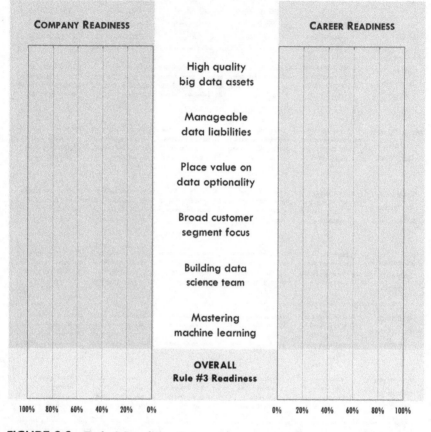

RULE #3: USE YOUR DATA AS CURRENCY
READINESS SUMMARY

COMPANY READINESS

CAREER READINESS

High quality
big data assets

Manageable
data liabilities

Place value on
data optionality

Broad customer
segment focus

Building data
science team

Mastering
machine learning

OVERALL
Rule #3 Readiness

100% 80% 60% 40% 20% 0%   0% 20% 40% 60% 80% 100%

FIGURE 6.6 Rule 3 Readiness Summary.

www.goliathsrevenge.com, this readiness summary will be produced for you automatically.

You are halfway there—three of the six rules completed. Take a breath, and then it's time to open up your innovation as TWC did using Rule 4: Accelerate through innovation networks.

Note

1. Bryson Koehler (former chief technology and information officer, The Weather Channel), in an interview with the authors, December 2017.

Chapter 7

Rule 4: Accelerate through Innovation Networks

It's rare that originality comes from insiders.

—Neil Blumenthal, *Warby Parker* cofounder

As you've worked through the first three rules of Goliath's Revenge, you have almost certainly committed your company to deliver more innovations on a faster timeline than your current capabilities make possible. The wrong answer to this mismatch is dialing back on your goals. You are in a race with other established companies, as well as with your industry's digital disruptors, to bring step-change customer outcomes to market.

Instead, learn from best-practice innovators such as NASA, Procter & Gamble, UnitedHealthcare, GlaxoSmithKline, and Under Armour. Put open innovation on equal footing with your internal efforts to achieve more in less time with lower risk. The payoff from orchestrating a network of innovation instead of building it all yourself can be profound.

In research by Wharton's Jerry Wind and IBM's Shanker Ramamurthy, network orchestrators that tap into the value of external partners enjoy market valuations of eight times revenue, versus five times revenue for technology creators and three times revenue for service providers. For perspective, the S&P 500 has historically valued large companies in the United States at a multiple of one and a half times revenue.

In spite of the attraction of open innovation networks, less than a third of large companies and less than half of smaller companies in our survey have fully embraced the concept. The shift from "only invented here" to "let the best ideas win" is not an easy one. It requires action on four fronts: overcoming the curse of "we know everything" (WKE), opening up innovation channels, becoming easy to innovate with, and expanding your corporate development toolkit.

Overcome the Curse of We Know Everything

WKE is a terminal illness for established companies and a natural byproduct of sustained commercial success and the adulation that follows it. You might recognize it by its dismissive cousin NIH (not invented here).

Inhibitors of Open Innovation

Your first task in pivoting your organization to an open innovation strategy is having a dispassionate discussion with your peers about which of the following eight inhibitors your company faces:

1. **Business model gravity.** External innovations that may challenge or cannibalize your current business model are dismissed out of hand.
2. **Engineering pride.** Internal innovators believe they can do it better and want the credit, resulting in external innovations that are never "up to our standards."

3. **Risk aversion.** Fear that external innovators present unacceptable financial, security, regulatory, compliance, or brand risks.
4. **Incentives mismatch.** Short-term compensation structures incent the people evaluating external innovations to dismiss their potentially longer-term payoffs.
5. **Scarce talent.** Significant talent gaps exist in your pool of scouts, dot-connectors, and solution navigators.
6. **Limited imagination.** External innovations seem far-fetched and beyond your comfort zone, particularly if they come from outside your industry.
7. **Grinding gears.** The cadence of your business is too slow to mesh with the rapid execution pace of those companies you want to work with.
8. **Standard operating procedure.** Your corporate standards around IP, data rights, and other issues are incompatible with those of startups.

Be honest. How many of these inhibitors are representative of your team, division, or company today? If it is just one or two, then you are in good shape to move ahead and address those inhibitors as you scale up your innovation ecosystem. If three or more of these inhibitors are active within your organization today, then you need to resolve them before proceeding with an open innovation model.

Procter & Gamble Makes the Pivot

In 2000, P&G CEO A. G. Lafley realized his internal R&D output was not delivering the growth shareholders expected. P&G needed to create the equivalent of a new $4-billion business every year. To understand the scale of that growth challenge, $4 billion is roughly the annual revenue of industry-leading companies such as ADT, Barnes & Noble, Boise Cascade, Symantec, Hyatt Hotels, and NASDAQ.

P&G made an aggressive shift toward open innovation. Its program, called Connect+Develop, amplified the innovation of P&G's 7,500 internal R&D employees with the efforts of 1.5 million scientists and inventors from around the world.

The results were dramatic. The proportion of externally led innovations jumped from 15% to 45% and included breakthrough products such as Swiffer and Crest SpinBrush, while R&D productivity yield improved by 60%. In 2004 P&G reported a 19% increase in sales, a 25% jump in earnings, and a total shareholder return of 24%.[1]

Open Up Innovation Channels

If your company is like the others in our research, you already have some channels through which external innovations can enter your company. Once you have addressed the inhibitors above, it is time to dramatically broaden your innovation channels to achieve an outcome like the one P&G accomplished.

As you can see from Figure 7.1, there are eight specific innovation channels that can add Big I and Little I ideas to your innovation funnel: research universities, strategic suppliers, strategic customers, private equity firms, startups, corporate venture groups, business incubators, and open innovation platforms.

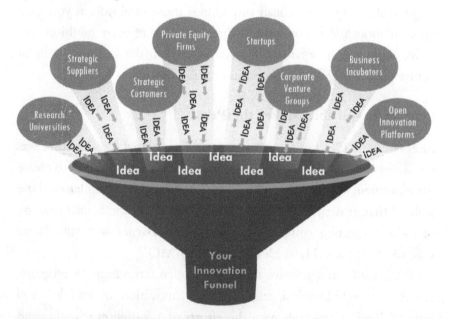

FIGURE 7.1 Channels of Open Innovation.

Note that activating an innovation channel is not the same as committing your company to adopting a specific innovation that channel might offer. Think about each of these channels as buying an option to evaluate new ideas that can augment your internal R&D efforts. (In Chapter 5, you put in place the capability to filter out the best ideas and act on them through either your Big I or Little I process.)

The Gives and Gets of Open Innovation Channels

In theory, having an innovation ecosystem looks like a no-brainer. Why wouldn't all of these innovative organizations want to partner with you? Well, there is no free lunch here. The more innovative a potential participant is, the more other companies will be lining up to work with them.

Developing a consistent flow of high-quality ideas requires being clear about what you are willing to give to get that kind of access. The more you give, the more likely your company is to get a preferential first look at that channel's innovative ideas before your competitors even get a chance to see them. This is a little like getting in early to a fantastic buffet so that you can fill your plate before the masses descend and pick it over.

You might remember the lyrics of a song from that popular kids' cartoon called *Barney*: "I love you, you love me, we're best friends like friends should be...." Well, you want to avoid what some call "barney" deals: that is, hollow announcements of professional admiration that lack the substance to produce any material advantage for either party.

See Figure 7.2 for a summary of what it takes to activate each of the open innovation channels and ensure that they deliver the idea flow you expect over the long term.

None of those gives may appear to be showstoppers. In fact, most have only limited up-front costs. However, you should sequence your efforts to open up these eight open innovation channels based on your readiness to make the unique commitment that each one requires.

CHANNEL	GIVES	GETS
Research Universities	• Research funding • Access to data / IP • Piloting opportunities	• First looks at research • New hire referrals • Spin out opportunities
Strategic Suppliers	• Revenue commitments • Co-innovation projects • Co-marketing funding	• Shared risk models • Investment funding • Path to scale
Strategic Customers	• Early innovation access • Discounted pricing • Limited-time exclusives	• Co-innovation partners • Market validation • Radiating references
Private Equity Firms	• Spin-out deal flow • Use case validation • Portfolio company exits	• First looks at startups • Big I co-investment • Spin-out destination
Startups	• Early market validation • Access to data • Investment capital	• Big I risk appetite • Entrepreneurial talent • Future M&A options
Corporate Venture Groups	• Access to data / IP • Revenue commitments • Radiating references	• Big I incubation option • Entrepreneurial talent • Disruption visibility
Business Incubators	• Access to data / IP • Early customer pilots • Co-investment funding	• Big I risk appetite • Entrepreneurial talent • Future M&A options
Open Innovation Platforms	• Hard problems to solve • Access to data / IP • Prize money	• Wisdom of crowds • Low-risk innovation • Entrepreneurial talent

FIGURE 7.2   The Gives and Gets of Open Innovation.

Become Easy to Innovate With

Open innovation is like having your cake and eating it too. You want
the maximum amount of innovation to be available to your team, group,
division, or company in the minimum amount of time. You also want
to keep your job by delivering on your near-term operational and
financial goals.

You can do both. Getting ecosystem partners to do some of the work serves to both amplify your returns and reduce your risks from the Big I and Little I process you installed back in Chapter 5. External innovators bring a sense of urgency, risk tolerance, and appropriate irreverence to your biggest opportunities.

However, most established companies struggle to ramp their innovation ecosystem up to a material scale before their attention shifts to the next important project. In dealing with startups, in particular, they fail to address the misaligned goals, mismatched resources, inconsistent stakeholder support, and corporate risk aversion that stands in the way of success. The beautiful music you were intending to play together ends up sounding as if AC/DC and the New York Philharmonic are on the same stage at the same time.

Make better music together by following these eight best practices from companies that are winning with open innovation: demonstrate commitment, set clear objectives, dedicate resources, empower an investment committee, adopt a lean process, minimize legal friction, build an innovation sandbox, and install a culture of exploration.

Demonstrate Commitment

Be clear up front about the percentage of your new product, service, and process innovations that you expect to come from startups. For example, General Mills' Connected Innovation Program was launched with a top-down mandate to boost the number of new innovation opportunities coming from outside innovators. The company went from 15% of its new product innovations coming from outside the company to 35% in just six years.

Set Clear Objectives

"Nice to meet you—let's do a pilot." Startups can die in pilot hell—working with established companies but failing to gain enough production deployments before their venture funding runs out. Don't engage in these open-ended pilots. Instead, define clear objectives up front for the business results your pilot must demonstrate and provide a provisional commitment to roll out the innovation if the startup delivers. This weeds out startups that are not yet ready to work with external customers. It also establishes your company's reputation in the venture community as worthy of first looks at future startups.

Dedicate Resources

Dedicated resources across areas such as technology, product management, operations, sales enablement, and channels are needed to support your company's work with startups. If this effort is only a part-time job, startups are going to move on to other companies willing to commit the resources needed to run at startup pace.

Empower an Investment Committee

Establish an investment committee with internal and external perspectives. Empower it to make investment and resource allocation decisions without multiple levels of syndication and signoffs. Internally, include business units, functional heads, R&D, corporate development, and strategy. Externally, look for technology leaders, market experts, and venture capitalists to make sure you don't pass on a potential breakthrough opportunity that falls within one of your corporate blind spots.

Adopt a Lean Process

Install a lean process to test, learn, pivot, and decide on the most valuable impact a given startup can make on your company. A large media company's innovation lab uses 30-, 60-, and 90-day sprints to cut through corporate inertia and focus engagements with startups. The innovation foundry of a global telecom company conducts monthly TelePresence meetings where vetted startups pitch how they can solve critical issues for the company, reducing the time-to-decision for both sides.

Minimize Legal Friction

Every startup has horror stories of 40-page contracts being imposed on them by established companies for $50,000 pilot deals. Without an in-house legal team, a big chunk of the value to the startup can be consumed by external lawyers negotiating corner-case scenarios. Be like a major Canadian bank, which cut its contract from 20 pages to 2, protected pre-engagement IP within the startup, and provided a clear path for handling joint IP.

Build an Innovation Sandbox

Develop a centralized innovation sandbox in which ecosystem partners can conduct research, test concepts, and pilot solutions on your infrastructure and de-identified data. For example, AT&T's Foundry provided access to a network test bed via APIs that represented the latest version of its communication network, but which was safely separated from its production systems. Data.gov is an example of how the US government is opening up its data to citizens and innovators alike. Initiated by former US CIO Vivek Kundra and President Obama, Data.gov now has over 100,000 data sets available in machine-readable format. It has already delivered innovations such as integrating product recall and health risk information into consumer shopping apps. If the federal government can stand up an innovation sandbox, what's stopping your company?

Install a Culture of Exploration

We left this one for last because it takes the longest to achieve. That means you should start immediately but plan for success in pockets of the organization. Pick the teams within your organization that are most change ready and try to get every employee on those teams to spend some part of their time exploring new ideas and the external partnerships that can deliver them. It does not have to be a major time commitment—even 10% would be half a day per week for each employee. Celebrate the successes in these early-adopting teams to spread the open innovation bug like a beneficial virus—quickly and organically. This approach is far better that some big announcement without enough action at the front lines.

So, you have prioritized the new innovation channels you are going to open up and have action plans in place for the eight areas above that are going to make your open innovation investments pay off. Now let's turn our attention to the unsung heroes of your open innovation program—your corporate development team.

Expand Your Corporate Development Toolkit

Every strategic initiative needs a focal point. Put your head of corporate development in the hot seat to coordinate open innovation across your company. If your organization is too small to have a corporate development team, then expanding your corporate development toolkit will ultimately be your CEO's responsibility.

Your toolkit should include some combination of six main structures: corporate venturing, IP licensing, corporate incubation, spin-outs, joint ventures, and acquisitions. For each one, we have included an example of a company using that particular tool effectively in its open innovation efforts.

Corporate Venturing: Intel Capital

In 2017, corporate VC teams deployed $37 billion of fresh capital to 1,268 deals. That represented 44% of all VC investments. Your corporate VC team must balance its focus across two mandates—achieving a competitive internal rate of return on the funds invested and accelerating innovation within your core business.

This can pay off handsomely. Research from Touchdown Ventures shows that the stock prices of companies that put corporate VC teams in place grow 50% faster than the overall market. Intel Capital represents the benchmark for how to leverage this aspect of your corporate development toolkit.

Over the past 25 years, Intel Capital has invested $15 billion across 1,500 companies, run 325 technology days to match startups with businesses, and had almost 500 exits (selling to realize gains/losses) through IPOs and acquisitions. Intel Capital delivers accelerated learning around new technologies, markets, and business models. Small checks in early funding rounds buy Intel a first look at a broad swath of disruptive innovations. Those real options can later be exercised through other aspects of the corporate development toolkit below.

Intellectual Property Licensing: Google and IBM

Established companies often have IP that could be more profitably commercialized by ecosystem partners than through internal investments. Start this process by hosting hackathons, sponsoring challenges, and standing up foundries that expose selected IP to your innovation ecosystem.

Some have taken the next step by open sourcing their IP as a way to attract the maximum possible innovation around it. Examples include Google (TensorFlow) and IBM (Watson and Hyperledger). Many engage in a form of the freemium business model with respect to their IP—open source a key portion of the IP with the option for ecosystem partners to step up to a full license over time.

Corporate Incubation: UnitedHealthcare

Internal business incubation is important for the most sensitive areas of your business, in which you need to retain absolute control of trade secrets and IP rights. Put an internal business incubator in place if your industry has these dynamics. Your incubator will simulate how a Big I idea might grow within an external venture capitalist's portfolio.

UnitedHealthcare is a good example. Back in 1996 it founded a subsidiary called Ingenix to incubate new analytic offerings from its massive claims records data set. That business delivered step-change customer outcomes through health insights and became a massive success. Now branded as OptumInsight, it is a $7 billion data and analytics powerhouse growing 20% per year. Talk about using your data as currency!

Spin-Outs: GE and Rabobank

Sting wrote the lyric, "If you love someone, set them free." Spin-outs are the commercial equivalent. Some Big I ideas are too risky, expensive, or distracting to pursue internally, yet your company will want to participate in the upside if they are eventually successful. Pushing those Big I opportunities into arm's-length companies allows them to tap into new sources of funding and talent while giving them the strategic flexibility required to prosper. If you really love them, you can buy them back later, once they are more mature.

Based on a decade of research in advanced microelectromechanical systems, GE spun out its high-reliability switch technology into a new venture in 2016. Yes, you just read the longest word in the book. These MEMS innovations are tiny machines less than a millimeter in size. Backed by $19 million in capital from GE Ventures, Corning, Microsemi, and Paladin Capital, the new venture (called Menlo Micro) is helping makers of medical equipment, wireless network devices, and Industrial IoT solutions design in MEMS-based switching systems. GE continued to add value by recruiting electronics industry veteran Russ Garcia as CEO and serving as an important Menlo Micro customer in the medical equipment and IoT markets.

For Rabobank, the "spin-out" was actually resisting the urge to spin in. In 2012, Rabobank bought 80% of a mobile app startup called MyOrder instead of acquiring the entire company. MyOrder's step-change customer outcome was helping consumers order and pay with their smartphones at over 11,000 restaurants, bars, cinemas, and car parks in the Netherlands. By leaving the venture structure in place, MyOrder's startup culture remained vibrant. New capabilities, such as shopkeeper analytics tool Sidekick, came quickly. Rabobank has continued to add value by aggressively selling the MyOrder solution to its business banking customers.

Joint Ventures: GlaxoSmithKline and McLaren

Joint ventures have a simple goal—combine crown jewels from two established companies to do something neither could do on its own. In math terms, add one plus one and get three. However, joint ventures require substantial effort to align objectives, create shared incentives, value respective contributions, negotiate IP rights, agree on ownership splits, and finalize governance rules. Without all of these, joint ventures are not worth the effort as Verizon + Redbox and Tiffany + Swatch have discovered.

The joint venture between pharma leader GSK and race car innovator McLaren is firing on all cylinders. During a Formula 1 weekend, McLaren analyzes one billion data points from 200 sensors placed on the car and driver. Through their joint venture, GSK has applied McLaren's unique predictive analytics and biotelemetry capability to everything from high-volume production efficiency to remote patient monitoring during clinical trials. It has produced a win-win—innovation acceleration for GSK and an entirely new line of business for McLaren.

Acquisitions: Under Armour

The statistics on the benefits from acquisitions are sobering—over 70% fail to achieve the objectives of the acquiring company. So, you should be using this tool in your corporate development toolkit under just two scenarios. One: you have been working with a target company using one of the structures above and it has matured to a point at which it can contribute substantial business value to your organization. Or two: a target company has unique, defensible, valuable assets or capabilities that could add to your crown jewels inventory and take you into multiple new businesses.

Under Armour provides an example of both scenarios playing out in parallel. In 2013, Wall Street analysts were scratching their heads when the company acquired MapMyFitness, MyFitnessPal, and Endomondo for a total of $560 million. Confusion reigned about what digital fitness apps had to do with being a world-class apparel company. However, Under Armour used those acquired companies as new crown jewels to launch an integrated fitness, nutrition, and sports apparel platform. The bold strategy paid off in two ways. In the near term, Under Armour made hyperpersonalized athletic-wear offers to its newly acquired 200 million users. Longer term, Under Armour is becoming an important part of the massive shift toward consumer-driven health decisions. Under Armour CEO Kevin Plank has identified digital fitness as a critical driver of future growth. Wall Street now gets it—the company's stock price has tripled in the three years following the acquisitions.

With these new corporate development tools ready, let's look at an organization that has successfully pivoted to open innovation: NASA.

NASA Opens Up

NASA's Space Life Sciences Directorate—now called the Human Health and Performance Directorate (HH&P)—is charged with keeping astronauts healthy and productive in space. Back in 2005, its R&D budget was cut by 45%. Necessity being the mother of invention, leader Jeff Davis decided to reshape HH&P's innovation culture and actively embrace external collaboration.

This meant overcoming years of internally focused R&D. To chart a new course, Davis and his team embarked on a visioning exercise to decide on a new path for HH&P.

Sometimes breakthroughs rely on being in the right place at the right time. In 2008, Davis attended an executive education class at Harvard Business School that included a session on open innovation taught by Karim Lakhani. Sitting in on that session convinced Davis to make open innovation a part of the newly developed HH&P ecosystem strategy.

NASA's HH&P engaged Dr. Lakhani to educate its workforce about this new approach to external innovation and demonstrate the viability of crowdsourcing platforms. The HH&P team identified 12 challenges to test the open innovation approach. After an open competition, HH&P selected InnoCentive and yet2. HH&P proved it could use NASA's brand and cool factor to attract innovators from around the world.

In just a few months, HH&P's first seven challenges drew 2,900 responses from 80 countries. One of the challenges demanded an algorithm that could predict solar events up to one day in advance with 50% accuracy—something internal NASA scientists had yet to achieve. The winning solution came from a retired radio frequency engineer and was 85% accurate up to eight hours in advance, a massive improvement.

This open innovation success has come full circle with NASA@ work—a global platform for internal challenges. It now has over 15,000 solvers working on new challenges, which are announced every two to four weeks. NASA@work has also energized internal employees to get involved in innovation efforts that go beyond their current roles.

Along the way, HH&P has worked hard to win over NASA employees who feared losing their identity as problem solvers and innovators in the pivot toward open innovation. Davis made sure employees recognized that crisply defining problems and evaluating potential breakthroughs are just as important to HH&P's success as inventing solutions.

The interactive Solution Mechanism Guide was developed to teach employees about open innovation and empower them to make decisions on when and how to use crowdsourcing platforms. In parallel, NASA hatched new recognition and reward programs that were proposed and ranked by employees.

NASA's openness to external innovation has both contributed to and benefited from the rapid growth of private space companies globally. NASA partnered with the XPRIZE Foundation to spur innovation for its lunar lander and space apps. The overall space-sector shift from a closed invention to an open innovation model has also helped open the floodgates of private sector investment into companies such as Elon Musk's SpaceX, Jeff Bezos's Blue Origin, and Richard Branson's Virgin Galactic.

NASA's leadership in harnessing both external and internal innovation has been widely recognized. In 2011, the US Office of Science and Technology Policy tapped NASA to establish a federal open-innovation capability called the Center of Excellence for Collaborative Innovation. Despite Davis and many members of the core team retiring or moving on, the engine they built around open innovation continues to thrive.[2]

Rule 4: Company and Career Readiness

It is time to understand how prepared your company and career are for Rule 4: Accelerate through innovation networks.

Company Readiness Self-Assessment

To complete your company readiness self-assessment, thoroughly read the grid in Figure 7.3, then identify the level of capability that your company has demonstrated for each cell in each row.

RULE #4: ACCELERATE VIA INNOVATION NETWORKS COMPANY SELF-ASSESSMENT GRID

	0-20% Minimal Capability	20-40% Limited Capability	40-60% Moderate Capability	60-80% Advanced Capability	80-100% World Class Capability
Beyond "We Know Everything"	Our culture is highly resistant to external innovations	6 of the 8 open innovation inhibitors are still in place	4 of the 8 open innovation inhibitors are still in place	2 of the 8 open innovation inhibitors are still in place	All 8 open innovation inhibitors have been resolved
Multiple innovation channels	Zero or 1 of the open innovation channels have been activated	2 of the 8 open innovation channels have been activated	4 of the 8 open innovation channels have been activated	6 of the 8 open innovation channels have been activated	All 8 open innovation channels have been activated
Right gives and gets	The vast majority of the ideas in our innovation funnel come from internal sources	At least 10% of the ideas in our innovation funnel come from external sources	At least 30% of the ideas in our innovation funnel come from external sources	At least 50% of the ideas in our innovation funnel come from external sources	Over 70% of the ideas in our innovation funnel come from external sources
Easy to innovate with	We are just starting out and none of the 8 best practices describe our company today	At least 2 of the 8 best practices apply to how we run our innovation network	At least 4 of the 8 best practices apply to how we run our innovation network	At least 6 of the 8 best practices apply to how we run our innovation network	Every one of the 8 best practices apply to how we run our innovation network
Robust innovation sandbox	We do not yet allow external access to sample data or our technology	Innovation sandbox is built on a one-off basis for specific external partners	Substantial sample data is available for startups to experiment with	Have now extended beyond data toward API-based access to our technology	Deep APIs, massive sample data sets, and valuable technology available today
Corporate development toolkit	We do not have a formal Corporate Development capability today	We have limited, ad hoc experience in Corporate Development today	We have substantial experience in 2 of the 6 Corporate Development tools	We have substantial experience in 4 of the 6 Corporate Development tools	We have substantial experience in each of the 6 Corporate Development tools

0%   20%   40%   60%   80%   100%

FIGURE 7.3   Rule 4 Company Self-Assessment Grid.

Career Readiness Self-Assessment

Repeat the exercise above with your career in mind. What roles are you playing in helping your company open up its innovation model? Mark your self-assessments on the grid shown in Figure 7.4.

RULE #4: ACCELERATE VIA INNOVATION NETWORKS CAREER SELF-ASSESSMENT GRID

	0–20% Minimal Capability	20–40% Limited Capability	40–60% Moderate Capability	60–80% Advanced Capability	80–100% World Class Capability
Beyond "We Know Everything"	Cannot understand why things need to keep changing so often	Understand that big changes are afoot but don't see my role in making them happen	I am naturally curious and a committed lifelong learner	I am well-versed on digital transformation and actively leading change in my area	Am well known for evangelizing new ideas across our company
Multiple innovation channels	Have not been involved in co-innovation projects with external partners	Have worked on co-innovation projects across 2 of the 8 innovation channels	Have worked on co-innovation projects across 4 of the 8 innovation channels	Have worked on co-innovation projects across 6 of the 8 innovation channels	Have worked on co-innovation projects across all 8 of the innovation channels
Right gives and gets	Not involved in adding innovation partners to our company's network	Provide support to the teams that are activating new innovation partners	Deeply involved in negotiating new partnerships with external innovators	Lead our company's efforts within one of the open innovation channels	Lead our company's efforts across multiple open innovation channels
Easy to innovate with	No previous experience in making our open innovation approach better	Have identified areas where our company can make open innovation easier	Active team member on multiple projects to streamline our open innovation process	Lead our company's efforts to design the friction out of open innovation	Am recognized across the industry as a thought leader on open innovation
Robust innovation sandbox	Not working as part of our open innovation sandbox teams	Member of one of our key sandbox teams – APIs, data sets, or technology tools	Lead one of our key sandbox teams – APIs, data sets, or technology tools	Drive our ongoing efforts to make our open innovation sandbox better	Lead our efforts to engage external innovators with our data and tools
Corporate development toolkit	No experience yet executing Corporate Development deals	Have worked on deal teams across 1 of our deal structures	Have worked on deal teams across multiple deal structures	Have led deals within 1 of our Corporate Development structures	Have led deals across multiple Corporate Development structures

0%   20%   40%   60%   80%   100%

FIGURE 7.4   Rule 4 Career Self-Assessment Grid.

Rule 4 Readiness Summary

Take a moment to fill in your Rule 4 readiness assessment, with your company results on the left side and career results on the right side of Figure 7.5. If you are completing your self-assessments online at www. goliathsrevenge.com, then this summary will be automatically generated for you.

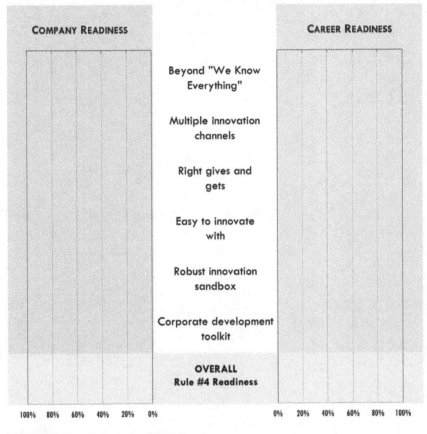

RULE #4: ACCELERATE VIA INNOVATION NETWORKS READINESS SUMMARY

COMPANY READINESS   CAREER READINESS

Beyond "We Know Everything"

Multiple innovation channels

Right gives and gets

Easy to innovate with

Robust innovation sandbox

Corporate development toolkit

OVERALL
Rule #4 Readiness

100% 80% 60% 40% 20% 0%   0% 20% 40% 60% 80% 100%

FIGURE 7.5   Rule 4 Readiness Summary.

Just two rules to go. Let's move on to the most important element that will propel you toward Goliath's Revenge—your talent.

Notes

1. Larry Huston and Nabil Sakkab, "Connect and Develop: Inside Procter & Gamble's New Model for Innovation," *Harvard Business Review* (March 2006).
2. Jeff Davis (former director of NASA's Human Health and Performance Directorate), in an interview with the authors, May 2018.

Chapter 8

Rule 5: Value Talent over Technology

It is incumbent on all of us to make sure we are building a world in which every individual has an opportunity to thrive.

—*Andrew Ng, Google Brain project founder*

So, you've validated your step-change customer outcomes, prioritized your Big I innovation opportunities, started actually putting your data to work, and opened up your innovation model. Take a breath. Celebrate the progress you've made in positioning your career and your company for Goliath's Revenge. You have two more rules to go and they are focused on the softer side of what separates the established companies that will succeed in a winner-takes-most world from those that will struggle.

When most people hear news about accelerating digital disruption, the rise of AI, or improvements in robotics, they think, "My company needs to get that technology deployed as soon as possible." It is a natural reaction. However, the necessary technology is actually widely available.

The hard part is translating those digital innovations into real business results, not science projects, or worse, white elephants. Doing so requires a clean-sheet approach to sourcing, developing, integrating, and retaining talent.

As you will see in the Goliath's Revenge survey results in Chapter 10, only 27% of small companies and 29% of large ones believe that they have the right digital talent. More than two-thirds of the companies surveyed identified either moderate or large talent gaps.

Time is of the essence. Having the right number of the right people with the right skills at the right time is likely the biggest determinant of your company's success. Successful Goliaths are taking six actions to make talent the centerpiece of their digital innovation: honoring institutional knowledge, going beyond 3D digital roles, committing to preemptive skill development, valuing venture general managers, optimizing the AI-human balance, and improving digital dexterity.

We will cover each of these areas in detail below. Before we jump in, though, let's start with an example of an organization getting it right in healthcare (an industry not often recognized for digital innovation): Penn Medicine.

How Penn Medicine Is Changing Healthcare

In 2012, Roy Rosin made the dramatic leap from being head of innovation at accounting software juggernaut Intuit in Silicon Valley to a healthcare system that was over 250 years old: Penn Medicine. Not only was the Philadelphia weather a major shock, but the entrenched barriers to innovation in healthcare were a stark contrast to the lean, continuous innovation model Rosin had installed at Intuit.

Rosin's hiring represented a major new direction for Penn Medicine. Innovation had traditionally meant undertaking world-class academic research to produce scientific breakthroughs. Frankly, the organization could have just rested on its laurels. Penn Medicine chose a different path—reinventing care delivery and bending the cost-value curve of healthcare by stealing a page from the Silicon Valley playbook.

The business model of healthcare in the United States has kept healthcare systems stuck in a volume-based model: more patients having more tests, procedures, and treatments means more revenue. Healthcare systems have wanted to deliver better patient outcomes through a blended AI-clinician model, but they've historically lacked the necessary digital innovation talent.

If there is one thing Silicon Valley is exceptional at, it is attracting talent and providing meaningful incentives for accelerated innovation. Rosin recognized that addressing the shortage of digitally savvy talent in healthcare would unlock better outcomes for both patients and providers.

Rosin brought a high EQ—emotional quotient—to the task. He sensed that bringing in a bunch of Silicon Valley whiz kids for his new innovation group would result in "organ rejection"— an extreme version of NIH. Instead, Rosin integrated the most respected clinicians at Penn Medicine with technical talent from Penn's own engineering program and business minds from Wharton. He augmented this team with external hires and specialized contractors only where needed.

Rosin built upon Penn's interdisciplinary strengths to create a culture of collaboration across groups that had rarely interacted on the topic of reimagining how care is delivered: business thinkers, technologists, designers, behavioral scientists, and clinicians. He invested time into resource grafting individuals with unique strengths into nimble teams. This proved easier than chasing the few people with both healthcare domain knowledge and deep technical know-how.

Rosin focused his team on two problems: stemming the runaway cost of healthcare (now 18% of US GDP) and flipping from reactively helping sick patients to proactively keeping people healthy. To get the most out of this team in the minimum amount of time, Rosin implemented the agile development methodology that most startups run in Silicon Valley: that is, get a beta to market fast, obtain real-world validation, and iterate toward a breakthrough solution.

Agile is a word seldom uttered in healthcare, the land of decade-long drug approval processes and this-is-how-we've-always-done-things inertia. Rosin also sponsored hackathons and innovation challenges to engage an even broader group of potential innovators in solving healthcare's most vexing problems.

Rosin's talent-first approach has already had a remarkable impact across three areas: channeling super-utilizers, reducing readmissions and morbidity due to pregnancy-related hypertension, and freeing up time for maternity ward nurses. Super-utilizers, such as low-income and homeless populations, consume a disproportionate share of healthcare. Limited preventative care drives abnormally high use of acute care services, such as emergency rooms. Penn's Shreya Kangovi led a team that developed IMPaCT, a community-healthcare model for addressing the complex family problems that delay care. Rosin's team gave Kangovi the tools and methodology to refine and package her model so it could scale and spread both across and beyond Penn. It has now attracted national attention and delivers roughly $2 in savings for every $1 invested for healthcare systems and agencies serving vulnerable populations.

Penn doctors knew that hypertension related to pregnancy was the top driver of seven-day obstetrical readmissions and obstetrical morbidities such as strokes, as well as 20% of maternal mortalities. But getting the requisite blood pressure readings after discharge was a major hurdle, leading to poor outcomes for patients. Katy Mahraj, an innovation leader on Rosin's team with skills in rapid experimentation and care redesign, was able to help top Penn physicians, who had insight into the patient context, develop a breakthrough solution. After iterating various testing protocols on women who had been discharged with a blood pressure cuff, the team deployed a novel, automated application in conjunction with the engineering team from Way to Health, a connected healthcare platform that had been developed at Penn. They recently conducted a randomized controlled trial demonstrating dramatically improved outcomes, with an 80% reduction in readmissions and the near-elimination of adverse health outcomes.

Finally, the pumping, tracking, and inventorying of mother's milk was a time-consuming, error-prone job for maternity nurses. It required 13,000 hours per year per NICU and had no reliable approach for tracking declines in the milk supply. A startup called Keriton was formed by connecting Penn engineering students with strong technical skills to lactation nurses who had deep insight into the problem. The team developed connected bottle sleeves with sensors, readers, and transmitters to automate the measurement and tracking of breast milk. It later pivoted from the early proof of concept to an entirely software-based system, automating the entire inventory and tracking process. The Keriton system ended up saving 7,000 hours of manual nursing work in a single NICU, increased milk received by 40%, reduced expirations by 50%, eliminated dangerous errors, and cut significant costs from labels and donor milk, delighting nurses and moms alike. This allowed maternity nurses to commit more of their time to high-value patient-care activities. Keriton has been recognized with numerous breakthrough innovation awards and recently attracted external investments from Dreamit Ventures and First Round Capital's Dorm Room Fund.

Successes like these have enabled Penn's Center for Health Care Innovation to expand into three discrete units. The Acceleration Lab is translating breakthrough care insights from Penn clinicians into care delivery as commercialized innovations. The Nudge Unit is applying Penn's behavioral science and design expertise to improving health outcomes. The Center for Digital Health is measuring the impact of digital healthcare innovations on patient populations.

One group, the PEACE team led by Dr. Courtney Schreiber, recently completed eight pilot projects on pregnancy complications in 90 days, a speed unheard of in regulated industries such as healthcare. That cadence of experimentation led to a specially designed clinic devised to be an alternative to the ER, which yielded a savings of $1,000 per incident along with a significantly improved patient experience. The formula of an unconventional leader plus cross-functional internal talent plus selective outside hires is paying off at Penn Medicine.

Unfortunately, few have enjoyed similar success. For every new chief digital officer (CDO) hired, another is being pushed out for a perceived lack of progress. So where are things going wrong? How can your company use talent to turn the tables on digital disruptors? Let's jump into the six talent priorities your company should be focused on.

Honor Institutional Knowledge

Established companies tend to overweight technical skills in their digital transformations. It feels like progress, announcing a big-name technology executive that is going to lead your organization into a digital future.

However, bringing in a CDO may be like wedging a Ferrari engine into a Yugo—the car makes a lot of noise but it's still slow. After revving hard for six months, your new CDO will be tired and ready to move on. Meanwhile, your core business will put another 100,000 miles on the odometer and ask, "What is all the fuss about?"

Aspiring Goliaths are installing a two-speed organizational model that values rapid learning at parity with near-term financial performance. They are integrating seasoned employees into teams seeded with talent from outside their company, and often from outside their industry. They are rewarding those teams with two-speed metrics that value both learning and business impact.

Honoring institutional knowledge prevents a cultural divide of new-hire haves and legacy employee have-nots that plays into the hands of digital disruptors. Make this principle the starting point of your talent strategy.

Go Beyond 3D Digital Roles

We have all heard some variant of "85% of the jobs of 2030 haven't been invented yet." If those projections are accurate, then why are companies sticking with yesterday's role definitions and career paths? Aspiring Goliaths are taking a different approach. They are hiring for two classes of digital roles—immediate and coming soon.

The immediate roles are what we call "3D"—design, development, and data science. Each is fundamental to executing on your transformation plan and positioning your company for digital success. 3D roles harden your core business in anticipation of digital disruption while powering the Big I innovation teams that you prioritized in Chapter 5.

In financial services, leaders such as Goldman Sachs and JPMorgan Chase have made substantial investments into hiring 3D talent, while regional banks have tended to outsource this work. Either approach can work. Just ensure you have enough internal 3D talent to allow for rapid experimentation and to make your company a smart buyer of external services.

Unfortunately, 3D talent is no longer enough. Your company is probably already late in hiring these coming-soon roles: product incubation managers, behavioral scientists, journey mappers, business modelers, solution finders, and emerging-technology specialists. These six roles are difficult to fill through an external contract, so now is the time to start staffing them inside your organization.

Product Incubation Managers

Too often, companies confuse project management with product management. In the environment of digital innovation, product management is the one in short supply, as product lifecycles shrink from decades to years and years to months. Layer in the complexity of disruptive technologies, emerging use cases, and new business models, and the pool of product management talent is even smaller.

Whether you are a pharmaceutical company commercializing digital medicine or a professional-services firm delivering a basic advice chat bot, these are not your traditional offers. They require special attention in terms of how they will be launched, priced, marketed, sold, and serviced.

Product incubation managers go beyond the typical product management skill set. They are trained in agile methodology, skilled at positioning intrinsic (rather than explicit) value, and savvy about the unique triggers of digital lead generation.

Behavioral Scientists

The most meaningful innovation opportunities live or die on whether people actually change their behavior. Your goal may be reducing the incidence of chronic disease, improving manufacturing plant safety, or lowering a city's carbon footprint. All of these innovation opportunities are rooted in cognitive psychology and behavior change.

In consumer markets, the emergence of passive data capture via sensors and wearables, combined with AI-based pattern discovery, is driving personalized nudges that shift behavior. Apple calls these "notifications," and you may have turned some of them off to avoid being nudged while you read this book.

Aspiring Goliaths such as Penn Medicine, Walmart, Morningstar, AIG, and Maritz have formed behavioral science groups to grow this capability. Move fast as both cognitive and behavioral scientists with specialty majors such as neuroscience or behavioral economics will soon be in short supply. The best candidates also have consulting experience working with business stakeholders on frontline behavior change.

Journey Mappers

The journey mapper role has a greater scope than traditional user experience designers. This new role integrates qualitative and quantitative inputs to create powerful stories that spur new thinking around persistent problems.

Your company may already be overwhelmed by endless breadcrumb trails of digital interaction data. You may have deployed machine and deep-learning tools to discover new patterns in all of that data. The missing link is often this journey mapper role.

Journey mappers apply a scientific, fact-based approach to understanding context and constructing user journeys. Rather than basing these journeys on a handful of generic personas and scenarios, they define user context at a personal level. Aided by adaptive user interfaces, video analysis, emotion detection, and an array of new sensors, journey mappers test alternative hypotheses, incorporate real-time feedback, and rapidly iterate to arrive at the optimal future user experience.

Journey mapper backgrounds include design, ethnography, observational research, data science, trend scouting, scenario development, and narrative creation.

Business Modelers

Given the complex and fast-changing business conditions that established companies are facing, they must continuously challenge their business model assumptions. As discussed in Chapter 5, business model innovation can drive significantly more value than either product or operational innovation alone.

While many companies develop business cases and estimate the ROI for potential innovations, few invest enough time in dynamic business model development and rigorous assumption testing.

Rapid experimentation and de-risking assumptions are critical in lean startup and discovery-driven planning. Business modelers develop adaptive financial models around reverse income statements that surface the most important assumptions. Your company can then execute the right experiments to finalize your future business model design.

Business modelers help maximize learning per dollar as your company implements an agile methodology. Without them, those sprints and minimum viable products are just random initiatives without a clear path to an attractive business return.

Great candidates for the business modeler role have strong finance backgrounds, experience in probabilistic models, familiarity with emerging technologies and venture creation, expertise in new business models, and an entrepreneurial mindset.

Solution Finders

As you saw with the NASA case study in Chapter 7, solution finders are just as important as inventors in pivoting to open innovation. Where specialists go deep in relatively narrow areas, solution finders are systems thinkers with a keen understanding of multiple disciplines. They connect the dots from emerging patterns to unmet needs and potential solutions.

Solution finders proactively cultivate innovation networks; leverage open innovation platforms, such as InnoCentive and Kaggle; and translate raw inventions into complete solutions that meet a defined need. In NASA's case, solution finders were already on the payroll and just needed to be recognized for the value their role could contribute to NASA's mission.

Companies with a traditional focus on internal R&D will likely need to hire these solution finders from the outside. Solution finders need to be skilled at leveraging external innovators, be collaborative with internal business units, have broad technology and business understanding, be experienced with open innovation platforms, and demonstrate a relentless focus on commercial impact.

Emerging Technology Specialists

With the digital landscape being reshaped by AI, IoT, blockchain, and immersive experiences, organizations require specialists capable of tracking, translating, and hype-testing these technologies over time. Emerging-technology specialists look over the horizon to identify how these disruptive technologies may impact your company, either positively or negatively.

In the case of AI, only 16% of companies are currently seeing the benefits from machine and deep-learning initiatives. It is not that these disruptive technologies don't work, it is more that AI is frequently applied to use cases that do not provide a clear ROI for the business—something that an AI specialist would be able to avoid.

These specialists require deep expertise within their technology domain as well as an appreciation for the most likely use cases and applications. They are often organized into centers of excellence so that their impact can be amplified across business units, but can also be multipliers as part of a business unit or function. Specialists need to focus on translating the art of the possible into business impact, not science fiction projects.

Invest in Preemptive Skill Development

The roles above are examples of how your company needs to evolve its talent strategy to turn the tables on digital disruptors. So how can you close your current talent gaps and get ahead of your future talent needs? The only way is through preemptive skill development.

Building capability at a material scale in these new roles is not easy. Candidates with the required skills are in short supply and universities are late in building dedicated majors in these new domains. To secure your talent future, consider four parallel models for preemptive skill development: internal development and mobility, external recruiting, partners and freelancers, and skill grafting.

Internal Development and Mobility

Here is a scary fact—42% of millennials will leave their jobs if they are not learning fast enough. Their generation has career-development impatience. Your company must provide career paths that allow talented young employees to experience a number of roles in a short time frame. This will lower attrition, accelerate learning, and get the right people in the right roles sooner.

This rapid-rotation approach requires aggressive mentoring and just-in-time training to ensure your people are productive. Invest in a train-the-trainer model as you grow your internal community or "tribe" in each new role. New social networks such as TalentSky are helping established companies better express their skill demand in these emerging areas and consider a broader pool of internal and external talent in staffing decisions.

External Recruiting

While external recruiting can be expensive, it is the fastest way to overcome your company's blind spots. Established companies often have more money than time in dealing with digital disruption. Therefore, it is worth taking the risk of getting some external hires wrong to accelerate your pace of innovation.

Aspiring Goliaths have tended to focus external hiring around key areas such as adjacent market entry. For example, when retail pharmacy CVS acquired Aetna in order to enter the market for health insurance it acquired a massive new talent base. Similarly, GM used both acquisitions and external recruiting to secure its path to Goliath's Revenge through electrification, autonomy, and shared transportation.

Partners and Freelancers

The imperative of time often makes partnering for the roles above an attractive option. While contract talent will likely cost two to three times as much per person as an internal employee, you can put that talent to work immediately.

Open innovation platforms such as Topcoder and Kaggle are important sources of on-demand talent in these new roles. With 92% of millennials wanting to work remotely, these gig economy workers do not even need a seat in your office to be effective. For example, companies such as PWC are tapping into this gig economy talent pool through their Talent Exchange platform.

Skill Grafting

The grafting of plants to improve survival rates, increase yield, and select for new attributes goes back four millennia to ancient China. Much like the grafting of plants, achieving the optimal talent mix that maximizes digital innovation yield is challenging. Done right, the payoff is extraordinary.

As you saw in the Penn Medicine case example, it is often easier to find two people with complementary skills and team them up than search for the needle-in-a-haystack domain-plus-technology hire. Many digital organizations are experimenting with paired programming models that do this at scale.

Google discovered that the success of product teams is as dependent on soft skills and personality mix as hard skills and technical experience. To make skill grafting work, put effort into the soft-skill side of integrating people from different functions, companies, and industries into high-performing teams.

Prioritize Your Talent Sourcing Options

We have now covered the first three actions in valuing talent over technology: honor institutional knowledge, go beyond 3D digital roles, and commit to preemptive skill development. Using Figure 8.1, decide how your organization will source talent for the nine roles outlined earlier.

		Expected Talent Sourcing Mix			
		Internal Development and Mobility	External Recruiting	Partners and Freelancers	Skill Grafting
Near-Term "3D" Roles	Designers	##%	##%	##%	##%
	Developers	##%	##%	##%	##%
	Data Scientists	##%	##%	##%	##%
Medium-Term New Digital Innovation Roles	Product Incubation Managers	##%	##%	##%	##%
	Behavioral Scientists	##%	##%	##%	##%
	Journey Mappers	##%	##%	##%	##%
	Business Modelers	##%	##%	##%	##%
	Solution Finders	##%	##%	##%	##%
	Emerging Technology Specialists	##%	##%	##%	##%

FIGURE 8.1   Preemptive Skill Development Plan.

Think about what percentage each talent source (the columns) should represent for each of the digital innovation roles (the rows). All rows should add to 100%. Once you are done, add up the columns to get a relative ranking of the importance of each preemptive skill-development approach for your business.

Value Venture General Managers

Most companies develop generalist employees that they hope can run a function or business unit over time. This approach often backfires. Corporate generalists watch their careers plateau due to a lack of digital skills. Talented specialists get pulled away from their unique area of expertise and are forced to become generalists. Both scenarios lead to frustration for the employee and a leadership chasm for the company.

Getting to the Balanced T

As shown in Figure 8.2, the ideal leadership profile in a rapidly digitizing world is what we call a "balanced T" venture general manager

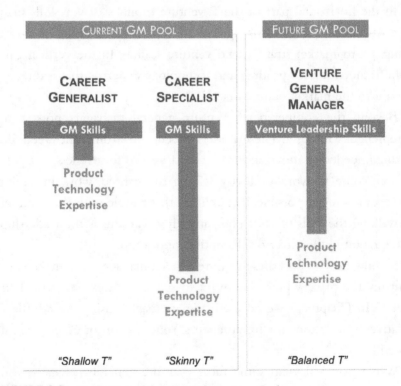

FIGURE 8.2   Evolution of the General Manager Role.

profile (right side of figure). The current development approach produces either the shallow T profile of too-broad generalists (far left) or the skinny T profile of converted specialists (middle).

Venture capitalists have always valued these balanced T venture general managers. While you can add quantity to make up for below-average quality in some jobs, this is not possible for leadership roles. Companies that have tried two-in-a-box leadership structures suffer from too-slow decision-making.

For example, one of the reasons Blackberry lost out in the market shift to smartphones was its dual-CEO structure. Apple simply ran circles around them with its single, buck-stops-here CEO. The importance of having a single leader is only increasing during this period of digital disruption in which time is the scarce commodity.

In the horizontal part of the T, venture capitalists favor skills such as capital raising, design thinking, lean startup execution, calculated risk taking, go-to-market strategy, and venture scaling. In the vertical part of the T, they look for product and technology expertise that is directly relevant to the market being pursued.

Beyond the competencies, venture general managers possess an entrepreneur's mindset. These leaders execute to a different creed: do anything needed to move an idea forward; ask for forgiveness, not permission; come to work each day willing to be fired; work in stealth mode for as long as possible. It is unlikely that people with this mindset are walking the halls of your company. However, this is the leadership profile required to deliver on disruptive innovation.

So how do you find these venture general managers and make your company the place where they want to spend the next stage of their careers? In Chapter 5 we covered one approach—using your Little I initiatives as auditions for intrapreneurs. Your version of *Shark Tank*, if you will.

While that will yield some future venture general managers, you almost certainly will need more of them to defend your current business and grow into adjacent markets. The second approach is to create a parallel organizational model in which venture general managers from the outside can coexist and succeed alongside your core business. Cisco provides an impressive example.

Cisco Builds a Venture General Manager Bench

Cisco's go-to innovation model has been to let Silicon Valley do most of the work: that is, let the VC community fund many competing companies, then allow Darwinian selection to cull the herd down to a few potential winners. Mike Volpe, former head of mergers and acquisitions, honed the model of acquiring one of the emerging leaders and then playing kingmaker by pushing that company's technology through Cisco's prodigious sales and channel ecosystems.

A happy byproduct of Cisco's codependent relationship with Silicon Valley has been an embarrassment of riches in terms of venture general manager talent. Cisco's former CEO, John Chambers, saw the second-order benefits of retaining the CEOs of acquired startups after the integrations of their companies were complete. Chambers viewed Cisco as having an unlimited set of market adjacencies, with its venture general manager capacity acting as the scarce resource in pursuing them.

At one point Cisco had over a hundred former CEOs working for the company. Chambers treated these venture general managers like a private equity firm treats their entrepreneurs in residence. Cisco paid them handsomely to wait for the right opportunity before deploying them to create a new market, grow an existing business, or run a newly acquired technology tuck-in.

These ex-CEOs all felt that they worked for Chambers, even if they had two or three layers of management in between them and Cisco's CEO. Chambers "lent them out" for leadership roles across the company but kept in touch, mentored them, and recognized their efforts. This deep pool of venture general managers was a critical driver for how Cisco grew beyond its networking roots into entirely new areas such as data centers, online collaboration, smart grid, and telepresence.

Now, your company may not have the luxury of retaining that many former CEOs on the payroll at any one time. If you had 10, you would be well on your way to Goliath's Revenge. The key is to see venture general managers as the most important role in delivering on your Big I aspirations.

Optimize the AI-Human Balance

According to Ray Kurzweil, founder of Singularity University and director of engineering at Google, AI will reach human levels by 2029 and surpass it by a billionfold by 2045. Every established company is in a footrace to increase its cognitive capacity ahead of competitors.

Corporate investments in machine learning and broad data access are growing exponentially. However, to truly keep up with the deluge of AI-based applications and innovation opportunities, you need to quickly find an equilibrium between machines and people.

To actually use your data as currency, you must classify which activities should be optimized for machines, which for humans, and which for a hybrid model. This classification involves difficult decisions around reskilling, talent shaping, and rightsizing your labor force in the face of an AI-dominant future. Putting off this classification effort allows your competitors time to gain an algorithmic advantage that will be hard to overcome later.

The Three Phases of AI Migration

In most industries, AI is just beginning to drive real business value. AI is being deployed in specific use cases: bots for customer service, robotic process automation, personalized marketing, suggestive selling, and adaptive forecasting.

Some industry-specific use cases, such as AI-based risk management and fraud monitoring in financial services, are also starting to pay off. Advanced organizations are even hiring chief artificial intelligence officers to coordinate their efforts.

As shown in Figure 8.3, the AI invasion is unfolding across three phases, each with the potential to shift the balance of power from humans toward machines. Managing this AI–human balance across these phases is going to require significant leadership focus.

Phase 1: Exploration

This is the honeymoon phase of AI adoption. AI has made great progress in areas such as natural language processing, where accuracy has gone from 77% to 95% in just five years. However, the human brain still

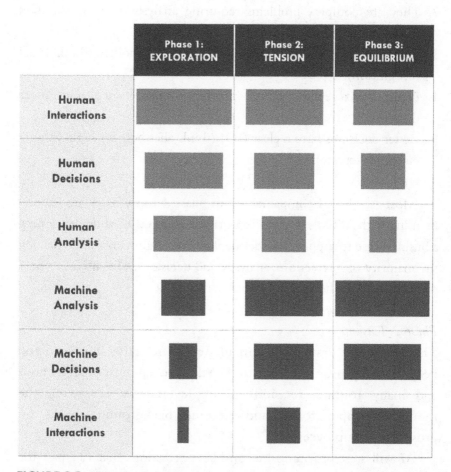

FIGURE 8.3 The Three Phases of the AI Invasion.

has 10 times the cognitive power of the world's fastest supercomputer (1,000 versus 100 petaflops). This will flip by 2020, given the current growth rate in computing power.

This exploration phase is focused on identifying near-term use cases, building the data sets required to train AI models, running pilots to validate the real-life benefits of AI, and redesigning business processes to fully leverage emerging AI applications.

Phase 1 use cases tend to share five characteristics:

1. They are repetitive tasks (think email spam filtering).
2. They are complex problems requiring analysis of many variables (think fraud detection).
3. Extensive data sets are available to train AI models (think facial recognition).
4. Errors are acceptable (think predictive maintenance, not cancer diagnosis).
5. Better decisions have a clear ROI (think chat bots for high-volume customer service).

Most established companies are in phase 1 today. They are experimenting with AI tools (such as TensorFlow and H2O) while developing a business case to support broader deployments. Humans are still driving the majority of interactions, analyses, and decisions. AI is used as a productivity tool for human 3D talent.

Phase 2: Tension

Things change dramatically in phase 2. Inevitably, machine and deep-learning progress leads to AI taking over most analysis tasks and many routine decisions. Examples include reviewing the inputs on paper forms and running background checks on prospective employees.

AI will start providing human-like interactions that can pass the Turing test as it takes on basic customer interactions and shared service functions. With potentially eight hundred million employees worldwide at risk of being displaced by automation, many employees will resist the push to automate their jobs.

Aspiring Goliaths are already putting in place social-responsibility plans for AI-driven worker displacement and reskilling. They are prioritizing growth opportunities that allow them to redeploy employees away from AI-ready routine tasks to roles requiring advanced soft skills, such as improving the customer experience, creating new product offerings, and designing operational improvements.

This might entail retail employees moving from back-of-store stockrooms to front-of-store customer-liaison roles. Truck drivers may need to become customer service reps. Financial planners may need to become financial coaches and relationship managers. You get the picture.

A lot of cheese is going to have to get moved in phase 2. If your company gets it right, AI and humans will start working together effectively and evolve toward a more fulfilling and productive future. Your talent management system will adjust to the gradual migration of tasks from humans to machines in parallel with a focus on new tasks that machines simply cannot do.

If you get it wrong, you and your company will get stuck in phase 2. The tension between minds and machines will freeze your organization in time. It will cut short your path to achieving Goliath's Revenge. Your company will get mired in philosophical discussions that validate the do-nothing option. You will fail to work through the ethical questions such as how long displaced employees should be given to build higher-order skills, when customers should be informed that their data is being used to train an AI application, and what to do if the AI model makes decisions with adverse consequences.

Phase 3: Equilibrium
In phase 3, established companies will achieve a new equilibrium in the respective roles of AI and humans. Use cases will be classified based on the potential for AI to deliver beyond-human results. Many of these will

require emotional intelligence, creativity, and nuanced interaction skills that are still far in the future as of this writing.

Successful Goliaths will be proactive in training their human workforce to fully leverage the machines to do more with the same rather than do the same with less. Corporate training will focus on next-level technical, problem-solving, and cognitive abilities, while company cultures will embrace a growth mindset instead of a defensive one.

Shortages in the 3D roles—designers, developers, and data scientists—will diminish in phase 3 as computers get better at writing code and building their own predictive models. Research from the University of Oxford suggests that the chance of programming roles being lost to automation is 48%. Product leaders, marketing experts, and user experience designers will no longer have to wait in line for scarce technical staff to respond to their requests. This will unlock the next leg of AI-powered growth in a self-reinforcing cycle.

As the AI invasion unfolds through these three phases, your best approach is going to be a proactive one. Once humans in routine jobs are displaced, it is too late to get the AI-human balance right. You need to already be executing your plan on how to redeploy your talent before the next wave of AI-driven change hits.

Improve Your Digital Dexterity

The final step in valuing talent over technology is increasing the digital dexterity of your leaders and teams. Digital is a moving target. It used to be about e-commerce and apps, but now it has morphed to include technologies such as AI, mixed reality, IoT, and blockchain.

Your company may still be thinking that a single CDO or CIO hire can cover the waterfront. That is like searching for a unicorn or a four-leafed clover: not impossible but highly unlikely. Few digital leaders in the world can stretch from the AI-based personalization of customer engagement to applying blockchain for global manufacturing compliance.

Aspiring Goliaths view digital as a team sport. They are asking each senior leader to adjust his or her focus and put these new rules into practice. See Figure 8.4 for examples of how senior executive roles are changing.

Evolving the individual roles of your senior team is a good start, but not enough to achieve Goliath's Revenge. An all-hands-on-deck sense of urgency is going to be required. We call that digital dexterity.

Growing Your Digital Dexterity

Digital dexterity is a measure of how well leaders and teams demonstrate technology awareness, customer focus, disruptive innovation, an experimental mindset, and a passion for rapid execution.

It is grounded in research on what underpins successful leaders and teams. As shown in Figure 8.5, digital dexterity focuses on the attributes an organization needs to have across digital strategists, digital innovators, and digital drivers.

Some of the drive factors and types shown in the figure's arrows represent standard attributes of individuals in high-performance teams.

	INFLUENCER	SHAPER
CHIEF INFORMATION OFFICER	Define and manage enabling digital infrastructure	Own all digital infrastructure and app portfolio
CHIEF MARKETING OFFICER	Set marketing related digital standards	Own all customer facing digital opportunities and incubator lab
CHIEF TECHNOLOGY OFFICER	Recommend digital architecture	Own digital product development and lab
CHIEF DIGITAL OFFICER	Evangelize digital possibilities, set standards	Lead overall digital portfolio and digital incubator/lab/ventures
CHIEF DATA OFFICER	Driving data access and modeling standards for digital	Digital used to fuel AI/data product portfolio and innovations
CHIEF PRODUCT / INNOVATION OFFICER	Integrate digital into product dev/innovation activities	Own digital product portfolio, lab and ecosystem/ventures
BUSINESS UNIT DIGITAL EXEC	Informs company digital portfolio with BU requirements	Owns development and mgmt. of digital portfolio for BU
CORPORATE VENTURES LEADER	Recommend and manage investments to support digital	Own digital ecosystem and external digital product incubation

FIGURE 8.4 The Digitization of Leadership Roles.

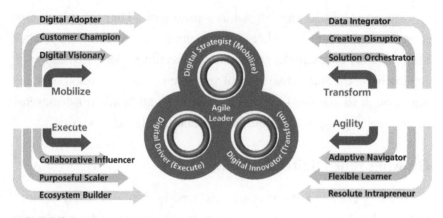

FIGURE 8.5   Drivers of Digital Dexterity.

SOURCE: Adapted from the Digital Dexterity Leadership Framework, Heidrick & Struggles, 2018.

However, several are worth extra focus as you think about expanding your organization's digital dexterity.

Let's start with the "purposeful scaler"—ruthlessly prioritizing, driving rapid action, and making swift decisions in delivering on the promise of innovation initiatives. Too many digital efforts have ended up in pilot hell with great demos but minimal business impact. Teams that include a purposeful scaler think beyond the demo or proof-of-concept from day one. Their innovations are built to scale.

Second is the "digital ecosystem builder"—tapping into a flexible, diverse pool of the best digital talent across internal groups and external partnerships to achieve outcomes that others view as impossible. Digital ecosystem builders seamlessly harness the best of the best across organizational boundaries. They possess charismatic leadership that inspires people in far-flung corners of your company to want to be part of their initiatives, even if that means night and weekend work.

Finally, the "flexible learner" and "adaptive navigator" have intense curiosity about new ways of working and a focus on swiftly adjusting to the constant changes afoot across the innovation landscape. Digital is moving so fast that proficient is no longer good enough. Team members need to have the mental agility and adaptive mindset to stay abreast of shifts in disruptive technologies, market boundaries, competitive offers, and customer expectations over time. They need to adjust their execution dynamically to reflect these external shifts.

Use the drive factors in Figure 8.5 as a checklist when you are assembling your talent into action teams around your most important Big I and Little I innovations. Seek a balance across those areas to maximize each team's digital dexterity.

Rule 5: Company and Career Readiness

So, you've thought through how to value talent over technology. Your organization is ready to honor institutional knowledge, go beyond 3D digital roles, commit to preemptive skill development, value venture general managers, optimize the AI-human balance, and improve your digital dexterity. Before we move on to the final new rule, it is time to complete your company and career self-assessments.

Company Readiness Self-Assessment

Let's start with your company's readiness for Rule 5. You are a professional at this exercise by now. Read the progression of options carefully before indicating how far your company has progressed on each row in Figure 8.6.

If you work in a large company, some parts of the organization may be further along on certain areas than others. Try to come up with an average assessment for each row that represents your company's overall talent readiness. You can always come back later and repeat the exercise for just your team or group.

Career Readiness Self-Assessment

Shift from the macro to the micro now. What is your individual contribution to your company's talent readiness? Again, be a tough grader as you complete the exercise in Figure 8.7. This is a tool for you to

RULE #5: VALUE TALENT OVER TECHNOLOGY
COMPANY SELF-ASSESSMENT GRID

	0-20% Minimal Capability	20-40% Limited Capability	40-60% Moderate Capability	60-80% Advanced Capability	80-100% World Class Capability
Honor institutional knowledge	Long-term employees are working to undermine the digital transformation	Seasoned employees and digital newcomers beginning to trust each other	Some teams collaborating well across veteran staff and new digital hires	Veteran staff and new digital hires investing substantial time to learn from each other	Veteran staff and outside digital hires working seamlessly to invent the future
Go beyond "3D" digital roles	Facing a major shortage of design, development, data science talent	Most required design, development, data science talent in place and productive	Significant talent in place for at least two of the six "beyond 3D" digital roles	Significant talent in place for at least four of the six "beyond 3D" digital roles	Significant talent in place for five or all six of the "beyond 3D" digital roles
Commit to pre-emptive skill development	Company is reactive in developing digital skills	Dependent on recruiting as main source of digital skills	Strong mobility programs developing skills internally	Fully leveraging partners and freelancers to fill skill gaps	Skill grafting delivering "one plus one equals five" talent
Value Venture General Managers	Venture GM role not well understood or valued	Aware that Venture GM pool is limiting growth	Modest pool of Venture GMs recycled across opportunities	Venture GM pool viewed as competitive advantage	Venture GMs driving multiple breakout growth plays
Optimize the AI-Human Balance	Human staff actively sabotaging AI rollouts to protect jobs	Human staff view AI with suspicion and worried for their jobs	Human staff in the midst of resetting roles due to rapidly improving AI	AI and Humans fully adjusted to the "new normal" – working well	Humans growing impact by proactively offloading basic work to AI
Improve your digital dexterity	None of the 12 drivers of digital dexterity in place	At least 3 of the 12 drivers of digital dexterity in place	At least 6 of the 12 drivers of digital dexterity in place	At least 9 of the 12 drivers of digital dexterity in place	All 12 drivers of digital dexterity in place and driving results

| 0% | 20% | 40% | 60% | 80% | 100% |

FIGURE 8.6   Rule 5 Company Self-Assessment Grid.

prioritize your ongoing professional development, so knowing where your gaps are is important.

Rule 5 Readiness Summary

Now that you've completed your company and career self-assessments for Rule 5, you can fill in your readiness summary in

RULE #5: VALUE TALENT OVER TECHNOLOGY
CAREER SELF-ASSESSMENT GRID

	0-20% Minimal Capability	20-40% Limited Capability	40-60% Moderate Capability	60-80% Advanced Capability	80-100% World Class Capability
Honor institutional knowledge	Sometimes viewed as divisive and political even if you are not really like that	Open to working with people from different organizations if required	Proven ability to work equally well with veteran staff and new digital hires alike	Viewed by peers as a great connector between disparate organizations	In-demand to lead teams that leverage long-term staff and new digital hires
Go beyond "3D" digital roles	No experience yet in the "3D" roles let alone the six new digital roles	Experience in at least one of the design, development, data science roles	Have completed job rotations in at least one of the six new digital roles	Have completed job rotations in at least two of the six new digital roles	Significant experience in at least three of the six new "beyond 3D" digital roles
Commit to pre-emptive skill development	Unclear on your professional skill gaps relative to future digital demand	Understand your skill gaps but have not done anything to address them	Have made a lateral career move to build your digital skill set	Have taken online courses on personal time to develop digital skills	Already worked in paired jobs for rapid skill development
Value Venture General Managers	Have no general manager skills to speak of	Have general manager skills but only in a mature business	Have led a successful innovation venture	Strong results leading many innovation teams	Peers seek your mentorship to build Venture GM skills
Optimize the AI-Human Balance	Act defensively when presented with AI projects and initiatives	View AI suspiciously as it regards your future career	Have led AI projects that delivered their promised results	Expert at getting AI and Humans working well	Viewed as AI innovator that is savvy about human impact
Improve your digital dexterity	Do not yet demonstrate any drivers of digital dexterity	Demonstrate at least 3 drivers of digital dexterity	Demonstrate at least 6 drivers of digital dexterity	Demonstrate at least 9 drivers of digital dexterity	Demonstrate all 12 drivers of digital dexterity

| 0% | 20% | 40% | 60% | 80% | 100% |

FIGURE 8.7   Rule 5 Career Self-Assessment Grid.

Figure 8.8. As with the previous rules, if you are doing these self-assessments online at www.goliathsrevenge.com, this readiness summary will be produced for you automatically.

It is time to move on to the final rule for turning the tables on digital disruptors: Reframe your purpose.

RULE #5: VALUE TALENT OVER TECHNOLOGY READINESS SUMMARY

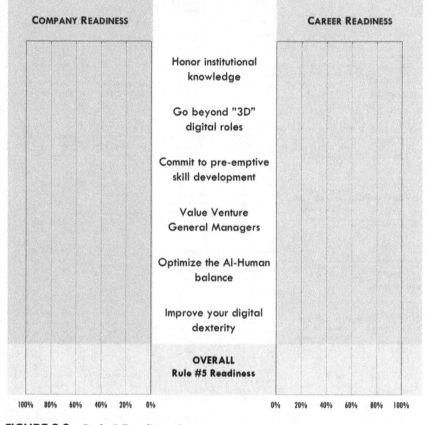

FIGURE 8.8   Rule 5 Readiness Summary.

Chapter 9

Rule 6: Reframe Your Purpose

Keep your eyes on the stars and keep your feet on the ground.

—*Theodore Roosevelt, US president*

Congratulations—you've made it to the sixth rule. Now we can imagine that you might have reservations about spending your time on reframing your purpose. We have all been through arm-waving visioning exercises that made our eyes roll and led to nothing of significance changing in the companies we've worked for. Keep an open mind, as the exercise of reframing your purpose is not one of those time wasters.

You see, reframing your purpose is really about opening up the range of growth options that your company is willing to consider. It is about raising your sights from your current industry position, business model, and product offerings to allow you and your peers to pursue the adjacent market opportunities that digital disruption creates.

It is also about engaging the next generation. In our research for *Goliath's Revenge*, we interviewed dozens of millennials to understand how they decide which companies to work for. The key finding is that this generation needs to feel that they are in service to a higher calling than market-share growth and stock-price appreciation. If they are the heart of your future workforce, then reframing your purpose is critical.

Doing so requires six actions: raise your sights, answer the Five Whys, embrace smart cannibalization, engage the next generation, align top down, and lead by example.

Raise Your Sights

Rule 6 is last for a reason. While the first five rules allow for rapid iteration and experimentation, established companies can't test their purpose and learn from those test results. If you get your purpose right, you will change your company forever in terms of its innovation opportunities, growth trajectory, and access to talent. If you miss the mark, you risk joining the rudderless companies orbiting the corporate world, losing energy with each passing year.

Reframing your purpose involves changes to both your mission and vision. Your mission shapes your organization's tone and culture. It focuses the energy of the company on how to deliver value to your customers day in and day out. Your vision defines your company's aspirational goal in terms of the big problems you solve and how solving those problems contributes to the greater good.

Powerful mission and vision statements act as important catalysts for innovation. Figure 9.1 provides examples of how strong statements of purpose can raise the sights of entire organizations.

Your purpose is why you exist as a company. Don't think about this in terms of the corporate doublespeak of large organizations. Even the smallest company needs to be crystal clear on its reason for being, and the idea that its purpose is broader than its current capabilities. Raising your sights literally provides room for your company, you, and your

	patagonia	**Linked in**	**CATERPILLAR**	**coinbase**
MISSION	Build the best product, cause no unnecessary harm, use business to inspire and implement solutions to the environmental crisis.	Connect the world's professionals to make them more productive and successful.	Enable economic growth through infrastructure and energy development, and to provide solutions that support communities and protect the planet.	Create an open financial system for the world.
VISION	A love of wild and beautiful places demands participation in the fight to save them, and to help reverse the steep decline in the overall environmental health of our planet.	Create economic opportunity for every member of the global workforce.	A world in which all of people's basic needs are fulfilled in an environmentally sustainable way and a company that improves the quality of the environment and the communities where we live and work.	Digital currency will bring about more innovation, efficiency, and equality of opportunity in the world by creating an open financial system.

FIGURE 9.1   Sample Mission and Vision Statements.

people to grow. It creates space for exploration, experimentation, and breakthrough innovation. It focuses your attention on serving the needs of existing and new customers alike.

Your company likely has a well-honed model for improving its existing products and current operations. However, innovation around how you make money is a much bigger leap. It opens up the potential risks and vulnerabilities inherent in your current business model. Only companies that have raised their sights have the courage required to pull it off.

Apple Raises Its Sights

An example might help. While you might think of Apple as a product innovation machine, that capability produced the flat line stock price of a company headed to its grave over its first two decades (Figure 9.2).

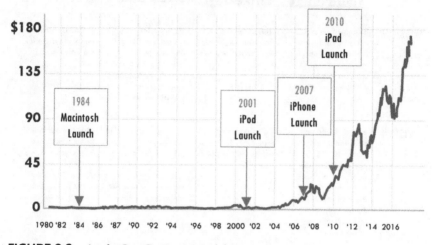

FIGURE 9.2   Apple Gets Business Model Innovation.

Only in 2001 did Apple's stock price head for the stars. That is the year that Apple raised its sights and was willing to take on business model innovation. While the Macintosh was an innovative product, the business model of personal computers was not changed by it.

With the iPod, Apple innovated the exponential growth of a two-sided business model. The iTunes application connected artists with the broad population of Apple device users in an entirely new way. With the iTunes Store's 99-cent-per-song business model, Apple broke apart the established business model of the music industry—the album. The iTunes innovation redefined the industry's gives and gets to deliver music lovers a step-change customer outcome: just the songs you love without the filler of the songs you don't.

The right side of Figure 9.2 tells a pretty convincing story. When Apple dropped "Computer" from its name in 2007, its sights were well and truly raised. Apple's broader purpose became changing people's lives for the better. The App Store was Apple's next business model innovation, helping it go from strength to strength on the path to becoming the first publicly traded company valued at over $1 trillion.

Aspiring Goliaths across other industries are following Apple's example and raising their sights. GM is morphing into a sustainable transportation leader that happens to include a highly efficient automotive manufacturing business. Discovery Insurance is migrating from a traditional insurance business model to an innovative one based on shared risks and rewards with its customers. Mastercard is broadening its purpose from running a credit card network to enabling modern payment ecosystems. Deere is evolving from manufacturing farm equipment to creating greater crop yield with precision agriculture.

All of these companies started with foresight about where the world is going and raised their sights about the role they could play in helping it get there. Take a moment to reflect on the digital transformation of your industry and the broader mission and vision that could unlock new innovation opportunities for your company.

Answer the Five Whys

Taiichi Ohno, founding father of what has become lean manufacturing, came up with the concept of the Five Whys as a way to understand a company's true purpose. Think of it as peeling back the layers of an onion to get to the core of why your company even exists. Start with "Why do we do what we do?" before going deeper into your answer with another why question, until you've drilled down to the core of your purpose. It generally takes five "why" questions to reach that core.

If you only get one shot at reframing your purpose, then the time required to answer each of the Five Whys is time well spent. Let's start with the example of a product we have all worn: sneakers. If your company were in the business of producing sneakers, then this might be how you would answer the Five Whys:

1. Why do we make sneakers? Because customers want sneakers.
2. Why do customers want sneakers? For their athletic activities.

3. Why do people engage in athletic activities? To compete and improve.
4. Why do people want to compete and improve? To be their personal best.
5. Why do people want to be their personal best? To feel good and inspire others.

Now, the purpose of this exercise is to unlock those market adjacencies we discussed in the previous rules. If you are going to set your sights on growth beyond your current core business, the Five Whys is the methodology for how to focus your organization on markets that are truly adjacent versus those that are just wishful thinking.

If you were to overlay that adjacent-market view onto the sneaker example above you would produce a market map, such as the one shown in Figure 9.3.

In line with this example, Nike's mission is "To bring innovation and inspiration to every athlete in the world." That broad purpose validates efforts by every Nike organization to innovate new business models far afield from sneakers and apparel. Examples include training services,

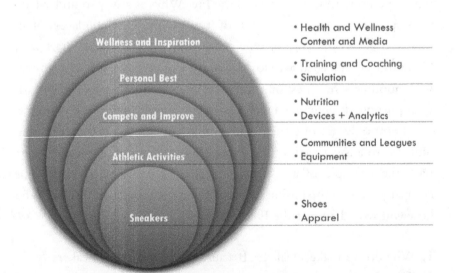

FIGURE 9.3 The Five Whys Broaden Market Reach.

fitness tracking devices, online gaming, nutrition counseling, athletic performance benchmarks, and innovative subscription business models (such as Peloton's).

Waze, the wildly popular traffic navigation application with over 65 million users in 185 countries, provides another example. If you ask the executives at Waze what the company's purpose is, you will find that it is not providing better traffic data. Waze is in service to giving people time back in their lives. It even celebrates how well it is doing—roughly 60 hours per year per customer. By framing its purpose so broadly, Waze is willing to explore additional services that can give customers back more time every day. Current examples include dynamically adjusting suggested routes based on customers' shopping lists and anticipating mealtimes to know when and where to preorder takeout food during a road trip.

Can you answer the Five Whys for your team, division, business unit, or whole company? Would your peers come up with similar answers? Take the time to find out.

Embrace Smart Cannibalization

When it comes to Big I disruptive innovation, most established companies are on the wrong end of the transition, on the road to becoming the disrupted instead of the disruptor. The paralyzing fear of cannibalizing their current profitable businesses is the single greatest risk they face in the digital age.

By now you know the lessons of what not to do by heart. Kodak invented the digital camera but chose not to commercialize it to protect film margins. Blockbuster lost out to Netflix by protecting the excess margins that came from late fees. Both went bankrupt.

Even when the fear of cannibalizing core businesses was not terminal, it delayed the success that established companies could have had sooner. Examples include Dell turning down an early chance to acquire Apple, Microsoft missing the opportunity to buy Google, and both Lockheed and Boeing underestimating the impact of the Predator drone on their core franchises.

The Two-Speed Organization Model

Embracing smart cannibalization requires a two-speed organization model that can fully participate in both the old wave and the next one. Your core business represents your speed-one organization. It is like a strong, powerful ocean liner—it is highly optimized for dependability, performance, efficiency, and profitability but has little ability to vary its speed or direction. Speed one is where your employees likely feel most comfortable and where the primary focus of your existing business metrics probably is.

Speed two represents keeping pace with digital disruption. Technologies such as AI, robotics, IoT, blockchain, and immersive experiences are changing the basis of competition in your industry. New competitors are emerging, while many of your traditional ones are falling behind. Establishing speed two requires a level of organizational agility that only a few established companies are able to muster today.

Here is your checklist of the five characteristics required to unlock speed two: culture of innovation, tribe of intrapreneurs, minimal administrative friction, access to crown jewels, and executive air cover. We have already covered these broadly in previous chapters, but take a moment now to consider whether your company is fully committed to them.

Culture of Innovation

Shaping and nurturing a culture of innovation is essential for both Little I improvements in your speed-one core business and Big I bets in your speed-two initiatives beyond it.

All employees must feel that they are helping deliver on your company's future vision and purpose. Your leadership team must be clear that a broad range of skills, areas of expertise, and backgrounds are critical to your company being able to thrive in the age of digital disruption.

Little I and Big I need to be rewarded in equal measure, so as not to shortchange either aspect of your two-speed organization model. Everyone needs to reap the spoils of your company achieving Goliath's Revenge.

Tribe of Intrapreneurs

Just hiring cool kids from the venture world in the hope of injecting start-up DNA into your company and buying your way to the two-speed organization model has a low chance of success. In fact, established companies are downsizing or mothballing their one-off innovation labs and design studios.

Follow the example of Mastercard and replace these one-off labs with a systematic program that can identify, develop, and retain employees with intrapreneurial qualities. That hidden-in-plain-sight talent is much more likely to be respectful of the core business and commit to your organization for the long term.

Using those internal entrepreneurial leaders as your base, you can then blend in outside talent to fuel disruptive ventures. That inside-out approach to developing two-speed organization talent gives your company the best chance of scaling beyond its legacy businesses.

Minimal Administrative Friction

Back in 1943, Kelly Johnson set up Lockheed's Skunk Works in Burbank, California, to rapidly develop a high-speed spy plane, which was the predecessor of the SR-71 Blackbird. Johnson erected a circus tent one mile from the main Lockheed facility and demanded that the group be able to establish its own rules for human resources, procurement, manufacturing, and quality in order to speed up the innovation cycle.

Johnson was ahead of his time. In most established companies, the finance, legal, procurement, and human resource functions have unintentionally erected strong barriers to innovation. Your fledgling two-speed organization can be easily overwhelmed by the administrative friction that these functions introduce into new ventures.

John Chambers and Marthin De Beer took a page from Johnson's playbook in setting up the Emerging Technology Group at Cisco. They put in place what were called rules of the road. Those rules conferred on Cisco's Big I new ventures a limited-time exemption from the standard operating procedures of the functions above. Those time limits accelerated Cisco's pace of innovation, as intrapreneurs wanted to take advantage of their opportunities to execute without the burden of excessive administrative friction.

Access to Crown Jewels

As discussed in Chapter 2, established companies often have more valuable crown jewels—self-funding innovation, brand reach, existing customer relationships, installed base, data sets, blocking patents, and standards influence—than they realize. However, those assets tend to be tightly coupled with the speed-one organizations that manage your core business.

To realize the full potential of your incumbent's advantage, you must overcome a combination of technological and process barriers. On the technology side, put in place a flexible infrastructure that mimics third-party clouds: that is, one that can be rapidly and easily provisioned through a set of consumable APIs. This maximizes the pace at which your ecosystem partners can tap into your data sets, algorithms, and applications as they develop and pilot innovative solutions. Your IT team must become an enabler for innovation instead of a gatekeeper. Your innovation sandbox (discussed in Chapter 7) will enable this iterative approach to innovation without putting your production systems and customer data at risk.

Your process challenges can be dealt with by standardizing the process for how pilots involving the assets of a speed-one organization are conducted. Think through the simplest gives and gets of your speed-one and speed-two teams to avoid one-off negotiations of political credit or revenue attributions. Next, apply lean thinking to your piloting program as you would with any other core business process. This combination allowed a Canadian bank to cut the time needed for initiating a pilot with an ecosystem partner from six months to just six weeks.

Executive Air Cover

When times get tough in the core business, leaders must resist the knee-jerk reaction to implement short-term financial measures. You've likely heard seemingly innocuous phrases such as "We are just tapping the brakes on that investment," "You can only have Sally and Frank if they can also cover their old jobs," and "The hiring freeze is just until we get through this quarter."

If you are looking for ways to kill your speed-two businesses, these are prime examples. Avoiding them requires air cover from your senior executive team. They are the ones who can avoid robbing the future to pay for the present.

Lou Gerstner's commitment to IBM's Emerging Business Opportunity incubator is a great example. IBM was in the midst of a gut-wrenching transformation from hardware manufacturer to software and services leader. Gerstner preserved the Big I bets within IBM's incubator through thick and thin. The company delivered the decade of protection and patient capital needed to allow Big I innovations (such as Watson) time to achieve their promise.

Pause here to reflect on which of these five enablers of a two-speed organization your company is capable of today. For the ones missing, can you at least identify who in your company is working to put them in place?

Engage the Next Generation

Today's 140 million so-called digital natives—the millennials and Gen Z'ers—represent 25% of the workforce and nearly $2 trillion of buying power. These are your future employees, and if your company is consumer facing, your future customers.

Digital natives are always connected and deeply mission driven. They are highly influenced by the social graph and exhibit a swarm-like behavior that multiplies their influence based on the relative size of their personal networks.

Digital natives use social networks to highlight major issues in the world around them but also believe that they have the power to address them. They are not afraid to speak up if they see something wrong with the status quo, particularly when their online networks affirm their opinions and reward their outspokenness.

This next generation tends to expect business leaders to weigh in on important issues, such as immigration, sexual harassment, racial discrimination, and climate change. They yearn to be part of efforts that make our world more inclusive, accepting, socially aware, and environmentally responsible. They hold themselves, their friends, and their employers accountable to these end goals.

Digital natives are at risk of painting all established companies with the same brush: being interested in profits at the expense of their employees and the planet. They don't see why it's so hard for companies to be both fiscally and socially responsible. They wonder why there are not more companies like Patagonia, which is helping to prevent deforestation; Warby Parker, which is helping to improve global eye care; and IKEA, which is actively hiring for diversity. In their eyes, it should be the standard for successful organizations to try to give back more than they take.

Reframe your purpose with digital natives in mind. They are the future and you want your updated mission and vision to stand the test of time. Digital natives think money is something you should earn if you do things that matter. Focus your purpose on why you matter to the world and digital natives will be flocking to your door to join the cause.

One way to achieve this is to express your reframed purpose in terms of your triple bottom line—that is, your social, environmental, and financial measures of success. Dow Jones even has its Sustainability Index, which measures how companies perform on this holistic set of measures.

Unilever, Patagonia, and Nestlé are excellent examples of this triple-bottom-line approach. Unilever is specifically developing products tailored to meet the needs of impoverished, developing parts of the world while preventing harm to our environment. Patagonia is extending the reach of its apparel brand with digital natives by promoting the recycling of clothing, equal access to opportunities, and sustainable manufacturing in an industry notorious for poor working conditions and damage to the environment. Nestlé is promoting water accessibility and sustainable food products for everyone on the planet.

Test your reframed purpose out with your kids and their friends. Make sure it passes the smell test for going beyond platitudes and committing your company to the triple bottom line, not a single one.

Align Top Down

Your reframed purpose will not mean much unless you can align your company, from the board level to the frontline staff. Bold statements of purpose open up the confidence to innovate, energize your employee base, and attract new customers, partners, and talent. However, by their nature, bold visions and missions stir up emotions and discomfort.

Carefully consider how to gain the top-down support and alignment needed to fully unleash the power of your new two-speed organization. Focus on the stakeholders who are listed next, in the order presented.

Your Leadership Team

In theory, your leadership team has been selected because each member has the right profile to drive the long-term success of the business. When change is modest and your industry is stable, this is usually true.

However, we live in times of dramatic and rapid change. Many of your leaders were likely promoted to their current roles based on their proven ability to drive your speed-one business. Those leaders may be the least likely ones to embrace the smart cannibalization required to position your company for a digital future.

It is time to assess your current leadership team in terms of foresight, adaptability, resilience, and learning. To live up to your reframed purpose, they are going to have to run the current business well and disrupt it as needed to deliver your future growth.

Your Board of Directors

Depending on your current board composition, you may have more or less work to do here. If your board is mainly composed of retired execs with deep expertise in your current industry and a traditional business model, then you will need to work early and often to educate them on the changing market landscape, customer behaviors, competition, and economics.

When he was CEO of Verizon, Ivan Seidenberg used a chunk of every board meeting to discuss emerging trends in wireless and digital media. He was working in advance to prepare his board for the major industry value shift from wireline and broadcast to wireless and content streaming. Seidenberg knew that sizable acquisitions would be needed and wanted his board knowledgeable and ready to act when the time came to pull the trigger.

In a midsized company, field trips with your board can be an effective way to give its members direct exposure to the pace of change and disruptive nature of digital attackers. Tom Gorman, former CEO of shared-logistics company Brambles, used this approach with incredible success. In particular, he brought his entire board and leadership team from their home base in Sydney, Australia, to Silicon Valley to meet with both established companies in the midst of digital transformation (such as GE and Cisco) and startups that could be part of Brambles' partner ecosystem. Those visits cemented the resolve of the board to form BXB Digital back in 2015.

Think of the investment in educating your board about digital disruption as air cover for your air cover: that is, support for decisions (such as the ones made by Gerstner at IBM and Chambers at Cisco) that protect speed-two organizations from financial gyrations in speed-one businesses.

Your Employees

As we discussed in Chapter 5, Big I disruptive innovation requires aligning employees in your core business with your long-term goals. It is easy for the team working on Big I initiatives to be viewed as a preferred class, thus creating tension and killing productivity in your core business.

A powerful purpose can bridge this divide by highlighting the equal importance of Little I and Big I in positioning your company for future growth and success. Your reframed purpose must stir the emotions of all employees and provide an attractive set of career paths that individuals can follow to maximize their impact over time.

To make your reframed purpose real for your employee base, communicate the burning platform outside-in, using specific customer examples and changes in the competitive landscape. Do not sugarcoat. After all, your employees all have Google in the palms of their hands. Remember that most people need to hear something new two or three times before they can internalize it. So, risk overcommunicating here to build a sense of urgency and validate the need for change.

Your Partners

Partners include your traditional vendors and channel partners, as well as those in the innovation ecosystem that you installed back in Chapter 7. The right partners are catalysts for delivering on your reframed purpose sooner.

In fact, they may already have their own initiatives underway to position themselves for Goliath's Revenge. Sharing hard-earned lessons, celebrating mutual successes, and building on each other's efforts will cement your partnerships for the long term.

Emerging winners are investing heavily here. IBM is incorporating AI and blockchain into supply chain innovations for industry leaders such as Dole and Maersk. GE is making big investments in its extensible platform, which makes machine learning and IoT more accessible to its industrial customers. TWC is innovating with companies such as Apple to capture more granular barometric data from user devices. Splunk is working with customers across nearly every industry to help them identify and unlock the latent value in their machine data.

Your Shareholders

More often than not, shareholders are inherited from previous eras of a company's history and take significant time to adjust to the new realities of digital disruption. As with other stakeholders, challenging themes, such as embracing smart cannibalization, need to be balanced with demonstrations of success from your innovation portfolio.

Shareholders with a growth orientation who plan to hold your stock for the long term will be in agreement with your reframed purpose and the investments you are making in disruptive innovation. Many short-term investors, such as hedge funds, will need to be convinced that you can successfully incubate new, growth businesses without missing your near-term financial commitments.

Help both groups understand how smart cannibalization gets ahead of value erosion to keep your top- and bottom-line growing. Some rotation in your shareholder base is to be expected. Your renewed commitment to the triple bottom line just may not resonate with the shareholders who feel that you can cut your way to greatness.

Your Customers

Last but not least, customers are a key audience when communicating your reframed purpose. As you are raising your sights, some customers could feel threatened. They may feel that any dollar spent innovating your way into adjacent markets is a dollar not spent on the next product or service developed for them.

As with your partners, identifying opportunities for cocreation with your best customers is a key part of reframing your business. Hitachi has invested heavily in such cocreation projects as a low-risk way to simultaneously innovate future offers and bring its long-standing industrial customers along.

On the other hand, there will likely be current customers that participate in a part of your business that is shrinking its way toward no longer being profitable. You need sufficient confidence in your reframed purpose that you are willing to part with those legacy customers when the time comes.

You may have other stakeholders, such as government agencies, regulators, associations, and NGOs. Go ahead and add them to the list. The key is building a broad web of support so that your reframed purpose sticks and is successful.

Lead by Example

In order for your troops to line up and march into the midst of digital competition, they will rightly expect your CEO and other leaders to be out in front leading the charge. These times of uncertainty will make your employees value leaders that walk the talk more than ever.

Future leaders must live their lives in a way that reflects the future purpose of the company. The days of your personal life staying separate from your professional one are long past. Leaders must be all in on your reframed purpose. Mary Barra is a great example of this, as she personally is leading the charge on GM's zero-zero-zero mandate—zero crashes, zero emissions, and zero congestion.

Achieving bold statements of purpose demands humility alongside the confidence. That is the only way for leaders to take the long view when not everything goes right. Former United Technologies CEO George

David had it right when he said, "You're going to be humbled by this job if you're in it long enough. Remember, it's about the company, not you—companies live for centuries and you're only a steward for 10 to 15 years." Henry Ford touched on a similar theme with "Obstacles are those frightful things you see when you take your eyes off your goal."

The most authentic leaders live their lives by a personal code that parallels and amplifies their companies' purpose. Crafting a personal statement of purpose is one of the most difficult things you will ever do. It needs to marry your unique talents, or superpowers, with the cause you feel emotionally in service to: that is, the one you would pursue even if you were not paid to do so.

Aristotle said, "Where your talents and the needs of the world cross, therein lies your vocation." In short, your legacy will be the results of applying what you are good at to the unmet needs of the world around you. Your personal statement of purpose will become a magnet for you to inspire and attract others to your cause.

As Bill and Melinda Gates have shown with their commitment to solving vexing humanitarian challenges, a personal statement of purpose crisply defined and well communicated can have truly global impact. Leaders that live by their own triple bottom line will be in great demand to run companies pursuing Goliath's Revenge.

Discovery Reframes Its Purpose[1]

Flying below the radar in South Africa, a radically new kind of insurance company has emerged, which is harnessing digital disruption and empowering end users to redefine what insurance companies do.

Adrian Gore does not fit the profile of a typical big company CEO. When he founded Discovery in 1992, South Africa had undergone a historic transformation from apartheid to a democratic system. This presented unique challenges in assessing the health risks of the newly integrated population. For example, there was just not enough historic data about the incidence of injury and disease by demographic segment to accurately price the insurance that Discovery would be underwriting.

Rather than cling to the old health insurance model of getting paid to manage risk, Gore turned the model on its head. He reframed the purpose of an insurance company to making members healthier and improving their lives.

Gore and his leadership team signaled to customers that they needed to be partners in managing their own health. In parallel, Discovery undertook a Big I disruption of epic proportions—reinventing the health insurance industry. Industry peers thought Gore was crazy. "Why mess with an industry business model that had served us all so well?" was a common refrain.

But not Alan Pollard. One of the first leaders Gore recruited to his cause, Pollard immediately realized the significance of Discovery's bold vision. By 1997, Gore, Pollard, and a tight-knit team of committed designers and developers came up with Vitality, a breakthrough insurance product that incentivized policyholders to live healthier lifestyles.

Pollard and team knew that lifestyle behaviors such as cigarette smoking, poor nutrition choices, and lack of physical activity were directly linked to the chronic diseases (such as diabetes) that cause over 50% of premature deaths. However, they were not naïve. They recognized that getting people to change deeply ingrained lifestyle habits is an incredibly challenging task.

Discovery engaged some of the world's top experts on what it takes to drive significant behavior change. It tapped into the emerging science of behavioral economics to devise Vitality's first-of-its-kind points-and-status rewards system for healthy activity. It went beyond health insurance to link its healthy-lives reward system to life insurance as well.

Vitality provided members with points for healthy activities (such as going to the gym) as well as discounts for purchasing healthy food options. It took off like wildfire with members, who were surprised and delighted that their insurance company would actually invest in their health.

The platform scaled rapidly to over 70,000 gym visits per day and hundreds of millions of healthy food purchases. This provided Vitality with a powerful first-mover advantage based on wellness data across large populations.

Discovery was on its way to the perpetual algorithmic advantage covered back in Chapter 3. It continued to refine the Vitality behavior-change model to maximize the healthiness of its covered population at minimum cost.

The rise of smartphones, wearable sensors, and health-related apps followed about a decade later. Vitality remained at the forefront of innovation, successfully integrating those emerging technologies into its program and furthering its reach, simplicity, and appeal.

In fact, Discovery became one of the first wellness companies to partner with Apple and utilize the breakthrough health-related innovations in the Apple Watch. Through the Vitality program, members are now able to purchase an Apple Watch with just a small up-front payment. They can then pay off the balance on their Apple Watch over the following 24 months by meeting specific physical activity targets communicated on the Watch or by using cash. This healthy lives barter has proved to be a step-change customer outcome with increased physical activity levels for over 60% of the members. A major win for Discovery, Apple, and the members themselves.

Discovery's reframed purpose did not stop with its core market of South Africa. The Vitality platform made possible international expansion. Discovery now participates in the most attractive global insurance markets in the world, through John Hancock in the United States, Manulife in Canada, Generali in Europe, AIA Group in Asia, and Ping An Insurance in China. These relationships, in turn, push more data into the Vitality platform to power the next leg of innovation.

In the United Kingdom, Vitality became the first life insurer whose premiums were adjusted based upon the healthy lifestyle choices of its members. Michael Porter of Harvard Business School cited Vitality as a shining example of a shared-value product: one for which both creator and user share in the risk and benefits of the disruptive solution.

Vitality is now providing a beachhead for Discovery to grow into additional insurance segments, such as automobile insurance. In that market, Vitality is helping users improve their so-called driving DNA to become safer drivers. Once again, Discovery's broad and compelling corporate purpose opened up an opportunity to grow. It partnered with two MIT professors with expertise in telematics to leverage its shared-value business model to launch a successful behavior-based auto insurance offering.

Gore challenged the established insurance industry mindset that getting users to change their behavior was just too hard. He reframed the purpose of insurance from managing risk to enabling healthy and safer lives. Gore led by example. He took the professional risk of publicly announcing Discovery's big innovation goals, creating a healthy pressure on his team to deliver on the company's Big I innovations.

Rule 6: Company and Career Readiness

What aspects of the Discovery case example can you put to work in your organization? Let's find out as you complete your company and career self-assessments for Rule 6: Reframe your purpose.

Company Readiness Self-Assessment

To complete your company readiness self-assessment, take the time to understand the calibration of minimal, limited, moderate, advanced, and world-class capabilities across each row in Figure 9.4.

Now, assess your company's demonstrated level of capability on each row. Try to think about your company as a whole, at least in this first

RULE #6: REFRAME YOUR PURPOSE
COMPANY SELF-ASSESSMENT GRID

	0-20% Minimal Capability	20-40% Limited Capability	40-60% Moderate Capability	60-80% Advanced Capability	80-100% World Class Capability
Raise your sights	We don't believe in all that mission / vision stuff here	Mission / vision too much about us; not enough about the world	Vision is clear but we haven't internalized it into our mission	Mission is right but vision may not be right for the long-term	Mission / vision so compelling that everyone can recite them
Answer the "Five Whys"	We struggle to even answer the superficial first "why"	Aligned at least 2 "whys" deep on why we do what we do	Aligned at least 3 "whys" deep on why we do what we do	Aligned at least 4 "whys" deep on why we do what we do	Aligned at least 5 "whys" deep on why we do what we do
Embrace smart cannibalization	We are on a path to be the Kodak of our industry	Only executing "speed two" model in adjacent markets; not our own	Speed two model has permission for smart cannibalization but just launched	Two-speed model in place but "haves and have nots" issues are still being worked on	Two-speed organizational model in place and delivering well
Engage the next generation	Do not think Digital Natives would enjoy working for our company	Beginning to get how Millennial and Gen Z employees are different	We support employees who want to make a difference outside of work	We've added either social or environmental goals to our financial ones	We live and breath our triple bottom line every day
Align top-down	Every group has its own mission and vision so no alignment at company level	Alignment is superficial today; not translated into day-to-day actions	Board and senior leaders aligned but has not reached the staff doing real work	Middle management to front line alignment in place but senior leaders are still TBD	Broad and deep alignment from Board to front-line to partners in place
Lead by example	Our leaders seem near-sighted; solely focused on delivering near-term profits	Our leaders might have strong personal purposes but I don't know what they are	Some leaders have strong personal purposes but others not so much	Our leaders have strong personal purposes but may not align to company	Leaders are genuinely authentic with company-aligned personal purposes

| 0% | 20% | 40% | 60% | 80% | 100% |

FIGURE 9.4 Rule 6 Company Self-Assessment Grid.

pass. If you want to also assess just your team, group, or division, you can come back later and repeat the exercise.

Career Readiness Self-Assessment

Narrow your aperture from your company to your career. What steps are you taking to reframe your personal sense of purpose? Mark your self-assessments on the grid shown in Figure 9.5.

RULE #6: REFRAME YOUR PURPOSE CAREER SELF-ASSESSMENT GRID

	0-20% Minimal Capability	20-40% Limited Capability	40-60% Moderate Capability	60-80% Advanced Capability	80-100% World Class Capability
Raise your sights	My team is just "heads down" trying to deliver on our performance metrics	My team is aligned to our company's purpose but does not have its own	My team has a draft statement of purpose that is still being refined	Mission / vision for my team is compelling but not sure if it aligns to our company overall	Mission / vision for my team is compelling and aligned to that of our company
Answer the "Five Whys"	Our company is doing this "Five Whys" effort but don't know how that effects me	My career path is built around helping our company deliver the 2nd "Why"	My career path is built around helping our company deliver the 3rd "Why"	My career path is built around helping our company deliver the 4th "Why"	My career path is built around helping our company deliver the 5th "Why"
Embrace smart cannibal-ization	If our company has a two-speed organization model, I don't know about it	I have had deep experience in speed one teams but not in speed two	I have had deep experience in speed two teams but not in speed one	Have worked in both speed one and two teams but am not equally proficient yet	I am ambidextrous; I have excelled in both speed one and speed two teams
Engage the next generation	Not sure what all the fuss is about with these social and environmental issues	Just starting to appreciate that Digital Natives are a breath of fresh air	I have adjusted my working style over time to better relate to Digital Natives	I am an active mentor to Digital Natives within and beyond my current team	I built our triple bottom line focus into how my team runs day-to-day
Align top-down	Don't think alignment is worth the effort; why can't everyone just do their jobs?	My team has started talking about alignment but not sure we can get there	I drive alignment within my team but not out to peers or up the organization chart	I drive alignment with my team and peers but have limited influence upward	I personally drive alignment within the 360 degree sphere around my role
Lead by example	These personal statements of purpose are just a waste of time	I am ready to commit time and energy to figuring out what my personal purpose is	Have ideas about my personal purpose but have not written it down in a formal way	My personal purpose is compelling but not sure if it aligns to our company very well	My personal purpose is compelling and aligned with our company's purpose

0%　　　20%　　　40%　　　60%　　　80%　　　100%

FIGURE 9.5 Rule 6 Career Self-Assessment Grid.

Rule 6 Readiness Summary

Now that you've completed your company and career self-assessments for this final rule, you can fill in your readiness summary in Figure 9.6. If you are doing your self-assessments online at www.goliathsrevenge. com, skip this step, as it will be completed automatically.

You've completed all six of the new rules that define success in pursuing Goliath's Revenge. It is time to bring it all together into

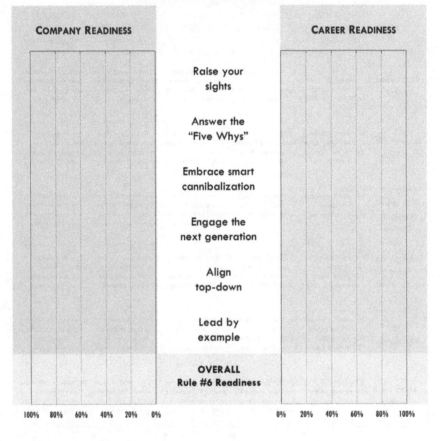

RULE #6: REFRAME YOUR PURPOSE READINESS SUMMARY

FIGURE 9.6   Rule 6 Readiness Summary.

an action plan for your company in Chapter 10 and for your career in Chapter 11.

Note

1. Alan Pollard (president of product and innovation, Vitality Group, Discovery Insurance), in an interview with the authors, March 2018.

Chapter 10

Company View: Your Disruptor's Playbook

It's okay to have butterflies. Just get them flying in formation.

—*Francisco López, musician*

Take a moment to celebrate how far you've come. You have inventoried the crown jewels that confer the incumbent's advantage on your company, understood why winners take most in digital competition, and self-assessed both your company and career relative to each of the six rules of Goliath's Revenge.

Now it is time to put that new knowledge to work and shift from thinking to doing. In this chapter you will learn how to build what we call a "disruptor's playbook" for your company, which will help turn the tables on your industry's digital disruptors. In the next chapter, you will narrow the focus to your career and the sequence in which you will close gaps in your professional readiness for a digital future.

On the company-strategy front, Francisco López has it right. Alignment of execution across functions, divisions, and geographies is paramount in making the changes needed to achieve Goliath's Revenge.

This is a team sport like football, not an individual one like tennis. It is not enough to have one group—a chosen few on your data science team or in your research labs, for example—executing your strategy. Established companies need to harness their collective skills, energy, and knowledge to out-innovate the digital disruptors.

You Are Not Too Late

Whether you work for a small, midsized, or large company, it is not too late to build a strategy to act on the six rules that we've laid out. You see, there are companies at all stages of readiness in dealing with digital disruption. In conducting the research for this book we interviewed and surveyed more than 50 organizations, across industries as diverse as automotive, healthcare, industrial equipment, defense, packaged consumer goods, hospitality, retail, recruiting, and telecommunications, to understand their readiness for Goliath's Revenge. Here is what we learned.

Balance Digital Offense and Defense

Figure 10.1 shows what we call a company's "digital innovation posture." As you can see, both small and large companies tend to have

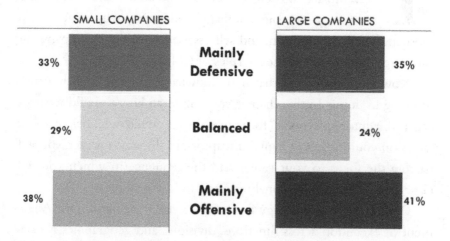

FIGURE 10.1 Digital Innovation Posture.

polarized their digital innovation efforts around either defending their current core business or growing into adjacent markets fast enough to offset declines in that business over time. Companies that have balanced their efforts between the two objectives are in the minority for both size groups.

We are greedy for you. As they say, the best defense is a good offense. Your disruptor's playbook must seek that balance. If you just try and wrap digital innovation around your current core business and traditional business model, you risk treating digital innovation like most burger chains treat ketchup: that is, like a condiment meant to make otherwise inferior ingredients taste palatable.

On the other hand, if you focus your six-rule execution solely on growing into adjacent markets, then you are going to face the show-me-the-money question. You are going to be at a company all-hands meeting where your CEO is presenting how fast your new digital business is growing in percentage terms, with a lingering realization that your shareholders only care about growth and profitability in absolute dollars. Too many companies miss this important detail, and it tends to get their senior leaders fired. Avoiding a 5% per year decline in your core business might mean more in absolute dollars in the near term than achieving 100% growth off of a small base in an adjacent market.

On this one, seek the middle ground—a portfolio of digital innovation investments that achieves a fifty-fifty balance between defending the core and growing into adjacent markets. This is the only way to align the long-term goals of your customers, employees, and partners with the frequently myopic orientation of your shareholders.

Fund Big I Innovation

In Chapter 5 we made the case that you should put in place an innovation portfolio management approach that succeeds at both Big I game-changing innovation and Little I incremental innovation. As you can see in Figure 10.2, slightly less than half of large companies and slightly

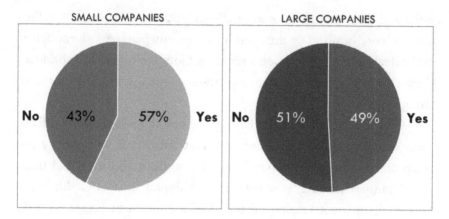

FIGURE 10.2   Willingness to Fund Big I Innovation.

more than half of smaller companies in the survey were willing to fund Big I innovation.

That means that half of your competitors are playing an incremental-only innovation game. This is like playing football—what we call soccer in the United States—and never taking a shot at the opponent's goal. That strategy only works when the buying criteria of your category are stable and competitive intensity is low. When winners take most, Big I innovation needs to be a foundational element of your investment approach.

As you might expect, those companies that are willing to pursue Big I innovation are also the ones most likely to have an aggressive grow-into-adjacent-markets focus. See Figure 10.3 for the breakdown.

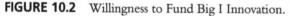

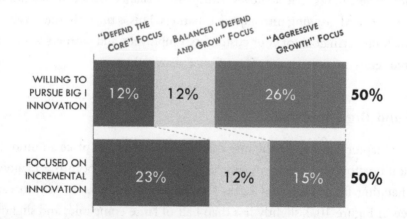

FIGURE 10.3   Big I Innovators Are Biased for Growth.

The corollary is also true. Established companies focused only on incremental innovation are doing the corporate equivalent of Muhammad Ali's rope-a-dope strategy. They are committing the vast majority of their digital innovation effort to defending themselves. Perhaps they feel that the Big I innovations in their core businesses were figured out a long time ago. Uber's reinvention of the taxi industry and Airbnb's competition with the hotel industry show that even long-stable segments of the economy are ripe for Big I innovation.

Leverage Your Data Assets

The underlying power of winner-takes-most dynamics is perpetual algorithmic advantage. In Chapter 6, you learned how to effectively use your data as currency to provide your company a path to this long-term source of market power and profitability. As you can see in Figure 10.4, very few of your competitors are making extensive use of their data assets today.

While smaller companies have a slight edge in terms of their willingness to invest in Big I innovation, they are well behind their larger competitors when it comes to leveraging their data for algorithmic advantage. In fact, nearly half of the small companies surveyed were

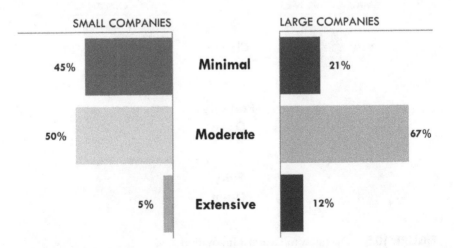

FIGURE 10.4 Data Leverage for Innovation.

making only minimal efforts to capitalize on their data today. Two-thirds of large companies were at least making moderate progress, following years of investments in data warehouses, business intelligence, analytics, and data science. The good news for companies large and small is that cloud deployment and business models are significantly reducing the cost of putting your data to work.

Open Up Your Innovation

The phrase "the wisdom of crowds" definitely applies to innovation, as you saw in the examples throughout Chapter 7. That is, no matter how large your company, the total innovation power of the external world dwarfs your internal team. However, as with your digital innovation posture, finding balance is the right approach. In Figure 10.5, you can see that only one-third of companies have found that balance so far.

On average, small companies are over-rotated toward external innovation and risk putting all their eggs in someone else's basket, while larger companies are more likely to be overly dependent on their internal R&D efforts.

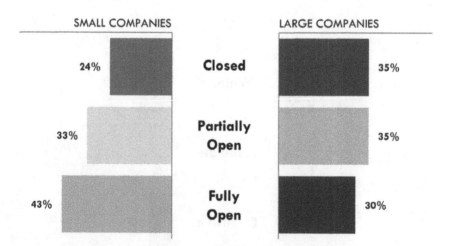

FIGURE 10.5 Openness to External Innovation.

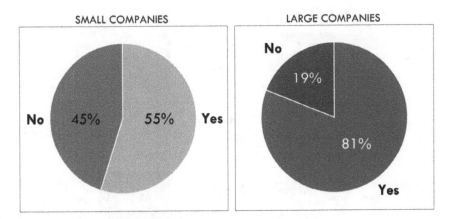

FIGURE 10.6   Formal Innovation Process in Place.

Install a Formal Innovation Process

One aspect of achieving balance in your digital innovation program is having a structured innovation process. As shown in Figure 10.6, most large companies have a formal innovation approach in place today, while almost half of smaller companies are still pursuing innovation in an ad hoc manner.

A key aspect of your disruptor's playbook will be your innovation portfolio management model and its associated phase-specific performance metrics. For some of you, this will improve on the innovation process you have today. For those starting from scratch, it will help you to start maximizing your return on innovation going forward.

Upgrade Your Talent

In Chapter 8 we showed you how the best established companies are valuing talent over technology in pursuit of Goliath's Revenge. If you feel as if that new rule is one of the most difficult to make progress on, you are not alone. As illustrated in Figure 10.7, fewer than 3 in 10 established companies feel that they have the right talent to compete in the digital age.

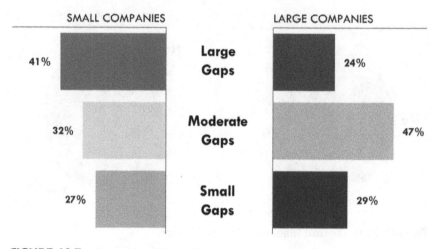

FIGURE 10.7   Innovation Talent Gaps.

41% of the small businesses in our survey had large gaps in their innovation talent pools, which is worrisome, given that small businesses represent approximately half of all employment within developed economies. That compares to just 24% of larger companies. As shown in Figure 10.8, this shortfall in the pool of innovation talent in small companies is partly made up through higher levels of employee engagement.

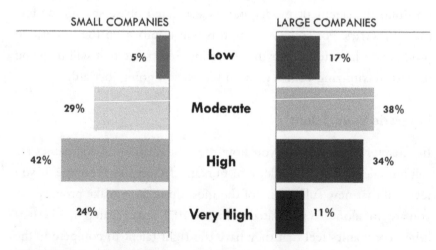

FIGURE 10.8   Employee Engagement Levels.

Small companies are more than twice as likely as large ones to report very high levels of employee engagement in their innovation initiatives. Over half of large companies report that their employee engagement is either low or moderate. Fixing this is critical, given the team effort required to deal with digital disruption and create a culture of innovation.

Align around Your New Purpose

In Chapter 9 you focused on reframing your professional and company purpose—raising your sights, if you will. In Figure 10.9, you can see that there remains much work to do in getting your peers flying in formation.

As you might expect, small companies have an easier time driving alignment than larger companies—they just have fewer moving parts. One-third of small companies feel that they have very strong alignment on their innovation strategy, which is almost double the percentage seen in larger companies. However, in half of large companies and nearly half of small ones, organizational alignment around their future innovation strategy is either weak or moderate. Given how fast the Davids in your industry are moving, a lack of organizational alignment is just not an option.

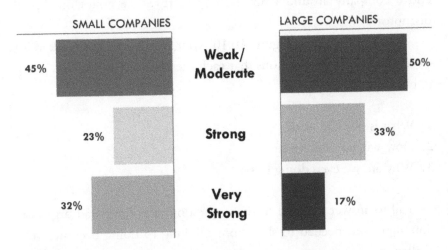

FIGURE 10.9 Organizational Alignment on Innovation Strategy.

Your Disruptor's Playbook

So how do you get your entire organization flying in formation? How do you take all of the principles and case examples from the six rules and put them to work in the cross-functional teams that make your company run? You need to integrate your decisions on how to pursue Goliath's Revenge into your version of the disruptor's playbook.

One of the most durable man-made structures in the world is the Parthenon. It sits proudly on a hill overlooking present-day Athens, Greece. Completed almost 2,500 years ago, it was a temple that also served as the city treasury—a place to store the gold. Through earthquakes, fires, wars, and marauding hordes, the Parthenon still stands today. You could be forgiven for feeling as if the digital disruptors in your industry are the modern equivalent of those marauding hordes, coming to steal your gold, your customers, and your job.

It is time for you to build a Goliath's Revenge Parthenon. That is, sequence and prioritize the initiatives that your company will undertake to defend its core business and grow into adjacent markets. In the next section, we will get into how you should prioritize your efforts. For now, let's start with the end in mind—aligning your entire company around your strategy to turn the tables on digital disruptors.

As you can see in Figure 10.10, your disruptor's playbook must clearly address three questions that each member of your team is going to be asking:

1. What is our end goal?
2. How will we achieve it?
3. Why are we even doing this?

Fail to answer any one of those questions and the broad organization alignment needed to shift from thinking to doing becomes very challenging.

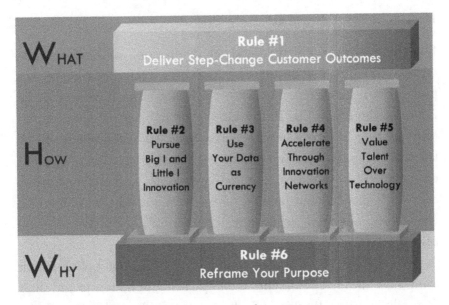

FIGURE 10.10   The Goliath's Revenge Parthenon.

As you reflected on each of the six rules, you may have come away thinking that they are not all at the same level of importance. But each rule plays a specific role in your disruptor's playbook.

What Is Our End Goal?

Rule 1 (Deliver step-change customer outcomes) is going to become your answer to the "what" question that will be on the mind of every member of your team. Digital disruptors are redefining the buying criteria of the categories that your company competes in. Sometimes they are even redefining the boundaries between industries. Broad organizational alignment requires a shared sense of the destination that your team is trying to get to before agreeing on the path you will take to get there. Rule 1 provides the framework you need to describe this destination from a customer-in point of view, using your stairway to value and whole offers by step. It is your BHAG.

How Will We Achieve It?

Once your team is united around the destination, you need to agree on how you are going to get there. As Figure 10.10 shows, Rules 2–5 play a critical supporting role here—the heavy lifting, if you will. Rule 2 (Pursue Big I and Little I innovation) seeks to broaden your portfolio of innovation initiatives beyond the incremental, slightly-better-than-last-year ones that your team is likely most comfortable with today. You cannot afford many Big I innovation investments, so this is the time to do your homework and pick the one or two areas that both leverage your crown jewels and deliver a major aspect of the customer-in outcome from Rule 1.

Rule 3 (Use your data as currency) is like a force multiplier—think about how air power multiplies the impact of ground troops and ships in a military battle. Putting your data to work will amplify the returns of your entire innovation portfolio. It will be a key element in driving the internal productivity improvements that help protect your margins. Data will also serve as a key aspect of the differentiation in your new whole offers as you deliver customer outcomes for each of the four buyer personas, attract new innovation partners, and steal market share from other aspiring Goliaths and Davids alike.

Rule 4 (Accelerate through innovation networks) addresses the time aspect of that "how" question. That is, how long it will take to get to the destination you've picked in Rule 1. Adopting John Chamber's "power of and" is the key here. It is not about whether external is "better" than internal innovation. It is simply about the pragmatic view that there are many paths to reaching your destination and that you and your team are going to take the most expeditious route. If that means leveraging an innovation from your internal research organization, data science team, or machine learning labs, then so be it. However, if an academic team within a leading university or a bunch of Red Bull-drinking coders in a startup or even the innovators within one of your smaller competitors can get you to your destination faster, then you need to be open to those strategic partnerships, cross-licensing agreements, minority investments, and potential acquisitions. Your answers on this rule will communicate more than you realize around how serious your company is in pursuing Goliath's Revenge.

Finally, Rule 5 (Value talent over technology) is a critical aspect of the answer to the "how" question for two reasons. First, the established companies that are already turning the tables on their industry's digital disruptors have doubled or tripled down on attracting, developing, and retaining talented people with digital-ready skill sets. As you saw in Chapter 8, this goes far beyond the 3Ds of design, development, and data science skills. It includes entirely new roles, such as product incubation manager, behavioral scientist, journey mapper, business modeler, solution finder, and emerging-technology specialist.

Second, valuing talent over technology will hold the fabric of your company together through this period of intense change. Helping people that already work for you build skills and competencies in these new areas sends a powerful message about "how" in the context of your company culture. It cements the guiding principle that long-time employees are still going to be valued if they demonstrate the openness and commitment required to play these new roles instead of clinging to the jobs of yesterday. This softer side of "how" is critical to avoiding an environment of haves and have-nots on your team. The external competitors are tough enough—you cannot allow internal competition to slow you down.

Why Are We Even Doing This?

If the "what" and "how" answers from your disruptor's playbook appeal to the heads of your teammates, then the "why" answers appeal to their hearts. The path to Goliath's Revenge is a three-to-five-year journey for most established companies. Sustaining the organizational alignment and change energy required for that period of time means going far beyond strategy and logic. You and your peers need to be inspired by a higher calling than your company's future market share, revenue growth, and profit margins.

Rule 6 (Reframe your purpose) is your answer to the "why" question. It raises your collective sights in terms of your company's mission and vision. This reframing of your purpose also establishes the clear rationale for change and validates why it is okay to borrow from the present to pay for the future. That smart cannibalization aspect of Rule 6 is critical. No company that is on the path to Goliath's Revenge has made progress without putting some sacred cows at risk.

Conversely, there are many examples of industry leaders whose fear of cannibalizing their current profit engines resulted in their demise. Blockbuster clung to its late fees for too long and Netflix put it out of business. Nokia and Motorola stayed wedded to the handset subsidies of national telecoms too long and missed the disruptive business model innovation of Apple and Google selling apps to end customers on smartphones.

This reframing of purpose gives upper-, middle-, and first-line managers the permission they need to be innovative. That means that if companies such as Schwab, Vanguard, Fidelity, Morgan Stanley, and TD Ameritrade need to put their high-margin wrap fees at risk to secure a position in the robo-advisor future of wealth management, their reframed purpose is the "why." In pursuing Goliath's Revenge, they have committed their entire organizations to playing the long game of helping their customers secure their financial futures, even if that causes some near-term pain on their quarterly earnings calls.

Mastercard Executes Its Disruptor's Playbook

Some star performers are living and breathing all six rules. Since going public in 2006, Mastercard stock has appreciated over 4,000%. This hypergrowth was built on continual improvement in Mastercard's core business and breakthrough innovations beyond it.

It all starts with Rule 1, delivering step-change outcomes to Mastercard's global network of customers. The unique Start Path program, orchestrated by innovation executive Deborah Barta, provides startups with operational expertise and commercial access. The goal is to get these startups in-market with Mastercard and its customers. For example, Mastercard's pilot with Mobeewave has turned smartphones into payment terminals across three different markets.

Back in Chapter 5, we outlined how Mastercard has become equally adept at capitalizing on both Big I and Little I innovation in Rule 2. Its unique "Take Initiative" program delivers CEO-level sponsorship and air cover for innovative ideas to blossom into breakthrough solutions and ventures.

For Rule 3, Mastercard turned data privacy and protection challenges into opportunities for new standards and security innovations for its 2.5 billion cardholders. The company analyzes anonymized transaction data to come up with future services and customer experiences.

Given that Mastercard was born as a network model, excelling through innovation ecosystems in Rule 4 is part of its DNA. Barta and her team have groomed Start Path ambassadors that allow Mastercard to stay abreast of the latest technologies and empower employees to make local connections with innovators worldwide.

For Rule 5, Mastercard continually anticipates the next wave of critical skills needed in its workforce. The company has developed its Innovation Masters program to support employees who are eager to develop their intrapreneurial talent. Mastercard also makes design-thinking workshops available globally to foster the outside-in perspective that best positions employees to work with external clients.

Mastercard is working tirelessly to digitize the 85% of the world's transactions that are still completed with cash. For Rule 6, there is a clear sense of purpose across Mastercard: doing well by doing good. In 2015 the company launched the Mastercard Labs for Financial Inclusion with support from the Bill and Melinda Gates Foundation. The goal is to bring more people into the financial mainstream through life-changing innovations in agriculture, microretail, and education.[1]

Companies such as Mastercard are driving continual reinvention and hypergrowth by putting all six rules of Goliath's Revenge to work. Now, let's think through how you will prioritize your own initiatives for each element of your Parthenon.

Prioritizing Your Initiatives

It is the time to get a return on the effort you invested in Chapters 4 through 9. You should now have six company self-assessment grids—one for each of the six rules—that you have taken the time to think about and complete. Pull those out and insert the overall readiness rating from the bottom of each grid onto your copy of Figure 10.11. If you completed your self-assessments online at www.goliathsrevenge.com, then your version of Figure 10.11 will be produced automatically.

This company readiness summary gives you a sense of how your current strategy and organizational capabilities match up against the six rules of Goliath's Revenge and how ready you are to build your Parthenon. A litmus test, of sorts. Remember that you should not feel discouraged if your readiness across the six rules is inconsistent. In fact, many of your peers have found that their overall readiness is currently below 50% on at least three of the rules, and well below the levels needed to successfully disrupt themselves.

This tool is less about giving yourself a grade than it is about deciding where your company should focus its efforts. In the near term, your company readiness summary will help you prioritize the innovation initiatives that you should invest in now. Over the medium term, it will drive a quarterly process of tracking your company's progress on each dimension of your disruptor's playbook.

As you look at your copy of Figure 10.11, you should have two goals in mind—building a strong foundation across every rule and establishing a world-class capability on at least one of them.

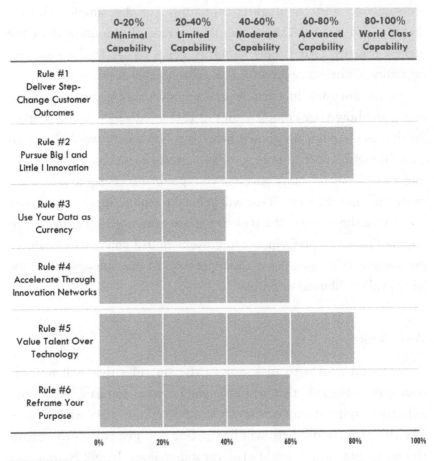

	0-20% Minimal Capability	20-40% Limited Capability	40-60% Moderate Capability	60-80% Advanced Capability	80-100% World Class Capability
Rule #1 Deliver Step- Change Customer Outcomes	■	■	■		
Rule #2 Pursue Big I and Little I Innovation	■	■	■	■	
Rule #3 Use Your Data as Currency	■	■			
Rule #4 Accelerate Through Innovation Networks	■	■	■		
Rule #5 Value Talent Over Technology	■	■	■	■	
Rule #6 Reframe Your Purpose	■	■	■		

0%   20%   40%   60%   80%   100%

FIGURE 10.11   Company Readiness Summary.

Your Foundation

Your highest priority in your disruptor's playbook must be the set of initiatives and investments required to get your company to at least the third column—that is, 40–60% readiness, or moderate capability—within each of the six rules. If you were a poker player, this is the ante that gets you in the game. If you do not ante, you do not play.

Achieving moderate capability for all six rules provides the platform for defending your core business in the near term, as well as for growing into adjacent markets over time. For the sample company shown in Figure 10.11, improving the leverage of data needs to be the highest priority. That sample company needs to get to the moderate capability performance level for Rule 3 as quickly as possible.

As we discussed in Chapter 6, there are many potential paths to improving how your company uses its data as currency. If you worked for the sample company shown here, your homework would be to go back through Chapter 6, review the success stories it contains, and structure a set of initiatives that can close your performance gap to at least the moderate capability level. That will generally require separate initiatives for each of the rows on the Rule 3 self-assessment grid (Figure 6.4) to achieve the overall performance improvement that you need. Obviously, the lower your starting point, the more rows of that rule-specific capability grid you'll need to act on.

Your Spike

Your second goal is to pick one of the six rules that will become your spike—the rule that will differentiate your company from your industry's digital-disruptor Davids and fellow aspiring Goliaths alike. The rule you choose here will be the one you prioritize investments around to get to the world-class capability level. It will be the part of your Parthenon that is different than the ones being built by your competitors.

In the example in Figure 10.11, both Rule 2 and Rule 5 represent opportunities for the sample company to achieve this competitive separation. For both Pursue Big I and Little I innovation and Value talent over technology, this sample company is already at the advanced-capability level that represents a 60–80% achievement standard against the readiness grids from Chapters 5 and 8, respectively.

As with building your foundation, the homework here is to go back to the chapters that discuss the rule candidates for your spike. Review the case examples of companies that are having success against that rule and examine your company's current readiness row by row on your copy of the rule-specific capability grid.

Your Plan

So, you have picked the one or two rules for which you are trying to get to moderate capability and the one new rule for which you are seeking to achieve a world-class capability level. It is time to build an action plan for each of the rules that you've prioritized.

Before you put pen to paper, think through the following four questions:

1. Can we apply the lessons from the case examples to our company by launching new initiatives that augment our rule-specific capabilities?
2. Do we have initiatives underway within a given row of the rule-specific capability grid that we could accelerate by adding talent or investment?
3. Which of our current initiatives are at odds with the rule-specific capabilities and should be stopped or refocused?
4. What portion of the human and financial capital needed for our new initiatives can we self-fund by shifting people and money between initiatives?

The answers to these questions will result in a draft list of the start, stop, and refocus decisions for each of the rules you have prioritized above. Figure 10.12 shows an example built around Rule 5 (Value talent over technology), in which our sample company aspires to go from moderate/advanced capability to world-class capability over time.

You should complete a copy of Figure 10.12 for each of the six rules. You will fill in the three right-hand columns for the rules that you have prioritized above and just the "stop" column (second from the right) for the other rule-specific action plans. That set of six action plans will represent your team's best thinking for how to shift from aspiring for Goliath's Revenge to actually building your Parthenon. Those plans

RULE-SPECIFIC ACTION PLAN EXAMPLE
RULE #5: VALUE TALENT OVER TECHNOLOGY

	Current Capability Level	Near-Term Capability Goal	New Initiatives To Start	Current Initiatives To Stop	Current Initiatives To Refocus
Honor institutional knowledge	Moderate Capability	Moderate Capability		• Initiative Name • Initiative Name	
Go beyond "3D" digital roles	Advanced Capability	Advanced Capability		• Initiative Name • Initiative Name	
Commit to pre-emptive skill development	Moderate Capability	World-Class Capability	• Initiative Name • Initiative Name	• Initiative Name • Initiative Name	• Initiative Name • Initiative Name
Value Venture General Managers	Moderate Capability	Moderate Capability		• Initiative Name • Initiative Name	
Optimize the AI-Human Balance	Advanced Capability	World-Class Capability	• Initiative Name • Initiative Name	• Initiative Name • Initiative Name	• Initiative Name • Initiative Name
Improve your digital dexterity	Moderate Capability	Moderate Capability		• Initiative Name • Initiative Name	

FIGURE 10.12   Rule 5 Action Plan Example.

establish which of the six rules you are acting on now and which dimensions of a given rule you are prioritizing to get in the game (moderate capability), get ahead of the game (advanced capability), and achieve competitive separation (world–class capability).

As you can see from the example, these action plans require you to identify specific initiatives to start, stop, and refocus for each of the capability rows that you plan to improve on. For the other rows in the grid, for which you are seeking just to maintain your current capability level, you will only be identifying initiatives in the "stop" column, in order to free up human and financial resources that can self-fund the new initiatives.

Now, it is far easier for established companies to start new initiatives than stop or refocus existing ones. Every established company has inertia and momentum. The strategic priorities of the past, and the initiatives that are their manifestation, take on lives of their own. Therefore, you and your team will say as much about your commitment to Goliath's Revenge through the initiatives you cancel, merge, or change as through the new initiatives that you announce and launch. So, don't be shy about those two right-hand columns of Figure 10.12.

The Feedback Loops

Depending on which of the rules you have prioritized, you may find that there are strong self-reinforcing dynamics at play. The sample company in Figure 10.12 is a good example, given its choice of pursuing world-class capability levels for Rules 2 and 5. Balancing continuous improvement Little I innovation programs with game-changing, disruptive Big I innovation efforts (Rule 2) almost always requires a significant shift in talent sourcing, development, compensation, and organization (Rule 5). The corollary is also true. Established companies willing to make bold, multiyear investments in Big I innovation put themselves into consideration for a class of talent that might not otherwise consider working for them.

For this sample company, these self-reinforcing dynamics might justify the significant investments needed to stretch all the way to world-class capability for Rules 2 and 5 in parallel. Such a goal would obviously require multiple new initiatives combined with deeper cuts in less strategic areas. Only once you've completed the rule-specific action plan templates can you step back and make sure that you have not bitten off more than you can chew.

Your Integrated Disruptor's Playbook

To summarize, the sample company has decided to advance one level (from limited to moderate capability) for Rule 3 while also improving by one level (from advanced to world-class capability) for both Rules 2 and 5. For each of these prioritized rules, the rule-specific action plans (such as the one shown in Figure 10.12) will summarize the initiative prioritization and resource allocation decisions that have been made in the three right-hand columns.

The sample company has decided to delay incremental capability investments for Rules 1, 4, and 6 until it achieves the desired progress for the other rules. It would complete rule-specific action plans for those deprioritized rules in order to identify initiatives to stop (second column from the right in Figure 10.12). As discussed above, explicitly deciding what to stop investing in going forward is just as important as chartering new initiatives.

This summary of your disruptor's playbook needs to be openly discussed, validated, and refined with your peers. People execute what they help shape, so be inclusive in how you build your company's plan. Taken together, the six rules can seem overwhelming. The old joke, "How do you eat an elephant? One bite at a time," is certainly applicable here. Far better to pick two to three rules and make meaningful progress within a quarter or two than to try and work across all six of them and have your organization be unable to sustain the energy required for the long term.

Making Mid-Course Adjustments

They say that no battle plan survives contact with the enemy. Your disruptor's playbook will not survive the pressures of digital competition without adjustments either. Now is the time to put in place the management cadence required to monitor shifts in the external environment (including the expectation ratchet from Chapter 3), track changes in your capability levels for each of the rules, and progress against the initiatives you've prioritized in your rule-specific action plans.

While every company is different, in Figure 10.13 we have outlined a starting point for establishing this management cadence around your disruptor's playbook.

We have assumed a calendar-based fiscal year in the draft management cadence, so you may need to adjust the months to reflect your fiscal year if it is different. We would propose that you invest in three types of cross-functional working sessions to track progress and adjust your disruptor's playbook as needed over time.

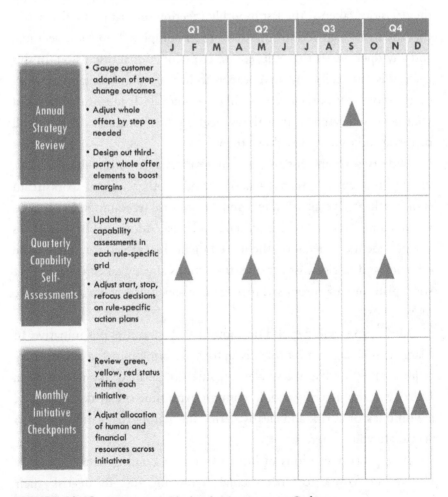

FIGURE 10.13   Disruptor's Playbook Management Cadence.

Monthly Initiative Checkpoints

Working from the bottom up, you and your team should be reviewing progress on each of the initiatives in each of your rule-specific action plans on a monthly basis. To simplify these reviews, put in place and enforce a standardized set of two to three slides that every initiative will use. This will allow the cross-functional team to rapidly absorb the summary of each initiative's progress without getting bogged down in unnecessary detail.

The first two slides should be the main focus. Slide one should list the decisions taken at the last monthly meeting on that particular initiative, the follow-up actions that have been completed on each decision, and any open issues that still require cross-functional discussion. In this cycle, it is critical for initiative leaders to have clear accountability to act on decisions from previous monthly checkpoints. It means that none of your peers will want to miss these meetings for fear that a decision will be made and executed without them.

Slide two should list the critical workstreams within the initiative, provide a green/yellow/red assessment of whether a given workstream is on track, at risk, or off track, and identify the recommended actions needed for those classified as off track or at risk. Additional backup slides can provide more detail on the impediments that are constraining those off-track and at-risk workstreams, the actions already taken on each "get well" plan, and any proposed management decisions needed to execute more quickly.

Ideally, you would spend no more than 15 minutes per initiative. In a large company, this monthly disruptor's playbook initiative review may require an entire day. In a smaller organization, it may take just an hour. Either way, the meeting should commit extra time on workstreams that are off track or at risk and clearly define the actions that can be taken to accelerate your progress.

Be especially cautious of initiative leaders coming to the monthly checkpoint to ask for incremental resourcing just to de-risk their execution against the plan. No program manager wants to come to a future meeting with the bad news of red and yellow assessments on critical workstreams. However, you want to put in place a culture of scrappiness that is capable of working efficiently and effectively against aggressive time frames in the face of limited resourcing.

Quarterly Capability Self-Assessments

The goal of all those initiatives is to advance your company's capabilities for your prioritized rules. On a quarterly schedule, you should step back from the initiative checkpoints to reassess your company's capabilities for each row of each rule-specific capability grid.

In total, those rule-specific grids represent 36 capabilities—six rows on each of six grids. We mentioned that the journey to Goliath's Revenge can be expected to take from three to five years for a typical established company—perhaps slightly less if your company is small and slightly more if your company is very large. For now, let's assume that your disruptor's playbook uses a four-year plan.

Because most established companies are starting from a point at which more than half of their capabilities are at the minimal or limited level of the grid, you can expect that you'll need to move at least 15 specific rows or capabilities up to the moderate level (see the "Your Foundation" section above). Additionally, you have chosen at least one of the rules to become your spike. For that rule, you are going to need at least four to five of the rows or capabilities to improve by multiple levels. So, assume that your spike represents 10 additional single-level capability improvements.

Overall, that means that you are going to require 25 single-level capability improvements in the execution of your disruptor's playbook over the 16 quarters of a four-year plan. Therefore, plan to advance two row-based capabilities by a single level every quarter. If that does not seem like much to ask, keep in mind that a single-level improvement in some of those capabilities may very well take three to four quarters to achieve.

These quarterly capability self-assessments will be full-day events. The prework, including an updated assessment of your company's current capabilities by row, should be distributed in advance. Use color coding to show where your capabilities were last quarter versus where they are this quarter. During the meeting itself, have the assigned leader for each rule talk through the rationale for the updated capability assessment and the contribution that each initiative made in achieving that progress.

Finally, discuss where progress on improving your capabilities for that rule is lagging behind schedule and what the root causes are for the misses involved. Update the rule-specific action plan to reflect the cross-functional team's shared view on start, stop, and refocus decisions at the initiative level and associated resourcing decisions for each initiative. Again, be sure to clearly capture what has been decided, so that the status of executing those decisions can kick off the next quarter's capability self-assessment meeting.

Annual Strategy Review

You need to strike the right balance between keeping your Goliath's Revenge strategy stable long enough to make real progress in executing it and not missing major market shifts that require the strategy itself to change. For most established companies, holding a strategy offsite annually is the optimal timing to reexamine at the fundamental basis of your strategy and the disruptor's playbook that is helping you execute it.

This annual strategy review is generally a multiday offsite with at least the top two levels of your company's leadership team. Cisco calls this process LRP—long-range planning. GE calls it GPB—growth playbook. Nearly every company already has some process in place for annual strategy reviews and next-fiscal-year budgeting. The goal here is to add a Goliath's Revenge focus to whatever your company calls that annual planning process.

The Goliath's Revenge agenda items should focus on three areas. First, remember that your strategy to turn the tables on digital disruptors is rooted in the step-change customer outcomes you prioritized back in Chapter 4. Once a year is the right interval to reach out to your customers and take stock of the impact you are having on their businesses (if you are B2B) or their lives (if you are B2C). The more you can quantify the value your customers are capturing from your step-change outcomes, the better the insight will be from this value-audit process. Are you delivering the 10X value that you laid out in your BHAG? If you're not 10X value, then how many X are you? Is your BHAG still right or did you aim either too high or too low? Now is the time to be honest with what you've learned over the past year and make the adjustments needed for the coming one.

Second, remember that you specified 10 to 12 whole offers across the four steps of your stairway to value (Figure 4.5). Take your market feedback down a level. Which of the whole offers, by step, are being rapidly adopted by customers for each of the four buyer personas? Which whole offers appear to be stalled, or worse, rejected by the customers you are targeting? How is the balance of customer adoption between steps 1 and 2, where you are primarily defending your current core business, versus steps 3 and 4, where you are growing beyond it? Use the annual strategy review to adjust your whole offer portfolio by step to reflect what the market is telling you.

Finally, revenue growth is not enough if you cannot also improve your margins and profitability over time. When we talked about the difference between an "offer" and a "whole offer," we gave you some examples of how you must orchestrate third-party capabilities to fill in the gaps in your own capabilities. (Think drivers and their cars from Uber's inexpensive, spontaneous trips whole offer.) Annually you want to be explicitly looking for opportunities to design out those third-party capabilities that helped you get to market quickly, but that are also a drain on your gross margins as your innovative new solutions scale up. Uber's heavy investment in self-driving cars is a great example of this, as the company seeks to rid itself of the expense and liability associated with human independent contractors and keep more of the money customers pay for rides within Uber itself. Every year, for every whole offer, you should be thinking the same way. What investments can you make that will help you capture a greater share of the profit pool in your industry?

That's it. You don't need a fourth set of meetings in your disruptor's playbook. A management cadence of 17 meetings a year spread across those three types—annual strategy review, quarterly capability self-assessments, and monthly initiative checkpoints—will put you well on your way to achieving Goliath's Revenge.

Note

1. Deborah Barta (SVP innovation channel management and startup engagement, Mastercard), in an interview with the authors, August 2018.

Chapter 11

Career View: Disrupt Yourself

Chance favors the prepared mind.

—*Louis Pasteur, inventor*

You have now completed the hard work of building the disruptor's playbook, which will position your company for Goliath's Revenge. Enough about the company. Let's talk about you and your career: specifically, how you can prioritize the roles you should pursue, the skills you should develop, and the plan you should execute to maximize your professional impact in this confusing time of digital disruption.

Roles change, people adjust. A century ago, farmers felt great about their chosen career, with one out of every three people working in agriculture. Today it is just one in a hundred. However, entirely new roles, such as automation engineer, agronomist, and biotech researcher, have been created that make that 1% still farming more and more productive.

Farming today looks nothing like it did a century ago. We feed many more people with a comparatively tiny workforce. Genetically modified seeds, robotic farming equipment, and AI-based crop planning have become the norm. Farmers sit in front of sophisticated computer interfaces to remotely control tractors based on sensor data and drone video. Algorithms decide where to plant what seed, and when to harvest the bounty in a way that maximizes yield and keeps the soil fertile.

This same story is playing out in every industry, with existing career paths being reshaped and new roles emerging. As philosopher Eric Hoffer said, "In times of change learners inherit the earth; while the learned find themselves beautifully equipped to deal with a world that no longer exists."

If you are reading this book, our bet is that you are a learner, so it is time to learn how to put Goliath's Revenge to work for your career. This means understanding your professional readiness as measured against the six rules, balancing your triple bottom line, writing your statement of purpose, and defining your personal action plan to deliver on your long-term goals.

Professional Readiness for the Six Rules

Pull out the career self-assessment grids that you completed at the end of Chapters 4 through 9 and fill in your overall assessment by rule on your copy of Figure 11.1. Again, if you completed the self-assessments online at www.goliathsrevenge.com, your career readiness summary will be produced automatically.

Don't be discouraged if your version of Figure 11.1 has more white space and smaller bars than the example shown here. You may be at an earlier stage in your career than that of the fictional employee in the example or have deep experience in a few rules but none in others. That is okay.

Go back and look at your source grids again. Reacquaint yourself with the specific aspects of the rules for which your capabilities are highly developed versus those for which you are just getting started. Interpreting those gaps correctly depends on your current level in your company.

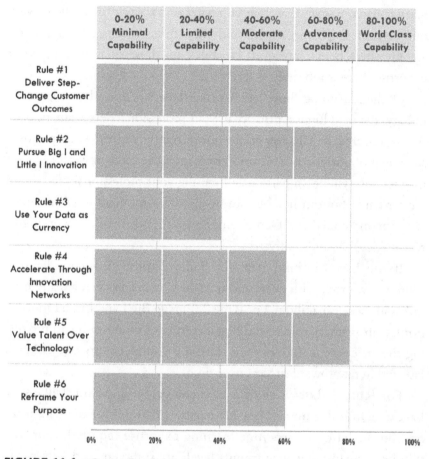

	0-20% Minimal Capability	20-40% Limited Capability	40-60% Moderate Capability	60-80% Advanced Capability	80-100% World Class Capability
Rule #1 Deliver Step- Change Customer Outcomes					
Rule #2 Pursue Big I and Little I Innovation					
Rule #3 Use Your Data as Currency					
Rule #4 Accelerate Through Innovation Networks					
Rule #5 Value Talent Over Technology					
Rule #6 Reframe Your Purpose					

FIGURE 11.1 Career Readiness Summary.

Senior Executive

If you are a CEO or senior executive, these grids are unforgiving. Recognize that your white space is going to be amplified throughout your company. The implications of your capability gaps vary dramatically by rule.

The "what" and "why" rules are nonnegotiable. Those are Rule 1 (Deliver step-change customer outcomes) and Rule 6 (Reframe your purpose), respectively. As a senior leader, it is your job to define the big, hairy, audacious goals that your company is in service to and help every one of your employees understand why those goals matter. So, if you are anywhere below advanced capability on those rules, building your expertise there is job one.

Of the remaining "how" rules, make Rule 5 (Value talent over technology) the next highest priority in your professional development plan. As we covered in Chapter 9, the more tightly aligned your personal statement of purpose is with your company's, the more powerful a talent magnet you will be. In particular, focusing your professional life around a clear triple bottom line—more on that in a moment—will resonate with the millennial and Gen Z employees that you will be working to recruit, develop, and motivate.

If you have capability gaps for Rules 2 through 4, consider surrounding yourself with peers and next-level managers that already have spikes in those capabilities. For Rule 2 (Pursue Big I and Little I innovation), your primary role is instilling a culture of innovation and providing the air cover that gives your team the confidence to take risk, fail fast, and iterate toward success over time.

For Rule 3 (Use your data as currency), you are most likely to have a technical team and outside partners that deliver the data integration, analytic, and machine learning expertise required. Your role will be ensuring that investments levels are sufficient and new capabilities are built rapidly enough to establish your company's algorithmic advantage. In parallel, get educated on the state of the art in machine and deep learning so that you can recognize great when you see it.

Finally, for Rule 4 (Accelerate through innovation networks), be sure to set the tone that NIH and WKE attitudes are career limiting going forward. Beyond that, you have almost certainly developed a sizable peer network on your path to becoming a senior executive. Continue to extend that network into the VC and startup realms to keep your finger on the pulse of over-the-horizon disruptive innovations that your team may not see coming.

Midlevel Manager

Middle management is where the battle for greatness is won or lost. Leaders with strong T-shaped capability profiles and deep institutional knowledge tend to reside at this layer of the organizational chart. This is also where legacy mindsets, cultures, and metrics can sometimes stifle even the most exciting innovation opportunities.

As a middle manager, focus your professional development on the "how" aspects of the new rules: that is, Rules 2 through 5. You are the last line of defense against your company failing to execute fast enough to achieve Goliath's Revenge. While you have influence on how your company prioritizes its step-change customer outcomes in Rule 1 and input to your company's reframed purpose in Rule 6, the final decisions likely come from your boss or your boss's boss.

For Rule 2, play to your strength. As you saw in Chapter 5, Big I and Little I innovations are equally valuable to your company's long-term success. So if you are gifted at driving the sustaining innovation that makes existing offers, experiences, and operations better, focus on leading Little I teams. On the other hand, if you wake up every day looking for the next high-risk/big-payoff breakthrough, then seek out opportunities to sponsor Big I initiatives, to mentor those teams, or to step out of your current role to act as a venture general manager for a disruptive innovation. At a minimum, get educated on innovation tools (such as design thinking) and new business-building methods (such as lean startup).

Rule 3 may well represent a mindset shift if you do not come from a data background. Build up your statistics and analytics skills through online and classroom-based executive education programs. While you may not be the one crunching data or building models, you need to appreciate how data and algorithms can automate routine processes for near-term profit improvement while acting as springboards for future disruptive innovations.

For Rule 4, build up your experience with external innovation networks by committing your organization to running small experiments on open innovation platforms (such as Topcoder or Kaggle). Consider becoming an expert yourself on those platforms by participating in challenges that fall within your specific expertise. As with senior executives, continue to broaden your professional network to include venture capitalists, startups, business incubators, and research universities that you think might impact your business over time. If you are a technologist, consider becoming more of a solution finder than an inventor, as the former role will be in ascendency once your company fully embraces open innovation.

For Rule 5, if you have a capability gap, then time is of the essence. You will be teaching the frontline managers how to source, recruit, develop, motivate, and retain talent over time. Investing personal time in preemptive skill development is always a good bet. It is like buying an option on your own stock. Finally, think through how to continually evolve the human-machine balance across your teams. Translating the "what" into the "how" is a moving target given the rapid progress in what AI and robotics are capable of. Stay nimble here.

Entry-Level Employee

Both authors of this book have kids that are recent college grads and working in their first or second jobs. So we have a good appreciation of the level of apprehension and uncertainty involved in planning a career that is sure to span multiple waves of digital disruption.

If you are just starting your career and have gotten this far in a business book, congratulations on thinking beyond your current role. As with the power of compounding in personal investing, any extra effort you apply now in expanding your skill set has the potential for big payoffs later. Each of the six rules provides an opportunity for this extra credit learning and accelerated professional development.

For Rule 1, take the time to internalize the stairway to value and buyer persona–based outcomes in Chapter 4. Regardless of your current role, if the opportunity presents itself to be part of customer- or partner-facing market-validation initiatives, jump at the chance. Those present the opportunity for you to build your own view around unmet customer needs and the disruptive innovation initiatives that could deliver on them. Overnight, you will be thinking about growth strategy in a way that employees with double your tenure are not yet able to.

For Rule 2, get involved with hackathons or innovation challenges, even if you do not have a technical background. The tools of data analytics and coding are getting so good that anyone can contribute to these teams. Seek out experiences in both Little I incremental improvement efforts and Big I disruptive innovation ventures. You might think that Big I is sexier and represents a better way to move your career ahead. Don't be that naïve. Established companies place massive value on delivering on their current-year financial goals, and most cannot get there without a steady stream of Little I successes. If you have entrepreneurial experience from your college days, make sure that your boss, mentor, and human resources representative knows about it to increase your odds of being selected for a Big I initiative.

For Rule 3, if you already have a strong statistics or data science background, you are ahead of the game and should pursue roles that leverage analytics and machine learning. If you have not developed these skills, invest your personal time now to gain at least a foundational understanding through online learning platforms (such as Coursera and Udacity).

For Rule 4, your recent academic pursuits actually give you a leg up. Keep in touch with professors doing interesting research and classmates headed to other innovative companies. By definition, you have a fresh network, so don't let it go stale. Continue to seek out opportunities to interact with people outside your company who are working on Big I and Little I initiatives. You never know when there will be an intersection between what they are working on and a new project you are asked to contribute to. Building partner networks and ecosystems is as much a mindset as it is a process. The more you can build this capability, the more valuable you will become to both current and prospective employers.

For Rule 5, you carry no baggage from a nondigital world. Use this perspective to look ahead and anticipate the roles that will be needed and that will excite you. In Chapter 8, we prioritized some for you to consider: product incubation managers, behavioral scientists, journey mappers, business modelers, solution finders, and emerging-technology specialists. If one or more of those strike a chord with you, then seek out people already in those jobs at your company, buy them lunch, and understand what those roles really entail.

Also, balance your T capability profile. If you are on a business track, think about accumulating more technology, data, and design skills. If you are on a technology track, build your competencies in product management and business modeling. This does not mean you should be a jack of all trades, master of none. By all means, develop deep expertise in an area that you could be famous for someday, but be well rounded too so that you can react quickly to the inevitable shifts that are coming your way.

For Rule 6, it is never too early to draft your personal statement of purpose (which we will cover later in this chapter). Chances are, you are still forming your views on the world and the kind of challenges that excite you. However, the old saying "If you don't know where you're going, then all roads will lead you there" definitely applies.

Balancing Your Triple Bottom Line

In a company context, the triple bottom line means balancing social, environmental, and financial measures of success. Here is the career version. See Figure 11.2 for a graphical representation of how you might think about balancing lifetime earnings, lifetime fulfillment, and social impact in each decade of your life.

This is about living a three-dimensional life. When you talk to people at a later stage of life who have enjoyed remarkable achievements in just one of those dimensions, they tend to have less satisfaction than people who have succeeded on at least two, and possibly all three.

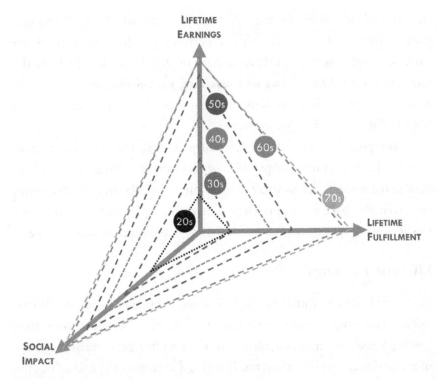

FIGURE 11.2 Growing Your Triple Bottom Line.

Conversely, people who try to make great leaps on all three dimensions in any given decade of their lives suffer from the high-stress situation of spreading themselves too thin.

Let's take an example—we will call her Joan. As depicted in the tri-angles of Figure 11.2, Joan chose to live her life as a series of majors and minors across the three dimensions of the triple bottom line. During the college and early career years of her twenties, Joan majored in social impact and ate a lot of microwaved ramen noodles with an egg added for cheap protein. Joan's thirties delivered a big jump in earnings as she joined a prestigious consulting firm; took on the tough tasks of an associate, then engagement manager; and generally hit her professional stride.

Now a partner, Joan's forties and fifties delivered big leaps in both earnings and fulfillment. Joan became increasingly motivated by how her consulting practice helped accelerate the careers of the executives she advised. She lived vicariously through their successes, as the best outside advisors tend to do. In her personal life, Joan prioritized her time to leave a lasting, positive impact on those she touched. As she looks out toward her sixties and seventies, Joan is planning an explicit rebalancing away from incremental earnings and toward big leaps in both fulfillment and social impact.

Now, your life will take a different path than the one shown here. Figure 11.2 is just an example of how to think about staging your lifetime achievements across these three dimensions. To help you plot your own triangles back to your twenties and create a plan out to your seventies, let's go deeper into what each of these triple bottom line axes mean.

Lifetime Earnings

Now, you might be thinking, "Why put money first of the three dimensions?" The simple reality is that it drives human behavior more than anything else. Like it or not, money is the most universal measuring stick of professional accomplishments. It is also a means to the end of buying the goods and services needed to improve our lives and grow our families. Four reasons that money matters follow.

A Necessary Evil

Let's face it—most advances in society have come about through capitalism. Individuals undertake education, entrepreneurs launch businesses, and investors take risks hoping to grow their wealth over time. Without this economic incentive system, few people would work as hard as they do.

The Market Price of Skills

Today's kids will mostly end up in jobs that haven't been invented yet. This makes it hard to differentiate attractive careers from those that will become commoditized. Markets can be brutally honest in rewarding scarce capabilities (such as AI today) and devaluing others. This makes earnings the default proxy for identifying which skills are in demand versus which are dying off.

The Fuel for Innovation

True entrepreneurs love asymmetric payoffs. They want to go big or go home. They are in the minority, in that they will accept a major reduction in salary if they can own a significant piece of the action. The promise of life-changing wealth, even if the odds are low, continues to draw new entrepreneurs to venture-backed companies. It is why Silicon Valley remains such a vibrant place.

Capital for a Bigger Game

Now, clearly you can make an impact by committing time to social impact projects. However, improving the prospects of thousands or millions of people requires significant resources. Building up your financial war chest by means of a successful career positions you to play that bigger game if you choose to. People such as Bill Gates and Warren Buffett are literally changing the world by funding projects that provide access to clean water, healthcare, and remote education.

Lifetime Fulfillment

Fulfillment is the achievement of something desired, promised, or predicted. It brings a sense of purpose to our lives. Fulfillment exists in both the professional and personal realms. Getting recognized for your incredible work on an important project and seeing your daughter lead her team to success in a playoff volleyball game could each move you along that horizontal axis of Figure 11.2. So, how can you advance your life in this dimension? We describe four ways to do just that next.

Create the Right Collisions

Like molecules bouncing around in a closed vessel, your life is full of seemingly random collisions with the people and experiences that shape who you will become. Yet these collisions are not nearly as random as you might think. Taking just four steps can increase your odds of having the right collisions: pursuing a diverse career path, having an independent point of view, building strong personal and professional relationships, and living by a statement of purpose that resonates with others. As the famous Roman philosopher Seneca said, "Luck is where opportunity meets preparation."

Stay Obsessed with Learning

Learning is like oxygen—once it stops, you're dead. In a world where the pace of change is accelerating and we are all racing to stay ahead of AI and automation, continuous learning is essential. However, you might have shut down your learning mode after college graduation. Sure, you might read books and engage in on-the-job training, but what was the last entirely new topic you immersed yourself in? Now, we are not saying that you should teach yourself rocket science, as Elon Musk did in his spare time. Just keep the flame of your intellectual curiosity burning to maximize your lifetime fulfillment.

Know When to Pivot

Mahatma Gandhi said, "You must be the change you want to see in the world." Go back and look at the progression of your triangles on your copy of Figure 11.2. Can you pinpoint the key decisions that drove advancement in one dimension at the expense of the other two? Maybe the decision was taking a year off from college to travel in Europe. Maybe it was leaving a job too early because you felt undervalued. Maybe it was taking on a big fund-raising role at your kids' school that led to a new professional relationship. Be explicit in identifying decisions to pivot toward the road less traveled. Just keep in mind the end goal of leading a fulfilling life and progressing toward your desired impact on the world around you.

View Risk as an Opportunity

If you've ever played poker, the surest way to go broke is to muck every hand because you do not think your cards are good enough to put any chips in the pot. Eventually, the blinds will kill you. Life is like that too.

Realize that most successes in life are built on the back of prior failures, so some of your pivots may very well take you down a dirt road. Think like a poker player. When presented with a potentially risky opportunity, think, "Is this the pot that I want to put all my chips into?" How big a return from accepting that risky opportunity might you get in terms of a jump in personal or professional fulfillment if your bet pays off? Be the person who can see beyond the risk all the way to the potential return.

Social Impact

Muhammad Ali once said, "Service to others is the rent you pay for your room here on earth." We all want to do things that matter. Some digital natives jump right into social entrepreneurship at a point in life that the previous generation was taking any job that could pay the bills. There is no right or wrong sequencing for this dimension of your triple bottom line triangle. That said, think about the following four actions that can lead you to accelerated social impact.

Do Stuff That Matters

This one is simple. Invest your talents and resources to solve problems that can elevate the human condition. If you need some inspiration around what those problems might be, here are seven priorities from the United Nations: access to clean water, women's rights and education, climate change, access to healthcare, food scarcity, human rights, and personal safety and security. Drive progress in any of those areas and you are certain to accelerate your social impact.

Have Contagious Passion

Wear your passion on your sleeve instead of hiding it. Making progress on any problem worth solving almost certainly takes a team. Apply all those leadership lessons you've learned in your professional life to this new domain of social impact. Inspire and mobilize others to pursue your idea for how to make a real impact on the world.

Look for Intersections

The dimensions of your triple bottom line triangle are mutually reinforcing. Seek out intersections between the social-impact axis and the other two. For example, take those new inspirational leadership skills that you developed solving your community's social challenges back to your day job. Use those new capabilities to become even more adept at inspiring people who don't work for you to get behind initiatives you are driving. Have a prepared mind to anticipate risks and opportunities. Be a dot connector that surfaces insights and sees the connections across industries needed to solve big problems in the world.

Live Your Values

Great people naturally gravitate to other great people. In driving social impact, be clear about how your personal value system aligns with the problem you've chosen to tackle. Seek out others who share your passion for solving that problem and have a value system and underlying motivation similar to your own. Your values are how you are going to translate your personal statement of purpose into a living, breathing compass for your life and not just an exercise in a book.

Now that you understand what each axis of the triple bottom line means, take a moment to think through how well you are progressing against your lifetime earnings, lifetime fulfillment, and social impact goals. See Figure 11.3 for a template.

Give yourself a 3 on any aspect of your triple bottom line that is progressing at the rate you expect. A 4 or 5 means that you are ahead of your goals, while a 1 or 2 means you are behind. Put a date in the corner of the tracker and come back to this a year from now to see if you've caught up in the areas where you felt you were not making the progress you wanted to.

Now, we understand that this is not a comfortable exercise and that the average person does not like discomfort. However, we are pretty sure that you are not reading this book in search of "average." Progress on each dimension of your triple bottom line replenishes your energy and

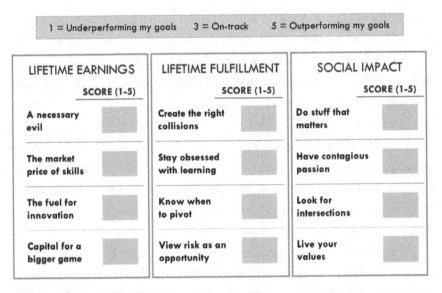

FIGURE 11.3   Tracking Your Triple Bottom Line.

pushes you forward. It validates the effort you've put in and the risks you've taken.

When developing the phonograph, Thomas Edison said, "I have not failed, I have just found 10,000 ways that don't work." If you've given yourself a few 1 or 2 scores in tracking your progress against your triple bottom line goals, that is okay. Chalk it up to experience and devote some time next month or next year toward that dimension of your life.

Navigating Choppy Waters

Picture yourself whitewater rafting with nine strangers and a guide. You are heading toward the churning gyrations of class five rapids. Your guide tells you to look down the river to see threats far enough in advance to maneuver around them. She says you need to use the current to your advantage so that you don't have to paddle so hard.

Before you left the shore, you made some important decisions that will have you end up either on the raft or under it. Did you spend the extra time needed to get in shape and develop the skills needed to be on this particular river? Who did you team up with, and how does their fitness level and skill set ready them for such a turbulent journey?

If this feels like the most-recent special project in your professional life, then you are not alone. Managing your career is a bit like that rafting trip. A few important decisions are within your control, but many are beyond it.

Scenario planning has been used for decades to make good decisions in the face of uncertainty. The goal is to make decisions that are roughly right instead of ones that are precisely wrong. Scenario planning stretches your thinking, challenges your assumptions, and keeps you moving forward when times are uncertain.

Shaping your life to progress against your triple bottom line goals requires that you anticipate the future currents that will push your career one way or the other. To bring us full-circle to the GM story that began this book, let's assume that your particular passion is the future of transportation.

To make good decisions about your career, consider the alternative scenarios for how the industry you want to work in is going to evolve. See Figure 11.4 for three plausible scenarios of how the car industry might look by 2023.

Scenario A	Scenario B	Scenario C
Same as it Ever Was	**Community Cars Rule**	**Autonomous Cars Rule**
• Gas powered cars still rule due to low oil prices	• Inexpensive fleets of cars and trucks proliferate	• Fully self-driving cars are affordable for all
• Electric and autonomous cars remain toys of the elite	• Cars are fully connected and accessed by mobile phones	• Taxi and Uber drivers are a thing of the past
• Driver assistance features become standard	• Community cars work in harmony with public transportation	• A new role of automotive concierge emerges
• Cars overall get safer and auto insurance premiums fall	• Urban car ownership plummets as on-demand goes mainstream	• Cars are optimized for the best entertainment experience
• Luxury cars remain an important status symbol	• Cars are no longer important status symbols	• Superfast 5G networks stream in immersive experiences

FIGURE 11.4   Car Industry 2023 Scenarios.

Scenario A	Scenario B	Scenario C
Same as it Ever Was	**Community Cars Rule**	**Autonomous Cars Rule**

COMMON SKILLS	• Remote Telemetry • Safety Engineering • Electric Powertrains	• Mobile App Design • Robotic Automation • Predictive Maintenance	• In-Car Entertainment • Branding • Online Marketing
SCENARIO-SPECIFIC SKILLS	• Industrial Design • Performance Engineering • New and Used Car Sales	• Schedule Optimization • Fleet Network Design • Ride-Sharing Coordination	• Machine Vision • Entertainment Curation • New and Used Car Sales

FIGURE 11.5   Skills by Future Scenario.

Now think through what types of roles, skills, and experiences will be most valued in each scenario. Some capabilities will be valuable no matter which industry-evolution scenario unfolds. Others will be valued only under one or two of those scenarios. See Figure 11.5 for examples of both for each of Figure 11.4's car industry scenarios.

So, if your career goal is shaping the future of the car industry, skills in areas such as remote telemetry, electric powertrains, or online marketing are going to be highly valued regardless of how the industry evolves. If you focus your skill development solely on areas such as fleet network design or machine vision for autonomous driving, then you are making a riskier bet on scenarios B or C, respectively.

When we get to your personal action plan below, make sure you consider this future view of the skills and capabilities likely to be most in demand in your industry. That is the only way to put the preemptive skill development we covered in Chapter 9 to work for you.

Your Purpose and Headline

Your purpose is what gets you out of bed every morning. It transcends any specific role you take on, skill you build, or company you work for. Now, hopefully there is significant alignment between your purpose and your company's (Chapter 9). That makes life easy. However, if your personal purpose is fundamentally incompatible with your company's purpose, then it is likely time to look for another job that is a better fit.

Your Statement of Purpose

Here are some examples of powerful statements of purpose at the individual level. They each answer the cosmic question, "Why was I put on this planet?"

- To make chronic disease and suffering a thing of the past through preventative healthcare.
- To unlock the potential in the world around me through innovation, leadership, and human understanding.
- To leave the planet a better place for our kids by eliminating industrial pollution.
- To improve financial literacy among those who need it most through technology and human interactions.

Pause here and write a draft of your statement of purpose. Keep it to a single sentence. Reflect on the impact you aspire to have over the course of your career. Your statement of purpose will serve as the destination point on your career GPS.

Your Future Headline

Now let's define a waypoint along your career journey. Assume it is five years from now and the editor of your industry's most important publication has called and wants to write a profile on the impact you've had. What do you want the headline to say?

Going back to the car industry scenarios, if you had committed your career to car-industry scenario B and worked in the public sector, your future headline might be:

"Mayor Joanne Smith made community car-sharing possible. Her tireless work on cutting red tape, rezoning parking lots, and promoting public investment in charging infrastructure cut Denver's traffic by 50% and its air pollution by 80%."

If you were a finance manager working to help shape the same scenario, your future headline might be:

"Innovator James Frederick developed a groundbreaking fractional ownership model that took car sharing mainstream. Individuals can get a return on their partial car ownership and credits to drive any car in the fleet."

Your future headline takes one or more scenarios for how your industry is likely to evolve and overlays your professional aspirations. It is a pithy way to answer the question, "What are you going to do about it?"

Come back to your statement of purpose and future headline at least annually to take stock of whether that long-term destination and midterm waypoint still make sense. If not, then adjust them to reflect that future version of you.

Your Personal Action Plan

This may all seem like a lot to think about: understanding your professional gaps against the six rules, setting your triple bottom line goals, thinking through which skills will be valued under multiple industry evolution scenarios, and finally writing your statement of purpose and future headline.

Stepping back, this all comes down to navigating your professional life through what are going to be very rough waters. Digital disruption can be disorienting. Simplify things by building an action plan that defines what you are actually going to do over the coming month, six months, and year. Don't go further out in time than that.

In each time frame, be specific in laying out the concrete steps you are going to take to advance your lifetime earnings, lifetime fulfillment, and social impact goals. This is not the time to be aspirational. Write your action plan in such a way that a friend could easily tell you whether you completed each action or not.

What does this look like in practice? Here is an example of how Jaclyn, a midlevel product manager within an established publishing company, might map out her personal action plan. Jaclyn aspires to be an internal venture leader on innovative new digital and AI product offerings but is currently managing a legacy publication.

One-Month Actions

- Update my personal statement of purpose.
- Enroll in an online user experience design course.
- Find a mentor with a new-ventures background.
- Research internal and external open innovation competitions.
- Thank five people who have helped guide my career so far.

Six-Month Actions

- Get feedback monthly from my new-ventures mentor.
- Have six lunches with people working in digital product development jobs.
- Complete online user experience design course.
- Enroll in entry-level machine learning certificate course at local college.
- Make it to at least 10 of my volleyball team's games.

One-Year Actions

- Network with startup leaders through college and company alumni networks.
- Complete an AI pilot to streamline the data cleansing aspects of my current role.
- Enter an internal innovation competition to learn and gain executive exposure.
- Land a digital product manager role in our digital innovation group.
- Commit 20 hours as a volunteer at my local animal rescue shelter.

Note that all of these are make or miss. That is, Jaclyn is holding herself accountable through actions that are crisply defined and on the path toward her long-term goals.

The Time Is Now

You can't wait forever. If you are in your twenties, you have boundless energy and the physical capacity to take on almost anything. You can work a 12-hour day, party all night, sleep on the floor, drink a Red Bull, and be ready to go tomorrow. You might lack the experience, personal network, and financial resources to have the full impact you aspire for, but your enthusiasm is high.

If you are in your fifties, you have lived through enough experiences to develop the pattern recognition that leads to wisdom. If you've been successful, you also have a broad network of personal and professional relationships to draw on. Finally, you may have substantial capital to deploy to the projects you care most about. However, you may no longer have the energy to pull all-nighters and work seven days a week.

While the slope of the curves or the point of their intersection might be different from what is depicted in Figure 11.6, some version of the longevity paradox holds true for most talented people.

You can have a major impact at 18 (like Mark Zuckerberg or Malala) or after 80 (like Warren Buffett and the Dalai Lama). The longevity

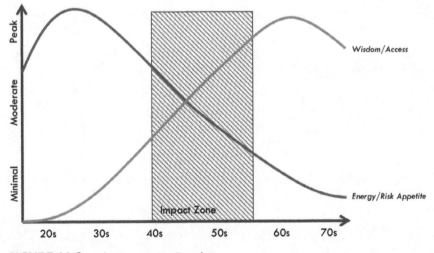

FIGURE 11.6 The Longevity Paradox.

paradox just means that you need to partner with someone at the other end of the age spectrum that can complement what you bring. Just start somewhere and you'll have the chance to leave a legacy of impact.

Now it's time to stop reading and get to work making your future headline a reality. Go be a disruptor inside your Goliath and beat David at his own game. Good luck!

Appendix: Goliath's Revenge Rule Templates

We have covered a lot of ground in getting you and your company ready to turn the tables on digital disruptors. To bring you back to the big picture, we have included the detailed definitions and assessment scorecards for each of the six rules in Figures A.1 and A.2, respectively.

Also, in Chapter 10 you built your disruptor's playbook around rule-specific action plans. To help you build those, we have included a blank action plan template for each new rule in Figures A.3 through A.8.

GOLIATH'S REVENGE NEW RULES DEFINITIONS

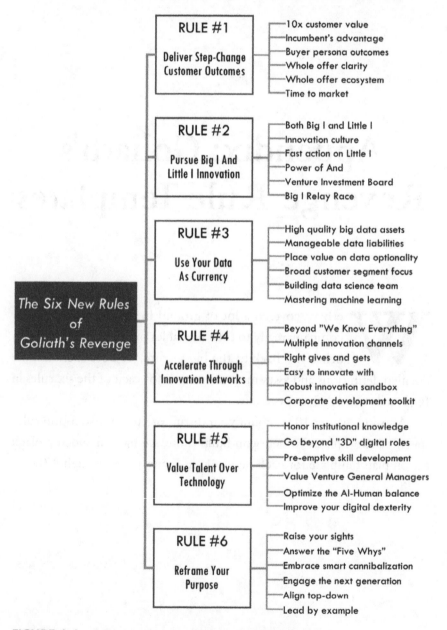

FIGURE A.1   Goliath's Revenge Rules: Detailed Definitions.

GOLIATH'S REVENGE NEW RULES ASSESSMENT

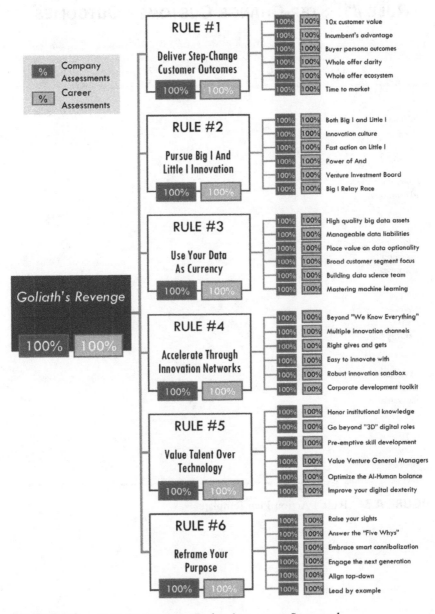

FIGURE A.2   Goliath's Revenge Rules: Assessment Scorecard.

RULE-SPECIFIC ACTION PLAN TEMPLATE
RULE #1: STEP-CHANGE CUSTOMER OUTCOMES

	Current Capability Level	Near-Term Capability Goal	New Initiatives To Start	Current Initiatives To Stop	Current Initiatives To Refocus
10X customer value					
Incumbent's advantage					
Buyer persona outcomes					
Whole offer clarity					
Whole offer ecosystem					
Time to market					

FIGURE A.3   Rule 1 Action Plan Template.

RULE-SPECIFIC ACTION PLAN TEMPLATE
RULE #2: PURSUE BIG I AND LITTLE I INNOVATION

	Current Capability Level	Near-Term Capability Goal	New Initiatives To Start	Current Initiatives To Stop	Current Initiatives To Refocus
Both Big I and Little I					
Innovation culture					
Fast action on Little I					
Power of And					
Venture Investment Board					
Big I Relay Race					

FIGURE A.4   Rule 2 Action Plan Template.

RULE-SPECIFIC ACTION PLAN TEMPLATE
RULE #3: USE YOUR DATA AS CURRENCY

	Current Capability Level	Near-Term Capability Goal	New Initiatives To Start	Current Initiatives To Stop	Current Initiatives To Refocus
High quality big data assets					
Manageable data liabilities					
Place value on data optionality					
Broad customer segment focus					
Building data science team					
Mastering machine learning					

FIGURE A.5   Rule 3 Action Plan Template.

RULE-SPECIFIC ACTION PLAN TEMPLATE
RULE #4: ACCELERATE VIA INNOVATION NETWORKS

	Current Capability Level	Near-Term Capability Goal	New Initiatives To Start	Current Initiatives To Stop	Current Initiatives To Refocus
Beyond "We Know Everything"					
Multiple innovation channels					
Right gives and gets					
Easy to innovate with					
Robust innovation sandbox					
Corporate development toolkit					

FIGURE A.6 Rule 4 Action Plan Template.

RULE-SPECIFIC ACTION PLAN TEMPLATE
RULE #5: VALUE TALENT OVER TECHNOLOGY

	Current Capability Level	Near-Term Capability Goal	New Initiatives To Start	Current Initiatives To Stop	Current Initiatives To Refocus
Honor institutional knowledge					
Go beyond "3D" digital roles					
Commit to pre-emptive skill development					
Value Venture General Managers					
Optimize the AI-Human Balance					
Improve your digital dexterity					

FIGURE A.7   Rule 5 Action Plan Template.

RULE-SPECIFIC ACTION PLAN TEMPLATE
RULE #6: REFRAME YOUR PURPOSE

	Current Capability Level	Near-Term Capability Goal	New Initiatives To Start	Current Initiatives To Stop	Current Initiatives To Refocus
Raise your sights					
Answer the "Five Whys"					
Embrace smart cannibal-ization					
Engage the next generation					
Align top-down					
Lead by example					

FIGURE A.8   Rule 6 Action Plan Template.

About the Authors

Todd Hewlin is managing director of TCG Advisors, a Silicon Valley consulting firm renowned for its work helping companies cross the chasm to breakout growth. Previously a partner at McKinsey and a senior executive at Symbol Technologies, Hewlin is regularly found in the boardroom of market leaders advising them on how to grow in a rapidly digitizing world. He is coauthor of *Consumption Economics* and *B4B* and a frequent keynote speaker at major industry events.

Scott Snyder leads digital and innovation consulting for Heidrick & Struggles and is a Senior Fellow of the Management Department of the Wharton School. Snyder is a recognized thought leader in digital transformation and innovation, having held leadership roles at GE and Lockheed Martin, launched three startups, and led technology and innovation for venture capital firm Safeguard. He is author of *The New World of Wireless* and has lectured at top institutions including Wharton, MIT, Babson, Duke, and INSEAD on emerging technologies, digital strategy, and innovation.

Index